TWO NATIONS UNDER GOD

The Deuteronomistic History of Solomon and the Dual Monarchies

Volume 2

HARVARD SEMITIC MUSEUM

HARVARD SEMITIC MONOGRAPHS

edited by
Frank Moore Cross

Number 53
TWO NATIONS UNDER GOD
The Deuteronomistic History of Solomon and the Dual Monarchies
Volume 2
The Reign of Jeroboam, the Fall of Israel, and the Reign of Josiah

by
Gary N. Knoppers

Gary N. Knoppers

TWO NATIONS UNDER GOD

The Deuteronomistic History of Solomon and the Dual Monarchies

Volume 2

The Reign of Jeroboam, the Fall of Israel, and the Reign of Josiah

Scholars Press
Atlanta, Georgia

TWO NATIONS UNDER GOD
The Deuteronomistic History of Solomon and the Dual Monarchies

Volume 2

The Reign of Jeroboam, the Fall of Israel, and the Reign of Josiah

by
Gary N. Knoppers

Library of Congress Cataloging in Publication Data
Knoppers, Gary N., 1956-
Two nations under God.
(Harvard Semitic monographs ; no. 52-53)
Includes bibliographical references and indexes.
Contents: v. 1. The reign of Solomon and the rise of Jeroboam—v. 2. The reign of Jeroboam, the fall of Israel, and the reign of Josiah.
1. Bible. O.T.—Kings—Criticism, Redaction. 2. Document (Biblical criticism) 3. Bible. O.T.—Kings— History of Biblical events. 4. Jews—History—953-586 B.C.—Historiography. 5. Solomon, King of Israel. I. Title. II. Title: 2 nations under God.
BS1335.2.K66 1993 222'.5066 93-37963
ISBN 1-55540-913-X (cloth : v. 1 : acid-free paper)

Printed in the United States of America
on acid-free paper

To My Parents:

Barthie Maria Boon Knoppers and

Nicolaas Bastiaan Knoppers

Alse alle dinghen selen vervaren,
So dal die edele minne waren
Ende hare clare gheheel openbaren,
  Als ghi in een nuwe beghin
Met minnen die minne seelt ane staren:
  'Siet, dit eest dat ic bin.'
(Hadewijch, *De Visioenen*).

TABLE OF CONTENTS

PREFACE

In researching and writing this book I was aided by colleagues, friends, and family. Frank Cross, the outgoing editor of Harvard Semitic Museum Monographs, has both consistently encouraged my interest in the Deuteronomistic History and provided me with lucid comments on each chapter in this volume. He continues to be a model of support for younger scholars in the field. Steven McKenzie, Hayim Tadmor, and John W. Wright each read chapters 2-6 and provided me with many helpful observations. Paul Hanson, Theodore Hiebert, and James Kugel critiqued earlier versions of chapters 2-4 and sharpened my understanding of critical issues. Sarah Foster and Dennis Ford at Scholars Press helped in editing this volume and preparing it for publication.

At Penn State I have enjoyed the support of many people but especially my colleagues Baruch Halpern, William Petersen, and Judith Van Herik, each of whom has encouraged me in pursuing this project. By carefully proofreading the manuscript Gisela March and Patricia Mateya saved me from many errors. I am indebted to Christopher Oves and especially to Prodromos Prodromidis for patiently assisting me in the compilation of indices. A travel to collections grant from the Institute for Arts and Humanistic Studies enabled me to make two important research trips. In the Spring of 1993 I received the Josephine Berry Weiss Faculty Fellowship in the Humanities from the Research and Graduate Studies Office in the College of Liberal Arts. This fellowship generously supplied me with both the time and the research support necessary to completing this work.

I owe a debt of gratitude to my family. My wife Laura has provided me with both intellectual and emotional support as I worked on this long project. My children Theresa and David present a welcome respite from and contrast to life in the academy. My parents have always stressed the value of education to their six children. I am most pleased to dedicate this book to them.

ACKNOWLEDGEMENTS

Portions of chapters 5 and 6 appeared in an earlier form in my article, "'There was None Like Him': Incomparability in the Books of Kings," *CBQ* 54 (1992) 411-31. I would like to thank the general editor of *CBQ* and the Executive Secretary of the Catholic Biblical Society of America for permission to incorporate this material into the present volume.

ABBREVIATIONS

The abbreviations used in this work follow those listed in the *Society of Biblical Literature Membership Directory and Handbook* (Decatur, GA: Society of Biblical Literature, 1993) with the following exceptions and additions.

acc	accusative
Ant.	Josephus, *The Jewish Antiquities*
Annals	D. D. Luckenbill, *The Annals of Sennacherib*
BN	*Biblische Notizen*
CE	the Ethiopic to Chronicles
CG	the majority Greek text of Chronicles
CG^{A}	Codex Alexandrinus to Chronicles
CG^{B}	Codex Vaticanus to Chronicles
CG^{L}	the Lucianic recension or the Lucianic manuscripts (be$_{2}$)
CG^{N}	Codex Basiliano-Vaticanus to Chronicles
CL	the Old Latin to Chronicles
CM	the Masoretic Text of Chronicles
cp.	compare
CS	the Syriac Peshiṭta to Chronicles
CT	the Targum to Chronicles
CV	the Vulgate to Chronicles
Diss.	dissertation
DN	divine name
Dtr^{1}	the Josianic Deuteronomist

Dtr^2	the exilic Deuteronomist
DtrH	the exilic, deuteronomistic historian
DtrP	the exilic, prophetic redactor of the Deuteronomistic History
DtrN	the exilic or early postexilic, nomistic redactor(s) of the Deuteronomistic History
E	the Elohist
FOTL	The Forms of the Old Testament Literature
Fs.	*Festschrift*
H	the Holiness Code
infin	infinitive
J	the Yahwist
Jer C	a series of speeches in the Book of Jeremiah with affinities to Deuteronomy and the Deuteronomistic History
KAI	H. Donner and W. Röllig, *Kanaanäische und aramäisches Inschriften*, vols. 1-3
KE	the Ethiopic to Kings
KG	the majority Greek text of Kings
KG^A	Codex Alexandrinus to Kings
KG^B	Codex Vaticanus to Kings
KG^L	the Lucianic recension or the majority of the Lucianic manuscripts (boc_2e_2)
KG^N	Codex Basiliano-Vaticanus to Kings
KM	the Masoretic Text of Kings
KS	the Syriac Peshiṭta to Kings
KT	Targum Jonathan to Kings
KTU	M. Dietrich, O. Loretz, and J. Sanmartín, *Die Keil-alphabetischen Texte aus Ugarit*.
KV	the Vulgate to Kings

Luc	Lucifer of Cagliari
masc	masculine
Mati'ilu	Treaty between Ashurnirari V of Assyria and Mati'ilu of Arpad
mss	manuscripts
n.	note
NJPS	New Jewish Publication Society translation (1985)
P	the Priestly writer(s)
part	participle
pl	plural
PN	personal name
pron	pronoun
4QKgs^{a}	the first copy of Kings from Qumrân Cave 4
6QKgs	the copy of Kings from Qumrân Cave 6
4QJer^{b}	the second copy of Jeremiah from Qumrân Cave 4
Rgns	ΒΑΣΙΛΕΙΩΝ, the Septuagintal Books of Reigns or Kingdoms
rell	*reliqui*, the rest of the selected Greek cursives
Sefîre	J. A. Fitzmyer, *The Aramaic Inscriptions of Sefîre*
sing	singular
SyrH	the Syro-Hexapla
trans.	translation
VTE	D. J. Wiseman, *The Vassal Treaties of Esarhaddon*

CHAPTER 1

INTRODUCTION

Nations, like men, have their infancy.
(Henry St. John, Viscount Bolingbroke,
On the Study of History, letter 4).

Studying the Bible from an academic vantage point inevitably raises questions of method and coverage. In the first volume of this work, I addressed the composition and coverage of primarily one era in the Deuteronomistic History -- the *floruit* of the united monarchy (the ascent and reign of Solomon) and its end (the demise of Solomon, the ascent of Jeroboam, and the assembly at Shechem).[1] The present volume concentrates on selected events in the divided monarchy -- the reign of Jeroboam, the fall of Israel, and the reign of Josiah. I argue that the Deuteronomist uses events in the early divided monarchy to frame the history of both Israel and Judah. In describing the sins of

[1] In vol. 1: chap. 1, I surveyed recent treatments of the textual history of Samuel-Kings and assessed arguments for the literary (dis)unity of the Deuteronomistic History. There is no need to repeat that discussion here. In the same chapter, I also show why the united monarchy and its decline were of such interest to later Israelite writers.

Jeroboam, the prophecies against Jeroboam, and the fall of Jeroboam, 1 Kings 12:26-14:18 actually explain and justify the fall of Israel and the reforms of Josiah two and three centuries later. Both the themes and the structure that the Deuteronomist imposes upon the history of the early divided monarchy evince a disproportionate concern with (northern) Israelite history and Israelite-Judahite relations. This concern is best explained as stemming from the late preexilic period, obviously a time of disaster for Israel, but also a time of great turmoil for Judah.

The selection of coverage in this work has both advantages and disadvantages. One obvious disadvantage from the standpoint of redaction criticism is that this work cannot address the composition and meaning of all the controversial passages and motifs in Kings, much less in the Deuteronomistic History.[2] But focused coverage also has its advantages. Given the textual, stylistic, formal, and thematic diversity of Kings, concentration upon the reigns of a few pivotal monarchs allows for the application of different methodologies -- textual criticism, source criticism, literary criticism, form criticism, and redaction criticism -- to resolve several critical issues.

Recourse to this somewhat eclectic approach in vol. 1 demonstrated the usefulness of a variety of interdependent scholarly tools to engage the major issues of composition, sources, style, point(s) of view, form, and purpose, which have dominated scholarly discussions of Solomon's reign, in particular, and the Deuteronomistic History, in

---

[2] Cf. Campbell (1986), Dietrich (1972), Friedman (1981a), Jones (1984), McKenzie (1991), O'Brien (1989), Nelson (1981a; 1987), Provan (1988), Würthwein (1977; 1984).

general.[3] By interdependence I do not mean that modern critical approaches (e.g., textual criticism, source criticism, form criticism, traditio-historical criticism, redaction criticism, and literary criticism) are entirely complementary. Few would claim that traditio-historical criticism can be easily harmonized with literary criticism. Nevertheless, I maintain that each of these methods offers its own potential for clarifying puzzling features in the text. Moreover, the application of one critical method can shed light on the problems encountered by the application of another. The significant differences in content and sequence between the LXX and the MT, for instance, provide important clues to the Deuteronomist's narrative strategy in portraying the inception of Solomon's reign.[4]

In volume 1 (chap. 2), I argued that the deuteronomistic depiction of Solomon's ascent and reign is more positive and coherent than many scholars have recognized. The Deuteronomist may well have employed a source, a "Court History of David" or a "Succession Narrative," to depict Solomon's rise to power (1 Kings 1-2), but this does not mean that the Deuteronomist's concern with Solomon begins only in the material he adds in 1 Kings 3-10. The Deuteronomist shapes and supplements his source, citing Nathan's promises (2 Sam 7:5-16) and David's prayer (2 Sam 7:18-29) to tie the reigns of David and Solomon closely together.[5]

---

[3] I say somewhat eclectic, because my work does not employ a number of the newer academic approaches to biblical criticism, such as structural criticism, poststructuralist criticism, reader-response criticism, and feminist criticism.

[4] When applied to the text of Samuel-Kings, the traditional distinction between lower and higher criticism is therefore misguided, if not completely erroneous.

[5] Engaging the diachronic dimension of the text can inform and enrich synchronic interpretations. See especially chaps. 4-5 in vol. 1.

Similarly, the very heterogeneity of Kings, which leads some interpreters to posit multiple redactions, may appear differently when viewed from the perspective of literary criticism. Although many commentators have cited the diversity of forms, perspectives, and styles of 1 Kings 1-11 as grounds for positing a series of redactions, I have argued that the Deuteronomist employs heterogeneity to achieve a limited number of discrete ends. Hence, the different senses of wisdom in 1 Kings 3-5 need not entail a series of editions of or additions to an *Ur*-text in which Solomon's wisdom is one dimensional. The Deuteronomist plays on the different connotations of royal wisdom in the traditions bequeathed to him to create a portrait of Solomon as a multi-talented sage.

Nor should scholars feel compelled to reduce the Deuteronomist's interest in Solomon to his accomplishment of one feat -- Solomon's construction and dedication of a central sanctuary. However important the temple is to the Deuteronomist, his concerns clearly include Solomon's wisdom, diplomacy, wealth, and leadership. The confluence of interests is not accidental. Consistent with ancient Near Eastern royal ideology, the Deuteronomist links Solomon's economic, diplomatic, and cultic successes to the attainment of rest, peace, and happiness for his people. Inasmuch as David is the Deuteronomist's ideal king, I argue that the first period of Solomon's rule is his ideal age. The reigns of David and Solomon complement one another in establishing Israel's normative institutions. Hence, one cannot appreciate the oscillation between regression and reform, a hallmark of the Deuteronomist's coverage of the dual monarchies, without recognizing what the Deuteronomist posits as form.

The issue of heterogeneity also affects the interpretation of Solomon's decline and Jeroboam's rise to power (vol.1: chaps. 4-5). Scholars have debated the nature, date, and purpose of the material dealing with Solomon and Jeroboam in 1 Kings 11-12. Examining the differences between the MT of 1 Kings 11-12, the LXX of 1 Kings 11-12, and the oft-neglected "supplement" of 3 Rgns 12:24a-z, elucidates distinctive features in the Deuteronomist's presentation. No other study has established that the Deuteronomist's commentary upon the transition to the divided monarchy belongs to his series of major reflections, speeches, and prayers by which he unifies his history. By orchestrating the division according to his standard typology of sin, punishment, and divine deliverance, the Deuteronomist endorses the creation of two nations under one God. A common heritage and a common cultic obligation to the Jerusalem temple characterize nascent Israel and Judah, but their separate polities are divinely ordained. This study reveals a consistency in the Deuteronomist's compositional technique, even though some critics have questioned the unity of the Deuteronomist's presentation of Judges and Kings.

Although I have used the insights of textual and literary critics to defend the basic unity of the Deuteronomist's history of Solomon (vol.1: chaps. 2-5), I disagree with the common assumption among literary critics that the Deuteronomistic History is an exilic creation.[6]

---

[6] This is true not only of (new) literary critics, such as Alter (1981; 1987), Long (1984; 1991b), Polzin (1980; 1989), and Savran (1987), but also of more traditional critics, such as Noth (1968; 1981), von Rad (1966b), and Wolff (1975). Members of the so-called Göttingen school also hold to exilic (or postexilic) authorship (Camp 1990; Dietrich 1972; Smend 1971; 1978; Spieckermann 1982, and Veijola 1975; 1977).

Most of the reign of Solomon is structured to address dominant concerns of the preexilic period. The Deuteronomist's recourse to the Davidic promises to defend Solomon's rise presupposes, for example, that the Davidic throne continues to endure, if not thrive (vol. 1: chap. 2). Similarly, the panegyric to Solomon in 1 Kings 3-10 is structurally and thematically best understood as the work of a Josianic Deuteronomist (vol. 1: chaps. 3-4). By constructing such a glorious period in Solomon's rule, the Josianic Deuteronomist (Dtr^1) promotes the enduring achievements of the Davidic monarchy in the late seventh century, an age in which kingship had been subject to a variety of searching critiques.

The deuteronomistic exaltation of Solomon in the first period of his reign and his excoriation of Solomon in the second period of his reign has important implications for understanding the deuteronomistic construction of the dual monarchies, the subject of this second volume. If Solomon has proved to be a controversial figure for both the Deuteronomist and Solomon's modern interpreters, this is no less true of Jeroboam. Some explain the variant coverage of Jeroboam through recourse to sources, incorporated but not overwritten in Kings. Others appeal to a series of multiple redactions to account for the divergent deuteronomistic comments upon his ascent and reign. I contend that the Deuteronomist, whatever the precise nature of his sources, developed a more sophisticated and elaborate narrative strategy in portraying Solomon's decline and Jeroboam's rise than most commentators have acknowledged.

First, blaming Solomon for disunion vindicates deuteronomistic standards, specifically the exclusive loyalty due the Jerusalem temple. Disunion paradoxically becomes an argument for both the elimination of foreign cults and for centralization. Second, the Deuteronomist construes the division to justify and adumbrate Josiah's reforms. If

Solomon's sins are more basic than the division between Israel and Judah, then redressing Solomon's sins can help to rectify the rift between the northern and southern tribes (chap. 6). Third, in the deuteronomistic record the course of the northern kingdom is a history of its own making (chaps. 2-4). Should the northern experiment fail, neither the Jerusalem temple nor the Davidic throne can be held responsible. Indeed, subsequent to the fall of the North to the Assyrians (2 Kgs 17:1-7aα, 18-19, 21-33; cf. 2 Kgs 18:9-12), the survival of Jerusalem and the Davidic line during the Assyrian crisis (2 Kgs 19:34; 20:5-6) confirm that YHWH's promises to chosen David and chosen city still obtain.[7]

The description of Jeroboam's cultus in 1 Kgs 12:26-33 forms the hinge in the Deuteronomist's treatment of Jeroboam (chap. 2). All preceding coverage of Jeroboam is positive; all succeeding coverage of Jeroboam is negative. Israel's great turning point ironically transpires at the beginning of its history. Many scholars have characterized the Deuteronomist's judgment of Jeroboam's innovations as a denunciation of Bethel and Dan from a Judahite perspective, but I maintain that the Deuteronomist's evaluation is more profound. By privileging Jeroboam's establishment of sanctuaries at Bethel and Dan with such critical coverage, the Deuteronomist tacitly acknowledges that the rivalry between Israelite and Judahite state-sponsored sanctuaries is an inner Israelite controversy. But the Deuteronomist impugns Jeroboam's counter-cultus as fundamentally un-Israelite. In

---

[7] Note the witnesses of 4QKgs and KG^{B} to 1 Kgs 8:16 and the testimony of 2 Chr 6:5-6 (Trebolle 1992:315-24). On the importance of Hezekiah's reign in the Deuteronomistic History compare the treatments of Camp (1990), Childs (1967), Gonçalves (1986), Knoppers (1992), McKenzie (1991), Provan (1988), and Seitz (1989). See also chap. 6.

the contrast he draws between the pan-Israelite acclamation of Solomon's temple and the aberrant nature of Jeroboam's counter-cultus, the Deuteronomist's very description of Jeroboam's cult casts doubt upon the prospects for the northern kingdom.

Recognizing the Deuteronomist's contempt for Jeroboam's cultic initiatives, commentators debate the presence of two successive prophetic condemnations of Jeroboam (1 Kgs 13:1-34; 14:1-18). Does this apparent doublet reflect a combination of sources, a succession of redactions, or the interpolation of one or more late pericopes? I argue that the Deuteronomist, consistent with his dictum that cult and kingdom are related but distinct phenomena, addresses the implications of Jeroboam's sacral initiatives in two successive stages: the prospects for this new cult (1 Kings 13) and the impact of this cult upon Jeroboam's kingdom (1 Kings 14). The Deuteronomist incorporates prophetic traditions, but he shapes these materials to his own ends. In 1 Kings 13 the Deuteronomist supplements prophetic traditions to heighten his denunciation of Jeroboam's Bethel cult (chap. 3). Jeroboam's recalcitrance, in the face of trenchant prophetic opposition becomes a deuteronomistic metonym for the decline of the Israelite monarchy. In the deuteronomistic record, the remarkable reversals in the tale of two prophets adumbrate the reversal effected by Josiah's cultic reforms. 1 Kings 13 ultimately functions as an *apologia* for the Josianic reform, elucidating his imperial program and marshalling historical support.

The Deuteronomist's differentiation between cult and kingdom illumines the Deuteronomist's editorial upon the fall of Israel in 2 Kings 17, long considered a *crux interpretum* in the Deuteronomistic History (chap. 3). 2 Kings 17 is not the Deuteronomist's last word on the future of the Israelite people, even though the exile of Israel marks the realization of Ahijah's judgment against Jeroboam.[8] This reflection carefully distinguishes between the political termination of Israel (2 Kgs 17:7aα, 18a, 21-23) and its continuing cultic life (2 Kgs 17:24-33). The northern kingdom falls to the Assyrians in 722 BCE, but the same catastrophe ironically leads to the reinvigoration of the Bethel cult enfranchised by Jeroboam. By detailing Israel's demise and tracing its cause to Jeroboam's investiture of the Bethel cultus, the Deuteronomist paradoxically sustains the Bethel cultus as an object of divine concern. The Deuteronomist's editorial is therefore more than an epitaph for Israel (contra Noth 1981:6). Reform is no less necessary in the aftermath of the Assyrian exile than in the two preceding centuries. The renascence of the Bethel cultus after the Assyrian exile renders the prophecies of the man of God and the Bethel prophet about the Bethel cultus and the northern sanctuaries more probable than ever (1 Kgs 13:2, 32).

In 1 Kings 14 the issue is not the fate of Jeroboam's cult, but the consequences of this cult upon the prospects for Jeroboam's lineage and realm (chap. 4). To be sure, 1 Kgs 14:1-18 is formally diverse, containing legendary motifs, a prophetic consultation story, three commissions (vv 2-3, 7, 12), and two judgment oracles (vv 7-11, 12-16). Comparison between the MT (1 Kgs 14:1-18) and the supplement (3 Rgns 12:24g-nα) reveals, however, that the formal complexity of 1 Kgs 14:1-18 enhances thematic development. Drawing upon traditions dealing with Jeroboam's sick son, the Deuteronomist creates a mixed genre to address the fate of the kingdom entrusted to Jeroboam. In this regard, the heavily edited judgment oracles of 1 Kgs 14:7-11, 12-16 play a critical role in northern history analogous

---

8 Contra Noth (1981:80, 89). See 1 Kgs 14:7-16 and the discussions in chaps. 3-4.

to the role of 2 Sam 7:5-16 in southern history. As the Deuteronomist links the fate of David, his seed, dynasty, temple, and people in 2 Sam 7:5-16, so he links the fate of Jeroboam, his son, dynasty, cultus, and people in 1 Kgs 14:7-16.

Both promise and threat affect later kings -- for good or for ill. Like David, Jeroboam is an archetypal figure -- the benchmark for later monarchs in his realm. Ahijah's judgments set the stage for the Deuteronomist's pessimistic coverage of northern political history. By transforming a tale about a sick child into the condemnation of an entire nation, the Deuteronomist dramatizes the sudden but decisive reversal of political fortunes effected by the inauguration of Jeroboam's cult. The demise of Jeroboam's son prefigures, even secures, the demise of Jeroboam's dynasty and kingdom (chap. 4).

The Deuteronomist's condemnation of Jeroboam also sheds new light upon his use of the Davidic promises. The deuteronomistic application of Nathan's dynastic oracle is primarily defensive, valididating Davidic kingship and ameliorating the implementation of divine wrath in Judah. The promises to David and the judgments against Jeroboam are therefore not opposites. The Deuteronomist predicates the people's livelihood upon royal support for the temple and concomitantly upon royal subjugation of all other sanctuaries. David is the exemplar of this concern for a central sanctuary and Jeroboam is the antithesis of this concern. Whether positively (David) or negatively (Jeroboam), the Deuteronomist promotes similar standards for both realms. In both Israel and Judah the movement of history is directed toward the need for pervasive reforms.

As scholars have long recognized, the Deuteronomist posits the impetus toward the implementation of such radical reforms as the discovery of "the scroll of the torah" in the reign of Josiah (2 Kgs

22:8).[9] The measures Josiah takes upon hearing the recitation of the torah scroll -- his consternation, his humble response to Huldah's oracle, and his covenant renewal -- underscore the crisis he faces in improving the plight of his people. Because Josiah's reforms recall the stipulations of Deuteronomy, Pentateuchal scholars, historians of ancient Israelite history and religion, and scholars of the Former Prophets all take great interest in the deuteronomistic presentation of Josiah. Yet I would dispute the prevailing assessment that Josiah's reign represents the triumph of Deuteronomy. Such a view only replicate the Deuteronomist's own presentation without taking into account important differences between deuteronomic and deuteronomistic ideology. Similarly, there are problems with the notion that an exilic or postexilic Deuteronomist basically invents the torah scroll story to project an image of Josiah as a paragon of piety. Such a reconstruction sidesteps the problems inherent in the Deuteronomist's paucity of references to torah during his history of the monarchy. The later one ascribes the deuteronomistic edition of 2 Kings 22-23, the more acute the discrepancy between the Deuteronomist's criteria of judgment for kingly conduct and his account of the discovery of the torah scroll becomes. In my view, the preexilic Deuteronomist (Dtr^1) employs a quasi anti-monarchical law code (*Ur-Deuteronomium*) to authorize massive royal reforms. Hence, Josiah's attempt at centralizing the Yahwistic cult and eradicating all non-Yahwistic cults denotes more the triumph of deuteronomistic ideology than the triumph of Deuteronomy.

---

[9] Chaps. 5-6. Even among those critics who favor the double redaction hypothesis, none has, to my knowledge, offered a comprehensive interpretation of Josiah's reign.

In the deuteronomistic construction of history, Josiah's reforms in Jerusalem, the countryside of Judah, and the former northern kingdom appear not as as revolutionary, but as a noble attempt to actualize the ancient law of the sanctuary (chap. 6). In so doing, Josiah reverses the unrequited transgressions committed by Solomon, by Jeroboam, and by his other southern and northern predecessors. The Josianic reforms restore the orthopraxis that should have been the legacy of the united kingdom. The exclusive prerogative of the central sanctuary, mandated on the Plains of Moab (Deuteronomy 12) and celebrated in Solomon's temple dedication (1 Kings 8), finally becomes a reality in the campaigns of Judah's greatest reformer king. Already in narrating the reigns of the united monarchy's last king and northern Israel's first king, the Deuteronomist proleptically sets the agenda for Judah's decline, Israel's ruin, and their salvation. In the Deuteronomistic History, the story of two nations under God ends with the reforms and national Passover of King Josiah of Judah.

CHAPTER 2

THE SINS OF JEROBOAM

All kings is mostly rapscallions.
(Mark Twain, *The Adventures of Huckleberry Finn*, chap. 23)

Introduction

1 Kings 12 seems to exhibit a range of contrasting themes. One pericope appears charitable to Jeroboam (1 Kgs 12:1-20), while another appears highly antagonistic toward him (1 Kgs 12:26-33). Critics describe the former passage as pro-Shechem (1 Kgs 12:1-20), while labelling the latter as anti-Bethel (1 Kgs 12:26-33). A contrast is sometimes drawn between the purportedly anti-Judah portions of 1 Kgs 12:1-20 (e.g., vv 3-4) and the purportedly pro-Judah orientation of 1 Kgs 12:21-24. Some account for this thematic complexity by appealing to sources -- pro-Jerusalem, anti-Jerusalem, pro-Shechem, anti-Shechem, pro-Bethel, anti-Bethel.[1]

---

1 Gray (1970:299-300); Grønbaek (1965:421-436); Debus (1967:19ff.); Noth (1968:239-319; 1981:61-70); Würthwein (1977:150ff.). There is an overlap between those who attribute heterogeneity to sources and those who attribute it to various deuteronomistic redactions.

> A recognition of this diversity of opinion can be accepted as a basis for analysing chapter 12; both attitudes have been preserved in the Israelite-Judean interpretation of history, and both have been deposited in different layers within this chapter. (Jones 1984:247).

The appeal to sources is, however, unsatisfactory. The Deuteronomist undoubtedly used a variety of older materials, but what were his purposes in including these sources and why did he arrange them in the manner he did? More important, this approach fails to explain the different deuteronomistic comments on people and events. Invoking a series of major redactions -- pre-deuteronomistic, deuteronomistic, or post-deuteronomistic -- also fails to resolve the issue of heterogeneity. Aside from engaging in the extremely subjective enterprise of attempting to divide stereotypical deuteronomistic phraseology into a variety of different strands, this approach fails to apprehend the role of dramatic tension and literary complexity within the narrative complex depicting Jeroboam's rise and fall.

In my judgment, the literary and thematic complexity in 1 Kings 12 represents deliberate artifice. The Deuteronomist composes this chapter according to an overarching design and purpose. He neither erases nor completely suppresses older traditions, but rather reformulates and explicates them to serve his own ends. In 1 Kgs 12:21-33 both Rehoboam and Jeroboam challenge the validity of a new order in which Israel and Judah are to be two nations -- politically separate but cultically yoked. Rehoboam abandons his martial attempt to reunite the kingdom when he encounters stiff prophetic opposition (1 Kgs

12:23-24); but Jeroboam never desists from his plan to sever his realm from the national cultus established by David and Solomon.

Introducing the independent state of Israel, 1 Kings 12:25-33 mark Jeroboam's violation of his royal charge. I will argue that the Deuteronomist goes beyond criticizing Jeroboam's new cultus from a Judahite perspective. 1 Kgs 12:26-33 is polemic with a purpose. The author views the state-sponsored cults at Bethel and Dan as essentially un-Israelite. Inasmuch as the Deuteronomist derives royal and national fate from cultic praxis, the very description of Jeroboam's cultus casts doubt upon the long-term prospects for the northern kingdom. The creation of sanctuaries at Bethel and Dan therefore constitutes the pivot in the Deuteronomist's presentation of both Jeroboam and his nascent realm.[2] All preceding coverage of Jeroboam is complimentary; all succeeding coverage is negative. One need not posit multiple redactions to explain the heterogeneous commentary on Jeroboam. The deuteronomistic coverage of Jeroboam is both intentionally complex and internally consistent.

I. THE SECESSION CHALLENGED BY REHOBOAM

In 1 Kings 11-12 the Deuteronomist repeatedly asserts that disunion instantiates divine will (1 Kgs 11:11-13, 29-38; 12:15). Although they are to remain cultically united, the twelve tribes now

---

2 Since my focus is on the composition of the text and the deuteronomistic portrait of Jeroboam, I will not directly address matters of archaeology and history. On the archaeological excavations at Dan, see Biran (1980; 1987) and Mazar (1990:495). On Bethel, see Ahlström (1982:57-62). Boling and Campbell (1987:265-70) discuss tenth-century Shechem.

comprise two nations. First Rehoboam (1 Kgs 12:21-24) and later Jeroboam (1 Kgs 12:26-33) challenge the validity of this arrangement. Following his retreat from the breakdown of negotiations at Shechem, Rehoboam musters 120,000 men (KG) against Israel. This attempt to contest Israel's defection is rebuffed by the man of God Shemaiah.

A. THE TEXT OF 1 KGS 12:21-24

> (21) When Rehoboam entered[A] Jerusalem, he assembled [B]the house[C] of Judah and Benjamin,[B] 120,000[D] picked soldiers of war, to fight with Israel to return the kingdom[E] to Rehoboam, son of Solomon. (22) And the word of YHWH[F] came to Shemaiah, the man of God, saying, (23) "Speak to Rehoboam,[G] king of Judah and to [H]all the house of Judah and Benjamin[H] [I]and to the rest of the people[I] saying: (24) 'Thus says YHWH: You must not go up and fight with your kinsmen.[J] Return each one to his home, because I have caused this thing to happen.'" And they listened to the word of YHWH and returned[KL] [M]according to the word of YHWH.[M]

Notes

A) So the *Qere*, CM, and the versions. The *Kethib* reads ויבאו.

B) CM omits כל (of KM) before בית יהודה and את-שבט before בנימן. I follow CM (*lectio brevior*).

C) Reading with KM. KG reads *την συναγωγην*.

D) Reading with KG^{B}. KM and CM have 180,000.

E) Following CM's הממלכה and not KM's המלוכה (*lectio facilior*).

F) I am following KG and CM (יהוה), rather than KM's אלהים.

G) Reading with 3 Rgns 12:24y (*lectio brevior*). KM and CM add explicating בן-שלמה, "son of Solomon."

H-H) The witnesses to Kings and Chronicles diverge here: 1 Kgs 12:23: כל בית יהודה ובנימן; 3 Rgns 12:24y: כל בית יהודה ובנימן; 2 Chr 11:3 (CM): כל ישׂראל ביהודה ובנימן; 2 Chr 11:3 (CG^{AB}): כל יהודה ובנימן. With the exception of CM 2 Chr 11:3, the formulation of which is problematic (Knoppers 1990:424), these readings may simply be ancient variants.

I-I) Reading with 3 Rgns 12:24y. 1 Kgs 12:23 lacks אל, whereas 2 Chr 11:3 lacks the entire locution, ואל יתר העם. At first glance this expression appears expansionary, but ואל יתר העם may have disappeared from the Chronicler's *Vorlage* by haplography through *homoioarkton* (ואל to ואל). Hence, the phrase should be retained.

J) Reading with 2 Chr 11:4. 1 Kgs 12:23 adds בני־ישׂראל, an explicating plus.

K) KG reads *και κατεπαυσαν* (= וישׁבו or וישׁבתו?), while 3 Rgns 12:24z reads the rare *και ανεσχον*, the *Vorlage* of which is unclear (Hatch and Redpath 1897:87). Both Greek texts may be trying to communicate the perceived sense of a peculiar Hebrew idiom (n. L).

L) 2 Chr 11:4 reads וישׁבו מלכת (the *lectio facilior*); however, KM's וישׁבו ללכת (the *lectio difficilior*) is probably the more primitive reading. The same phrase appears in KM 1 Kgs 13:17, לא־תשׁוב ללכת, "you shall not return."

M-M) For כדבר יהוה (KM and 3 Rgns 12:24z), CM has אל־ירבעם.

B. THE COMPOSITION OF 1 KGS 12:21-24

The pericope recording Rehoboam's aborted designs on recovering the united monarchy is also found in the supplement (3 Rgns 12:24x-z).[3] The supplement provides, however, more background information. 3 Rgns 12:24x describes Rehoboam mustering his troops to fight against Jeroboam at Shechem. This provides an explicit rationale for Jeroboam's fortifying Shechem (1 Kgs 12:25). 3 Rgns 12:24x also depicts Rehoboam undertaking this expedition "at the beginning of the year."

Most commentators believe that 1 Kgs 12:21-24 is a late addition to the Deuteronomistic History, even though the passage appears in both the MT and in the supplement.[4] A few commentators disagree, but provide surprisingly little, if any, defense for their views.[5] Grønbaek (1965:423) and Trebolle (1980:122-25,164) present a mediating position. They argue that v 21 has links to v 25 and is therefore integral to the composition. In my judgment, 1 Kgs 12:21-24 is a unit inserted and shaped by the Deuteronomist. Since my view is that of the minority, I will argue my position in two stages. I will begin by explaining why the arguments for 1 Kgs 12:21-24 being a

---

3 Trebolle argues that 3 Rgns 12:24x-z was the last section added to the supplement (1980:148-49, 183).

4 Burney (1920:173); Campbell (1986:189); Debus (1967:34); Dietrich (1972:114); Jepsen (1956:102); Jones (1984:248, 254-55); Kittel (1900:105); Noth (1968:279-80); Vanoni (1984:53, 189-94); Würthwein (1977:160-61).

5 See, for instance, Montgomery (1951:251) and De Vries (1985:158). An exception is Nielsen, whose discussion of this text is extensive (1959:202-205). A late dating of this passage for Nielsen means ascribing it to the Deuteronomist (1959:208). Gray believes that the passage could stem from either the preexilic or the exilic Deuteronomist (1970:308-309). Cohn (1985b) and Walsh (1989) include this text in their literary analyses of 1 Kings 12, but do not discuss traditio-historical issues.

late insertion are inadequate. I will then provide evidence for viewing the pericope as an integral part of the deuteronomistic presentation.

Rehoboam's entrance (ויבא [*Qere*]) into Jerusalem (1 Kgs 12:21) is often cited as duplicating Rehoboam's flight to Jerusalem in 1 Kgs 12:18. But it is more likely that 1 Kgs 12:21 resumes the story of Rehoboam's flight.[6] References to "the house of Judah" (1 Kgs 12:21, 23) and to "the house of Israel" (1 Kgs 12:21) are not marks of lateness (contra Nielsen 1959:204). Quite the opposite may be true. The Deuteronomistic History sometimes downplays tribal distinctions in favor of a North/South typology. Other texts within this history also mention the house of Judah or the house of Israel. For instance, David first becomes king when the men of Judah anoint him over "the house of Judah" (2 Sam 2:4).[7] It is the Chronicler, not the Deuteronomist, as Japhet points out, who consistently presents a much more tribal understanding of "Israel" (1989:291-94).

The reference to "Benjamin" (KG, CM) or to "the tribe of Benjamin" (KM) in 1 Kgs 12:21 is unusual, but need not be late.[8] Judahite-Benjaminite relations are a preexilic, exilic, and postexilic

---

6 Frisch (1988:466). The use of ויבא is circumstantial (NJPS): "When Rehoboam entered Jerusalem, he assembled...."

7 See also 2 Sam 2:7, 10, 11. References to the "house of Israel" include 1 Sam 7:2, 3; 2 Sam 1:12; 6:5, 15; 12:8, 16:3, and 1 Kgs 20:31. There is also one reference to "the house of Benjamin" (2 Sam 3:19). As we have seen in vol. 1, both the MT and the supplement mention Jeroboam's appointment over "the house of Joseph" (1 Kgs 11:28; 3 Rgns 12:24b). Herrmann discusses the institutional role of "the house of Judah" and "the house of Israel" in the constitution of the Davidic state (1984:269-71).

8 Contra Kittel (1900:105), Noth (1968:279), and Würthwein (1977:161). See note B above.

issue (Bright 1981:235; Donner 1977:391, 476-77). Nor does the reference to Benjamin represent an attempt, overtly at least, to solve the twelve tribes, ten tribes, one tribe conundrum of 1 Kgs 11:13, 31-38.[9] Instead, the phrase, "the house of Judah, Benjamin, and the rest of the people" implies completeness (1 Kgs 12:23).[10] The later mention of Jeroboam and Rehoboam being continually at war (1 Kgs 14:30//15:6 [KM]) is a problem in and of itself, because the deuteronomistic treatment of Rehoboam and Jeroboam (1 Kings 12:1-14:29) does not mention any such wars.[11] That Rehoboam refrained from hostilities immediately following the division, therefore, does not present any special contextual difficulties.

Probably the strongest biblical evidence for dating this pericope late is the appearance of the name שׁמעיה. Noth notes that the name Shemaiah is popular in the postexilic period and suggests that its use in 1 Kgs 12:21-24 implies a late date for this pericope (1968:280). Yet the name is not restricted to postexilic texts. It occurs in preexilic and exilic biblical texts (Jer 26:20; 29:24, 31, 32; 36:12). The name שׁמעיהו (or שׁמעיה) is also very common on preexilic Hebrew bullae

---

9 If the reference was an interpretation of, or resolution to, the twelve tribe problem, one would expect the text to say, "the tribe of Judah and the tribe of Benjamin."

10 Contra Grønbaek (1965). Noth (1930) notes the twelve tribe system presupposed by 2 Sam 19:44. If so, the description is typological ($10 + 1 \neq 12$). Kallai (1978:256-57) recognizes the schematic use of Judah and Israel elsewhere in Samuel-Kings, but contends that 1 Kgs 12:21 presents a historically accurate picture of the people and territory under Rehoboam's control.

11 That 1 Kgs 14:30 is often interpreted as referring to razzias (e.g., Noth 1968:280) underscores the problem. Chronicles does, of course, offer an instance of a civil war (2 Chr 13:2-20), but the combatants are Jeroboam and Abijah.

and seals (Avigad 1986:#29, 33, 38, 64, 162, 163, 179; Tigay 1986:62-63, 88). Finally, I do not see 1 Kgs 12:21-24 as manifesting "pro-Judaean and pro-David" sentiments not in keeping with the anti-Judahite tenor of much of 1 Kgs 12:1-20 (Nielsen 1959:204; Jones 1984:248). First, the postexilic period does not have any monopoly on pro-Judahite sentiment.[12] Second, inasmuch as Shemaiah's rebuke of Rehoboam is rather sharp (see below), one could make a case for an anti-Judahite *Tendenz*. In any case, one should explore how the passage, whatever its origins and *Tendenz*, functions within its context. A contrast between the reactions of Israelites and Judahites to disunion may well represent deliberate narrative strategy on the part of the Deuteronomist. Heterogeneity, and not homogeneity, may be the Deuteronomist's intent.

C. REHOBOAM'S CHALLENGE IN LITERARY CONTEXT

In my judgment, Grønbaek and Trebolle are right to see a connection between 1 Kgs 12:21 and Jeroboam's fortifications in 1 Kgs 12:25. Without the presence of at least 1 Kgs 12:21, if not the entire pericope of 1 Kgs 12:21-24, there is no clear transition from the conclusion to the assembly of Shechem, "there was none left to the house of David except the tribe of Judah alone" (1 Kgs 12:20), to Jeroboam's building ventures in 1 Kgs 12:25. In addition to the connection between 1 Kgs 12:21 and 1 Kgs 12:25, there are a number of other links between 1 Kgs 12:21-24 and its context. Both 1 Kgs 12:1-

---

12 Because the Deuteronomist incorporates, recontextualizes, and edits materials with a variety of ideological tendencies, it seems precarious to isolate and date any particular account on the basis of ideology alone.

20 and 1 Kgs 12:21-24 portray the northern and southern tribes as reviving institutions of the league to determine their future (Tadmor 1982:253-57; Reviv 1985:59-63). Whereas the northern tribes gather in an assembly (העדה) at Shechem to negotiate their fate, Rehoboam gathers (קהל) his people in Jerusalem to decide their fate (1 Kgs 12:20-21).[13] Rehoboam initially acts to restore the kingdom to himself (1 Kgs 12:21). Jeroboam subsequently enacts cultic innovations because of his concern that the kingdom will return to Rehoboam (1 Kgs 12:26).

The word plays on the root שׁוב in 1 Kgs 12:21, 24 resonate with the word plays on the same root in the surrounding narratives.[14] The reference to Rehoboam being the son of Solomon (1 Kgs 12:23) plays on Rehoboam's dubious distinction as the prophesied one from whom YHWH takes the kingdom. Shemaiah's reference to "the rest of the people" (1 Kgs 12:23) alludes to the earlier assertion (1 Kgs 12:17) that Rehoboam ruled over "the Israelites who lived in the cities of Judah" (contra Debus 1967:34). The continuities between 1 Kgs 12:21-24 and its context are more significant than the discontinuities. The latter can, I believe, best be explained as the result of the Deuteronomist shaping, but not effacing, his sources. 1 Kgs 12:21-24 presumes 1 Kgs 12:1-20 and forms a bridge to 1 Kgs 12:25-33. The pericope therefore comprises an integral part of the larger narrative complex depicting Jeroboam's rise and fall.

---

13 The LXX even refers to this convention as *την συναγωγην* (1 Kgs 12:21). See the above section on textual criticism.

14 See Cohn (1985b:30-31), Lemke (1976:310-12), Walsh (1989:361-63), and below.

D. SHEMAIAH'S RATIFICATION OF DISUNION

If 1 Kgs 12:21-24 originally stems from a pro-Judahite source, the placement of this pericope within 1 Kings 12 serves a dramatically different purpose. Despite experiencing rejection by the northern representatives, witnessing the stoning of his chief of forced labor, and narrowly escaping with his own life, Rehoboam does not accept failure. Upon his arrival in Jerusalem, he convenes his own assembly, a martial counter-assembly to the political assembly at Shechem (1 Kgs 12:21).[15] From Rehoboam's point of view, he, the son of Solomon, has a right to restore the kingdom (להשיב את-המלכה) to himself (1 Kgs 12:21).[16] But, from a deuteronomistic standpoint, Rehoboam's status as the son of Solomon is a dubious distinction. His reign is the divinely appointed occasion for disunion and his patrimony includes only one tribe (1 Kgs 11:12, 31-36; 12:15, 20). Hence, YHWH's commissioning formula for Shemaiah is pointedly addressed to "Rehoboam, king of Judah" (1 Kgs 12:23).

To appreciate the significance of Shemaiah's rebuke of Rehoboam, one has to distinguish between what the reader knows and what Rehoboam does or does not know. Shemaiah's oracle restates to Rehoboam what Solomon (1 Kgs 11:11-13), Ahijah (1 Kgs 11:29-38), Jeroboam (1 Kgs 11:29-38), and readers already comprehend, that the

---

15 Hölscher points out that the verb קהל also has martial overtones in Josh 22:12; Judg 20:1; 2 Sam 20:14; 2 Chr 20:26 (1923:182-83).

16 The Chronicler also plays on Rehoboam's status as the son of Solomon. His point is, however, completely different from that of the Deuteronomist (2 Chr 13:4-8). For the Chronicler, Rehoboam's Davidic pedigree precludes Jeroboam from having any right to a separate kingdom (Knoppers 1990:437-39).

division explicitly conforms to divine will. In the context of coverage focused upon the northern kingdom, Shemaiah's prohibition not only attests to the validity of the secession, it also defends it. In returning home Rehoboam concedes this divinely sanctioned state of affairs.

Conclusions

The source for 1 Kgs 12:1-20* may stem from a completely different tradition than the source for 1 Kgs 12:21-24. If so, the Deuteronomist exploits the *Tendenz* of each source by juxtaposing them. The Deuteronomist's inclusion and shaping of these episodes evinces logic. In deuteronomistic perspective, events in the North (1 Kgs 12:1-20) and the South (1 Kgs 12:21-24) converge in securing Israel's secession. Israel and Judah now comprise two related, but distinct nations (1 Kgs 12:24). Because Rehoboam and his people obey the prophetic word by dispersing and returning home, the conditions under which Jeroboam can work toward the realization of the dynastic promises made to him in 1 Kgs 11:37-38 have been guaranteed. Rehoboam's designs on a reunited kingdom have been thwarted and Jeroboam, in turn, is free to devote his attention to consolidating his rule and governing his new realm.

II. THE CULTIC SECESSION OF JEROBOAM

Like Rehoboam before him, Jeroboam attempts to subvert an arrangement in which Israel is to be politically, but not cultically, detached from Judah. Rehoboam sought political reunification, but Jeroboam's concerns are different. Jeroboam fears political reunification because of the cultic unity extant in Judah and Israel.

A. THE TEXT OF 1 KGS 12:26-33

(26) And Jeroboam said in his heart, "Now[A] the kingdom will revert to the house of David. (27) If this people go up to offer sacrifices[B] in the house of YHWH in Jerusalem, then the heart of the people[C] will return to their lord,[D] Rehoboam, king of Judah.[EF] (28) After taking counsel[G] he[H] made two golden calves and said[I] to the people,[J] "You have been going up to Jerusalem long enough. Here are your gods,[K] O Israel, who brought[L] you up from the land of Egypt!" (29) And he placed one in Bethel and the other he stationed in Dan. (30) [M]And the people journeyed before the one[N] to Dan and before the other to Bethel.[N] (31) [O]Then Jeroboam established cult places[P] and appointed priests from all sectors of the people who were not of Levitic descent. (32) And Jeroboam made a feast on the fifteenth day of the eighth month, like the feast which[Q] is in Judah.[R] (33) [S]And he ascended the altar to burn incense.

Notes

A) Reading with KM, mss oa$_2$c$_2$e$_2$, and Lucifer. KG^{AB} expands to *ιδου* (*sub obeliscus* SyrH) *νυν*.

B) Reading with KM the pl. KG^{B}, KE, and Lucifer read the sing. Mss b*i*oc$_2$e$_2$ read *τας θυσιας αυτων*.

C) Reading with KG^{AB}. KM adds the explicating הזה.

D) Whereas KM has אל־אדניהם, KG expands to *προς Κυριον και κυριον αυτων*.

E) KM and KG^{B} read והרגוני ("and they will kill me"); however, a few Hebrew mss, KG^{L} (ioc$_2$e$_2$), and Lucifer lack והרגוני (n. F).

F) KM adds ושבו אל־רחבעם מלך יהודה ("and they shall return to Rehoboam, king of Judah"). But a few mss and KG^{AB} lack this phrase. As Trebolle points out (1989b:292-93), an editor has inserted והרגני ושבו אל־רחבעם מלך יהודה through *Wiederaufnahme* (from ושב אל־רחבעם מלך יהודה to ושבו אל־רחבעם מלך יהודה).

G) KG^{A} has וילך instead of KM's ויעץ. KG^{B} has both, while Lucifer reads *tunc igitur Hieroboas cogitauit*. We read with KM (*lectio brevior*).

H) KG^{AB} and KM have המלך, while Lucifer and mss boc_2e_2 have ירבעם. KG^{N} omits, while Aquila, Symmachus, Theodotion, and SyrH have המלך *sub asteriscus*. The subject is likely explicative.

I) Mss boc_2e_2 add explicating ירבעם.

J) Reading with KG (see GKC #133c). KM reads אלהם.

K) KG interprets the ambiguous אלהיך as pl (*οι*) *θεοι*.

L) Montgomery (1951:258) and others emend to the sing העלך on the grounds that Jeroboam most likely did not conceive of his actions as being polytheistic. (Cp. the formulations of this confession in Neh 9:18 [sing] and Exod 32:4 [pl], both of which refer to Aaron's calf). The versions, like the MT, read the pl. Technically אלהים is a pl formation and occasionally takes a pl attributive adj (Deut 5:23; Josh 24:19; 1 Sam 17:26, 36; Jer 10:10; 23:36; GKC #132h) or a pl vb (Gen 20:13 {in conversation with a non-Israelite}; 31:53; 35:7; 2 Sam 7:23). Three considerations suggest, however, that a pl translation is warranted. First, as Donner (1973:47) points out, the Yahwistic confession always employs the sing vb: עלה (e.g., Judg 6:13; 1 Sam 12:6; 2 Kgs 17:36; Jer 16:14; 23:7) or יצא (e.g., Exod 16:6; Deut 1:27; 6:12, 23; 7:8, 19; 1 Kgs 9:9; 2 Chr 7:22). Exod 32:4, 8 and 1 Kgs 12:28 are therefore exceptional. Second, the antecedent to אלהיך in 1 Kgs 12:28 is pl (see below). Third, the deuteronomistic castigation of Jeroboam in 1 Kgs 14:9 states: "and you made for yourself other gods" (ותעשׂה־לך אלהים אחרים). The deuteronomistic employment of אלהים אחרים clearly has a pl designation (Josh 23:16; 24:2, 16; Judg 2:12, 17, 19; 1 Kgs 11:4, 10, etc.). Hence, whatever sources the Deuteronomist may have had at his disposal, he understands אלהים as pl.

M) KM, 6QKgs, and KG^{AB} have ויהי הדבר הזה לחטאת at the beginning of v 30. Mss bioc$_2$e$_2$ have ויהי הדבר הזה לחטאת ישׂראל ("and this thing became Israel's sin"). Many commentators excise v 30a as a late gloss. The issue is complex. The standard formulation of Jeroboam's sin in 1 Kgs 13:34 (cf. 14:10; 15:29; 2 Kgs 17:22-23) is לחטאת (בית) ירבעם. Neither tradition duplicates the common idiom. Nevertheless, v 30a does seem to be intrusive. The author(s) of this phrase in the MT (and its variant in KG^{L}) may have been informed by descriptions of both the sin of Jeroboam (לחטאת בית ירבעם) and the sin of Israel (גדולה חטאה [Exod 32:21, 30]; חטא [Exod 32:31, 32, 34]; חטאתכם [Deut 9:21]).

N-N) KM and 6QKgs, which read לפני האחד עד־דן, have evidently suffered a haplography. The Old Latin and mss boc$_2$e$_2$ read *προ προσωπου της μιας εως Δαν και προ προσωπου της αλλης εις Βαιθηλ*. Jepsen (in *BHS*) and others posit a haplography by *homoioteleuton*, but this involves rearranging the order of KG^{L} and KL. I would suggest a more parsimonious solution: a haplography by *homoioarkton* (from לפני האחד עד to לפני האחד עד).

O) A reading appearing before the beginning of v 31 in KL, the margin of the SyrH and two Greek mss (gι) expands to *και ειασαν τον οικον κυριου*.

P) Reading (tentatively) בית במות of KM and KL as a composite pl (GKC #124r). My translation follows that of the NJPS. The pl of both nouns appears in KG and KV: בתי במות (cf. 1 Kgs 13:32; 2 Kgs 17:29, 32; 23:19).

Q) Reading with KM. KG adds בארץ.

R) KM and KG continue with: ויעל על-המזבח (KG אשר) כן עשׂה לזבח לעגלים אשר-עשׂה והעמיד בבית אל את-כהני הבמות אשר עשׂה ("and he ascended the altar. So he did in Bethel to sacrifice to the calves which he had made. And he installed in Bethel priests of the high places which he built"). Along with Trebolle (1989b:290), I regard v 32b as an expansion inserted through repetitive resumption (from ויעל על-המזבח in v 32b to ויעל על-המזבח at the beginning of v 33). Trebolle's text-critical observations can be strengthened by comparing the assertion in v 32b with deuteronomistic condemnations of Jeroboam. The Deuteronomists assail Jeroboam for making the golden calves at Bethel and Dan (1 Kgs 14:9; 2 Kgs 10:29) and for leading the Israelites to worship Ba'l and the host of heaven (2 Kgs 17:16). Nevertheless, they never accuse Jeroboam of sacrificing to the golden calves.[17] 1 Kgs 12:32b was likely added by a later editor.

S) KM and KG read at the beginning of 1 Kgs 12:33: ויעל על-המזבח אשר-עשׂה (KM adds בבית-אל) בחמשה עשר יום בחדש השמיני בחדש[18] אשר-בדא מלבד[19] ויעשׂ חג לבני ישראל ("and he ascended the altar on the fifteenth day of the eighth month, which he had devised alone/from his own heart. And he made the feast for the Israelites").

---

[17] I do not view 2 Kgs 17:16 as intrinsic to the first edition of the Deuteronomistic History. In the preexilic version of Kings, Ahab introduces and sponsors Ba'l worship in Israel (1 Kgs 16:30-33). 2 Kgs 17:16 is the contribution of a later Deuteronomist (chap. 3).

[18] KG reads *εν τη εορτη* (= בחג).

[19] Some Hebrew mss, the *Qere*, and the versions have a divergent reading מלבו, reflecting an orthographic confusion between *dālet* and *waw*.

As Dietrich (1972:115) demonstrates, 1 Kgs 12:33 repeats much, but not all, of 1 Kgs 12:32. In my judgment, it is quite significant that those portions of v 32 (כן עשה בבית-אל לזבח לעגלים אשר עשה והעמיד בבית אל את-כהני הבמות אשר עשה) not repeated in v 33 essentially comprise the insertion identified in note R. Hence, recognition of an insertion by repetitive resumption in v 32 (note O) elucidates, in turn, the compositional history of v 33. In my judgment, there were two successive additions made to vv 32-33, both by *Wiederaufnahme*. The first, v 33 (except ויעל על-המזבח להקטיר at the end of the verse) was inserted in v 32b following כחג אשר ביהודה. This interpolation explains the origin of Jeroboam's altar (המזבח אשר-עשה) and insists, lest anyone confuse the Judahite calendar with the Israelite calendar, that the feast Jeroboam established was his own creation (בחדש אשר-בדא מלבד). This interpolation repeats v 32a, but in inverse order.

<u>1 Kgs 12:32</u>	<u>1 Kgs 12:33</u>
1) חג	3) בחמשה עשר יום
2) בחדש השמיני	2) בחדש השמיני
3) בחמשה-עשר יום לחדש	1) חג

Yet the author of v 33 did not repeat v 32b because he did not have v 32b in his *Vorlage*. The second addition (v 32b), also introduced through repetitive resumption (starting with ויעל על-המזבח in v 32b), ridicules Jeroboam for sacrificing to his calves. The resulting text has Jeroboam ascending (but never descending!) the altar three times, a fact almost all translations (e.g., NRSV, NJPS, REB) obscure.

B. THE COMPOSITION OF 1 KGS 12:25-33

As the variants to 1 Kgs 12:25-33 indicate, the compositional history of this pivotal passage is complex. Even the limits of this text are a function of how scholars construe the relationship between textual criticism and literary criticism. The present form of 1 Kgs 12:25-33 obviously has a close connection to 1 Kgs 13:1-3, the confrontation between a Judean prophet and Jeroboam at the Bethel altar, but is the connection early or late, intrinsic to the original account or redactional? 1 Kgs 12:25 begins a new section, but critics disagree whether the section ends with v 30 (Hölscher 1952:387-89), with v 31 (Montgomery 1951:259), with v 32 (Noth 1968:268; Gray 1970:311-13; Hoffmann 1980:63), or with v 33 (Burney 1920:176).

A few scholars contend that this entire pericope is the work of one author, but their arguments are unconvincing. Burney, for instance, believes that all of vv 25-33 (except v 32b) stem from a source (1920:176-77). Given the text-critical variants to this passage and the awkward transitions and repetitions within it, this view is overly simplistic. Some scholars see no source material whatsoever in 1 Kgs 12:26-33, but, like Burney, attribute the passage to a single author -- the Deuteronomist.[20] 1 Kgs 12:25-33 is, however, surprisingly bereft of deuteronomistic style and clichés.[21] O'Brien

---

20 Hoffmann (1980:64-69); Van Seters (1981:170-74; 1983:314); McKenzie (1991:52). Debus (1967:37) ascribes v 25 to a historical notice and vv 26-32 to later Judean polemic.

21 Except for 1 Kgs 12:30a (ויהי הדבר הזה לחטאת), none of the statements in this pericope appear in standard lists of deuteronomistic phraseology (e.g., Carpenter 1902:399-408, Driver 1914:98-102, Hölscher 1914:382-84, and Weinfeld 1972:320-65).

(1989:186-87) shows that the so-called Yahwistic confession (1 Kgs 12:28) appears in a variety of biblical books and is not the property of any one movement or school. Moreover, the southern perspective evinced in vv 26-27 is not necessarily deuteronomistic (contra Hoffmann 1980:67-68). Even the presence of two or possibly three deuteronomistic phrases does not prove deuteronomistic composition of the whole (*pace* McKenzie 1991:57).

Older studies, which extend Pentateuchal source criticism into Kings (e.g., Hölscher 1952:389; Mowinckel 1935:343), assign much of this passage to E. Recent scholars employ different sigla, but also discern at least two layers in 1 Kgs 12:25-33. Most trace the core of this source minimally to vv 28-29. Noth (1968:229-72, 280) attributes v 25 to a northern annalistic source; vv 26-29, 30b, and 31-32 to pre-deuteronomistic Judahite tradition; and v 30a to post-deuteronomistic addition.[22] De Vaux attributes vv 25-29a, 30b-31, and 32a to a source and vv 29b, 30a, and 32b-33 to later insertions (1971:98-99). Similarly, Jones (1984:248, 260-61) attributes vv 26-29 to source material and vv 30-33 to later additions.

Other scholars, while agreeing that 1 Kgs 12:26-33 evinces at least two stages of editing, contend that at least one of these stages is deuteronomistic. Even though this assessment seems sound, commentators debate which verses are deuteronomistic. Gray attributes most of vv 25-32 to a source and v 33 to the Deuteronomist (1970:312). Nielsen assigns 1 Kgs 12:25, 26-27*, 28*, 29a, 30b*,

22 In his previous study, Noth assigned vv 26-31 to the prophetic cycle centered on Ahijah (1981:69-70). Given that Noth (1962:246) believes that the original author of Exodus 32 had access to this Ahijah cycle, his revised view of 1 Kgs 12:26-31 undercuts his argument for the priority of 1 Kgs 12:26-33 over Exodus 32*.

31*, and 32a to his "Shechem II tradition" and vv 27 (אל ארניהם), 30a, 31a, and 33 to deuteronomistic and Judahite redaction.[23] Dietrich ascribes vv 28-29 to a source, vv 30-32 (and vv 26-27 in their present form) to DtrH, and v 33 to a later glossator (1972:114-119, 138). Würthwein assigns vv 28a and 29 to a source, but sees v 30b as an explanatory gloss on v 29b (1977:162). Campbell (1986:90), followed in part by O'Brien, ascribes vv 25, 28a, and 29 to the Prophetic Record, vv 26-27, 32 to the Southern Document, and vv 30a, 33 to deuteronomistic authorship.[24]

I agree that deuteronomistic editing is present in this pericope, but I do not believe that the evidence warrants ascribing as much material to the Deuteronomist(s) as Nielsen and Dietrich do. On the basis of style and idiom, the following expressions are the maximum that I think can be traced to the Deuteronomist.

בית דוד
(1 Kgs 12:26; cf. 1 Sam 19:11; 2 Sam 3:1, 6; 1 Kgs 12:20).
בית במות
(1 Kgs 12:31; cf. 1 Kgs 13:32; 2 Kgs 17:29, 32; 23:19).

The contextualization of these clichés suggests that the following statements can be attributed to the Deuteronomist.

עתה תשׁוב הממלכה לבית דוד	(1 Kgs 12:26)
ויעשׂ את־בית במות	(1 Kgs 12:31)

23 Nielsen also believes this deuteronomistic editor was responsible for rearranging v 32 into its present form (1959:207-208).

24 O'Brien contends, over against Campbell, that 1 Kgs 12:31, 32b-33 belong to a later redaction of the Deuteronomistic History and that v 30a is an even later addition (1989:264).

The original text (1 Kgs 12:26-29*, 30b, 31-32a) is coherent without these additions. One can conclude that the Deuteronomist's editing in 1 Kgs 12:25-33 is light. Both additions reflect predominant concerns in the deuteronomistic typology of the divided monarchy.

C. THE LITERARY STRUCTURE OF 1 KGS 12:26-33

An examination of the pericope's literary framework reveals three sections of unequal length. The first (v 25) documents Jeroboam's fortifications and establishment of a royal residence. There is no commentary upon or explanation of these actions.[25] The second section (vv 26-27) provides a rationale for Jeroboam's cultic initiatives. The third and longest section (vv 28-33) highlights five major royal actions.[26]

A) ויעש שני עגלי זהב (v 28)

---

25 Some historians see Jeroboam's actions as a defensive response to the invasion of Sheshonq, rather than as a response to Rehoboam's designs on recovering the united monarchy (1 Kgs 12:21-24; 14:25-26; Aharoni 1979:323-30; Gray 1970:311-12; Noth 1938:277-304; Mazar 1957:57-66; Soggin 1984:198; Kitchen 1986:298-300, 432-47). This point may be historically valid, but one should distinguish between the *bruta facta* of history and literary (re)presentation. The placement of this statement associates Jeroboam's actions with the establishment of his kingdom, rather than with a foreign invasion.

26 Hoffmann contends that the individual items in the second half of the pericope correspond to and elaborate upon their respective counterparts in the first half (1980:63-70). My presentation is indebted to his analysis. However, because of both text-critical and literary-critical factors, Hoffmann's formulation of this structure varies substantially from the one I am offering here.

B) וישׂם את-האחד בבית-אל ואת-האחד נתן בדן (v 29)
C) ויעשׂ את-בית במות (v 31)
D) ויעשׂ כהני מקצות העם (v 31)
E) ויעשׂ חג בחדשׁ השׁמיני בחמשׁה-עשׂר יום לחדשׁ (v 32)

The recurrent refrain ויעשׂ (or וישׂם) reinforces the implication that Jeroboam is responsible for all of these innovations. All of Jeroboam's actions are followed by comments on their significance.

A^1) הנה אלהיך ישׂראל העלוך מארץ מצרים (v 28)
B^1) וילכו העם לפני האחד עד בית-אל ולפני האחד עד דן (v 30)
C^1) ויעל על-המזבח הקטיר (v 33)
D^1) מקצות העם אשר לא-היו מבני לוי (v 31)
E^1) כחג אשר ביהודה (v 32)

Each comment details the nature or effects of Jeroboam's initiatives. Having portrayed Jeroboam's manufacture of the calves, the author imputes their role -- the iconography at Bethel and Dan is to lure the people away from Jerusalem. After Jeroboam stations the calves at Bethel and Dan, the people begin pilgrimages to these sites. Jeroboam appoints a priesthood, but its members are not of Levitic descent.[27] Jeroboam decrees a national festival that emulates the

[27] Given the relative lack of attention devoted to the composition of the priesthood in the Deuteronomistic History, this assertion is intriguing. Cross (1973:199) sees an older Mushite, anti-Aaronid polemic underlying the account of 1 Kgs 12:26-30 and ascribes 1 Kgs 12:31ff. to the Deuteronomist. Similarly, Weinfeld interprets the verse as anti-Aaronid polemic (1991:425). Halpern construes Jeroboam's actions as an attempt to control the Levite priesthood (1976:31-42). Allan (1974:356) suggests that Jeroboam appointed a non-Levitic priesthood, because the Levites were seen as agents of the Jerusalem government. White argues the contrary position, that

festival in Judah. Having (re)invested various cult places, Jeroboam himself ascends the Bethel altar.

D. A CULTUS MISBEGOTTEN

Historically, a cogent argument has been made that in instituting his reforms, Jeroboam attempted to out-archaize David (Wellhausen 1885:283; Cross 1973:73-74). Jeroboam's goal was undoubtedly to reorganize and preserve a cult, not to create a new one *ex nihilo*. Whether the issue is iconography (Albright 1968:43, 197-98; Debus 1967:42-47), location (Nielsen 1959:37-294, 323-46; Halpern 1988:229), priesthood, or festival (de Vaux 1971:106-107; Talmon 1958:48-74), there is good reason to believe that Jeroboam's cultus was essentially conservative, especially when contrasted with the religious innovations of David and Solomon in Jerusalem.

To this can be added a further consideration -- Jeroboam's right as king to establish and sustain various sanctuaries within his realm. Far from being innovative and impious, royal support of religious institutions was the norm throughout the ancient Near East.[28] Indeed, it has been suggested that Jeroboam established state sanctuaries at the strategic locations of Bethel and Dan to ingratiate himself with his subjects (Halpern 1988:229). A king's (re)construction of a sanctuary or palace exemplified vigor, administrative skill, and authority.

Jeroboam actually restored the Levitical priesthood (1990:149). As stated above, I do not believe that 1 Kgs 12:31 should be assigned to the hand of the Deuteronomist. The Deuteronomist's judgment on Jeroboam's sacerdotal initiatives is reflected in 1 Kgs 13:33 (chap. 3).

28 Frankfort (1948:267-74); Würthwein (1977:163-65); Clifford (1979:137-45); Gray (1985:53-62, 92-102); Hurowitz (1992:32-128).

Royal support for and restoration of sanctuaries projected an image of piety and success to present and future generations (Gray 1969:289-302; Lackenbacher 1990). The more elaborate and opulent the temple, the more likely the temple (and its royal patron) would serve as a conduit for divine blessings to the people and the land (Oppenheim 1977:95-97). Conversely, a king's neglect of cults within his own state could connote weakness, if not impiety and impotence.

The Deuteronomist's presentation of Jeroboam's cultus as anomalous is therefore itself an anomaly. The very criterion of evaluation is peculiar to the deuteronomistic construction of Israelite and Judahite history. Understanding the Deuteronomist's *Tendenz* resolves critical *cruces* in his presentation of Jeroboam's cultus. The Deuteronomist does not comment upon or criticize Jeroboam for (re)building Shechem and establishing Penuel as his royal residence (1 Kgs 12:25). In the deuteronomistic presentation, such political and martial maneuvers are completely in keeping with Jeroboam's geo-political responsibilities.[29] But if affairs of polity and security are intrinsic to Jeroboam's royal prerogatives, affairs of cult are an entirely different matter. For the Deuteronomist there could only be one central sanctuary: "the place where YHWH said he would make his name dwell," and that long hoped for sanctuary was the temple in Jerusalem.[30] In the deuteronomistic configuration of history, both Judah and Israel find blessing only through Zion.

---

[29] 1 Kgs 12:25 need not therefore be seen as a dangling historical notice without any connection to the surrounding material (*pace* Gray 1970:311-14, Montgomery 1951:254, and Noth 1968:280-81).

[30] Deut 12:21; 2 Sam 7:7-12; 1 Kgs 2:3; 3:6; 5:3-5; 6:1; 8; 9:3; 11:38, etc.

Jeroboam's decision to (re)establish sanctuaries at Bethel and Dan therefore requires rationalization. The explanation given (1 Kgs 12:26-27) does not portray Jeroboam's investiture of Bethel and Dan as reflecting any deficiency or heteropraxis on the part of the Jerusalem temple cultus. On the contrary, 1 Kgs 12:26-27 indirectly compliments the Solomonic temple. Jerusalem's allure to Israelites motivates Jeroboam to act. It is ironic that Jeroboam establishes a cult not as an act of piety, but because he doubts the durability of an arrangement in which Israel is to be politically, but not cultically, separated from Judah, an arrangement which has been repeatedly vouchsafed to him in both prophecy (1 Kgs 11:29-38) and history (1 Kgs 12:1-20). YHWH's sanctioning the political division between Israel and Judah fails to impress Jeroboam.

Jeroboam's actions appear reprehensible, given his mandate. Playing on the multivalency of שׁוב ("to turn, repent, return, restore"), the author depicts both Rehoboam and Jeroboam attempting to avoid the implications of the new *status quo* (Cohn 1985b:23-25; Frisch 1988:466-67). While Rehoboam tries to restore (שׁוב) unity to the fractured kingdom militarily and is told to return (שׁוב) home, Jeroboam is afraid that if his people return (שׁוב) to Jerusalem to sacrifice, then their hearts will also return (שׁוב) to Rehoboam.

The pericope, whatever its precise origins, serves deuteronomistic propaganda well. The passage purports to be descriptive, but its mode is caricature. 1 Kgs 12:26-33 portrays Jeroboam's cultus as a sham. In other biblical texts the trope of divine command is repeatedly employed to sanction the debut of cultic institutions. Hence, Moses' construction of the ark (Exod 25:10-22 [P]), the tent of meeting (Exod 33:7-11 [E]), and other sacred paraphernalia proceeds at divine behest and adheres to divinely ordained specifications.[31] Similarly, the Deuteronomist repeatedly engages Nathan's dynastic oracle as divine sanction for the establishment of a temple in Jerusalem (vol. 1). Not surprisingly, the Deuteronomist devotes much attention to Solomon's diligence in constructing this central shrine. No such divine impetus or human diligence appears anywhere in 1 Kgs 12:26-33. Jeroboam's actions convey anxiety (1 Kgs 12:26-27), rather than royal vigor and administrative skill.

That YHWH's name occurs only once in the cardinal passage describing the constitution of the northern cultus is revealing. Even then, the use of YHWH implicitly indicts Jeroboam. Rather than divine mandate, human anxiety motivates Jeroboam's enfranchisement of Bethel and Dan. Jeroboam's trepidations about his people's sacrificing at "the temple of YHWH in Jerusalem" assume that the Jerusalem temple is YHWH's temple (1 Kgs 12:27). Jeroboam's only reference to YHWH's name therefore reinforces the association of YHWH with Jerusalem and not with Bethel and Dan.

The only other use of a term for deity (אלהים) occurs in a noticeable deviation from Israel's historical confession. Jeroboam says of his golden calves: "Here are your gods, O Israel, who brought you up from the land of Egypt!" (1 Kgs 12:28). The import of Jeroboam's exclamation has, of course, divided scholars over the centuries.[32]

---

31 The recent debates about the dating of P need not deter us. Along with Clifford (1971), Friedman (1981a:44-136), and Cross (1981), I do not see the Priestly writer as inventing this description out of whole cloth. When the Deuteronomist wrote, he was undoubtedly aware of a variety of traditions promoting Israelite cultic objects. See the section on Solomon's dedication of the temple in vol. 1.

32 The dispute involves literary and historical issues, which are not always properly distinguished by scholars. Both historical and literary approaches are worthwhile forms of inquiry (chap. 1), but reconstructing the history of Jeroboam's cult is not tantamount to

Jeroboam's terse assertion is ambiguous. Are the calves divine pedestals for YHWH, akin to the cherubim in the Jerusalem temple?[33] Or are the calves representations of a divine attribute or deity (Bailey 1971:100-101)? If the latter, with which god(s) is Aaron's calf and Jeroboam's calves associated -- Apis (Pfeiffer 1961:75), Ba'l (Provan 1988:64), Hathor (Danelius 1967:95-114, 204-23), YHWH (Albright 1968:171-72; Donner 1973:48-50; Kaufmann 1960:270), Sin (Bailey 1971:104-15), or a deified Moses (Sasson 1968:384-87)? The author does not elaborate.

I would argue that the author obfuscates the origins and nature of Jeroboam's religion. He scorns Jeroboam's iconography, positing as much distance between it and the iconography in Jerusalem as possible. Israel's historical confession, with four notable exceptions (Exod 32:4, 8; 1 Kgs 12:28; Neh 9:18), always has YHWH as subject.[34] Moreover, the Deuteronomist indirectly acknowledges the Yahwistic nature of Jeroboam's Bethel cultus when he depicts the troubles that attend the implementation of foreign religious practices after the fall of the northern kingdom (2 Kgs 17:24-33).[35] The

---

reconstructing the portrayal of these reforms in 1 Kgs 12:26-33. My interest in this chapter is focused on the latter (the Deuteronomist's depiction of Jeroboam's sacral initiatives).

33 Albright (1948:229); Cassuto (1967:409); Cross (1973:74); de Vaux (1971:101-103); Kaufmann (1960:271); Obbink (1929:264-79), Noth (1960:233); Zevit (1985:61-62); Moore (1990:424).

34 See Donner (1973:47), Moore (1990:421-24), and the earlier section on textual criticism.

35 The association between YHWH and the golden calf is also patent in Aaron's announcement, "tomorrow shall be a feast for YHWH" (Exod 32:5).

Assyrian sponsored immigrants in Samaria are afflicted by YHWH's appointed lions, because they "did not worship YHWH...and did not know the custom of the god(s) of the land" (2 Kgs 17:24-26). The Assyrian king arranges for a priest from Samaria to be re-imported into the former northern kingdom to deal with this confusion. This priest settles in Bethel(!) and teaches these settlers how to fear YHWH (ויהי מורה אתם איך ייראו את־יהוה; 2 Kgs 17:28). The immigrants then worship YHWH as well as their own deities (2 Kgs 17:33).[36]

The omission of YHWH as subject in 1 Kgs 12:28 is therefore neither accidental nor inconsequential (*pace* Moore 1990:421-24). Historically, Jeroboam may have conceived of the calves as pedestals for YHWH. But the author depicts the calves neither as pedestals nor as divine attributes. The antecedent to אלהיך is שני עגלי זהב.[37] Hence, the antecedent, the noun, and the verb agree. The author of 1 Kgs 12:28 has Jeroboam identifying the two golden calves with the god(s) of the exodus. The significance of this correlation should not be downplayed. The cherubim sometimes enthrone YHWH (e.g., 1 Sam 4:4; 2 Sam 6:2; 2 Kgs 19:5; Ps 80:2; 99:1) and the ark occasionally functions as YHWH's footstool (e.g., Ps 132:7; 1 Chr 28:2). But never does an Israelite author equate the ark or the cherubim with deity.[38]

---

36 A later addition (vv 34-40) to 2 Kings 17 corrects this "slip" of the Deuteronomist by pronouncing that "they do not fear YHWH (אינם יראים את־יהוה) nor do they act according to the statutes, customs, torah, and commandment which YHWH commanded the sons of Jacob, whom he named Israel" (2 Kgs 17:34).

37 The deictic particle הנה at the beginning of v 28b also calls attention to שני עגלי זהב (Lambdin 1971:168-70).

38 Statements by non-Israelites are another matter. See, for instance, the remark of the Philistines in 1 Sam 4:7 concerning the arrival of the ark: "God (אלהים) has come (בא) into the camp."

1 Kgs 12:26-33 are ingenious polemic. When Jeroboam advocates that the Israelites venerate his golden calves, the inescapable implication is that Jeroboam's cult is simultaneously idolatrous and dyotheistic, if not polytheistic.[39] Yet, if the writer is familiar with the nature of iconography, why does he deliberately blur the distinction between the golden calves and the deity they enthrone or represent? Why does the author associate Jeroboam's images with idolatry and dyotheism? The claim of most scholars that 1 Kgs 12:26-33 criticize Jeroboam's cult from a Judahite perspective is well-taken, but does not go far enough. The author assumes the centrality of Jerusalem and portrays one of Jeroboam's initiatives (the festival) as an imitation of Judahite practice. Yet identifying the writer's outlook is not the same as identifying his purpose. In my judgment, the writer's critique of Jeroboam's reforms is more profound.

The pericope describing Jeroboam's (re)investiture of Bethel and Dan occupies a prominent position in the Deuteronomist's coverage of the northern kingdom, even serving as an introduction to northern history. The Deuteronomist could have devoted greater coverage to Jeroboam's fortifications (1 Kgs 12:25) or to his wars (1 Kgs 14:19), but he privileges Jeroboam's cult. The establishment (1 Kgs 12:26-33), continuation (1 Kings 13), and punishment (1 Kgs 14:7-18) of Jeroboam's sins dominate the deuteronomistic portrayal of Jeroboam's tenure. In indulging Jeroboam with this attention, the Deuteronomist concedes the antiquity and appeal of the sanctuaries at Bethel and

39 The author's play on the nature and use of cultic imagery is deft. Compare the assertion this author imputes to Jeroboam with the blunt charge the Deuteronomist imputes to Ahijah, "you [Jeroboam] have gone and made for yourself other gods" (1 Kgs 14:9).

Dan. If the tauromorphic iconography at Bethel and Dan was not popular and well-established, there would be no need to accommodate these shrines with such critical coverage. Moreover, by associating Jeroboam's calves with the god(s) of Sinai, the Deuteronomist tacitly acknowledges that the struggle between David and Jeroboam is an inner-Israelite controversy.

The Deuteronomist attempts, however, to blunt the appeal of Bethel, Dan, and the high places by depicting Jeroboam's cultic initiatives as perversions of an established orthopraxis. The Solomonic temple perpetuates, incorporates, and succeeds the Mosaic institutions of ark, sacrifice, priesthood, and festival (1 Kings 8). But Jeroboam's cultus revives and perpetuates Aaron's apostasy.[40] The cult of David and Solomon is authentic and primary; the cult of Jeroboam is counterfeit and secondary. The author goes beyond condemning the northern cultus as non-Judahite. He claims that Jeroboam's cult is fundamentally un-Israelite.

Conclusions

The differences between the depictions of the Jerusalem temple and the state sanctuaries at Bethel and Dan elucidate why Jeroboam's sins are a *Leitmotiv* in Kings. Jeroboam's establishment of a cultus is a supreme act of apostasy. The northern cultus at Bethel and Dan is founded by an Israelite and serves an Israelite clientele, yet it perverts authentic Israelite sacral rites and incorporates an alien understanding of cultic iconography. The coverage the Deuteronomist accords to the

[40] My forthcoming study of the differences between the portrayals of Aaron's calf and Jeroboam's calves in the David Noel Freedman *Festschrift* treats these matters in much greater detail.

cultic acts of Israel's first king is critical to his history of the monarchy. The Deuteronomist casts aspersions on the entire course of northern history by reifying Jeroboam's sectarian initiatives. At Mt. Sinai Moses' eradication of the golden calf removes the threat posed by Aaron's cultic innovation (Exodus 32). The threat posed by Jeroboam's revival of Aaron's innovation is, however, not removed. The sins of Jeroboam are formative. Even Jehu's reforms fail to eliminate Jeroboam's taurine images (2 Kgs 10:29). In this respect, the establishment of the Jerusalem temple and the establishment of a northern cultus are similar. Both are definitive. The effects of these state-sponsored acts are quite dissimilar. Solomon establishes his people on a firm footing, but Jeroboam imperils the future of his people. In deuteronomistic historiography, Israel can never succeed as long as Jeroboam's sins are left unaddressed. When Jeroboam's successors perpetuate his innovations, they damage their cause.

It is unlikely, given the deuteronomistic preoccupation with the adverse effects of Jeroboam's state-sponsored cult, that the description of this cult was written at a time (i.e., the Babylonian exile) when the Jerusalem temple no longer existed. The detailed coverage of Jeroboam, the invective against him, and the insistence that Jeroboam had no right to challenge the Jerusalem cultus would be most surprising were the Deuteronomist writing after Jerusalem's destruction. Temple supporters could exalt the inviolability of Jerusalem in the aftermath of the Assyrian crisis (2 Kgs 19:34; 20:6), but it would make little sense to deride Jeroboam's bull iconography, priesthood, sanctuaries, pilgrimage, and festival in the aftermath of Judah's own humiliation in 586 BCE.

The imperialism inherent in the Deuteronomist's coverage can also be best explained by recognizing that the Deuteronomist is waging a preexilic battle. The implication that the temple has a claim to the allegiance of all twelve tribes makes the most sense in the context of the late eighth-seventh centuries BCE, that is, after the northern kingdom had already fallen. In the dialectic between Jeroboam's sins and the Jerusalem cultus -- so central to the deuteronomistic construction of monarchical history -- there can be no synthesis. The very depiction of Jeroboam's sins points toward the continuing relevance of the Jerusalem temple for all who would associate themselves with the name Israel. That history is unkind to the northern kingdom is not surprising. The Deuteronomist structures the course of the dual monarchies so that the Jerusalem temple wins vindication at the expense of Israel's demise.

CHAPTER 3

JEROBOAM, PROPHECY, AND JOSIAH

Prognostics do not always prove prophecies,--
at least the wisest prophets make sure of the event first.
(Horace Walpole, *Letters, To Thomas Walpole*,
19 February, 1785.)

Introduction

The description of Jeroboam's cultus in 1 Kgs 12:26-33 forms the basis of the Deuteronomist's denunciations of Jeroboam. Consistent with his derivation of political events from royal cultic policy, the Deuteronomist addresses the implications of Jeroboam's sacral initiatives in two successive stages: the prospects for this new cult (1 Kings 13) and the impact of this cult upon Jeroboam's kingdom (1 Kings 14). Dtr[1] condemns Jeroboam for his influential "sins" and pays little attention to his personality. It therefore seems unlikely that an original diatribe against Jeroboam has been replaced by the present narrative of 1 Kings 13 (*pace* Würthwein 1973:183). From the perspective of the Deuteronomist, the fate of Jeroboam (1 Kgs 14:1-18) is secondary to the fate of the cultus he founded (1 Kgs 13:1-34).

But if the Deuteronomist is concerned with the prospects for Jeroboam's cult, why would he include the prophetic narratives in 1

Kings 13? What possible advantage does such inclusion hold for his history? Equally fascinating, in my view, are the recontextualization of and commentary upon these legends at the beginning and end of 1 Kings 13. Is this editorialization incidental and ancillary to the legends or does it develop motifs within them in new ways? I advocate the latter interpretation. The Deuteronomist plays on the series of sudden reversals depicted within his sources to underscore the ultimate demise of the Bethel sanctuary. No sooner has Jeroboam established the cults at Bethel and Dan then he witnesses both a prophetic repudiation of the Bethel cultus and a prophetic pledge of Josianic retribution. The Deuteronomist embellishes older prophetic legends with a view to the larger aims of his work.

The Deuteronomist's attention to redressing Jeroboam's sin is narrowly construed, involving neither the fate of the cultus at Dan nor the golden calves themselves. Instead, the Deuteronomist targets the Bethel altar, the high places, and their illegitimate priests. By narrowing the issue, he establishes a continuity in northern religious practice, despite Israel's exile, extending to the time of Josiah (Halpern 1988:249-50). The triumph of the divine word in the lives of southern and northern prophets points toward the triumph of the divine word in the reign of Josiah. The mention of Josiah in 1 Kgs 13:2 unifies the history of the divided monarchy, bracketing the beginning and the end of an independent northern cultus.

I. TRADITION HISTORY AND TEXTUAL CRITICISM

Two major views dominate the traditio-historical discussion of 1 Kings 13. Some scholars contend that most or all of 1 Kings 13 is a secondary insertion into Kings.[1] Most scholars argue the contrary position, that the prophetic legends within 1 Kings 13 were inserted by the Deuteronomist.[2] Two features of 1 Kings 12-13 dominate the debate. First, the closing verses of 1 Kings 12 and 1 Kings 13 parallel each other. Second, there is another parallel within 1 Kings 13. Beginning with a declamation concerning the Bethel altar by a southern prophet (vv 1-3), the story embedded in 1 Kings 13 ends with a northern prophet's commentary on the southern prophet's prophecy (v 32). Scholars disagree whether one or both of these parallels are deuteronomistic. To focus the discussion, I will concentrate on the opening and the closing verses of 1 Kings 13.

A. THE TEXT OF 1 KGS 13:1-3

> (1) And behold a man of God from Judah came by the word of YHWH[A] to Bethel, while Jeroboam was standing by the altar[B] to sacrifice. (2) He proclaimed against the altar, "Altar, altar,[C] thus says YHWH, behold a man shall be born to the house of David, Josiah by name, and he shall sacrifice upon you the priests of the high places, those who burn incense upon you, and he shall burn[D] upon you human bones. (3) And[E] this is the

---

1 Wellhausen (1885:283); Eissfeldt (1965:290); Debus (1967:35); Provan (1988:81); McKenzie (1991:55). For Lemke (1976:301-26) and O'Brien (1989:187) the addition is by a later Deuteronomist.

2 Burney (1920:179); Campbell (1986:90-91); Crenshaw (1971:43); de Vaux (1971:109); Dietrich (1972:120); Dozeman (1982:380); Eynikel (1990:236); Gray (1963:294); Gressmann (1921:247); Gross (1979:106); Klopfenstein (1966:652); Long (1984:143-52); Montgomery (1951:259); Nielsen (1959:207-208); Noth (1968:294-95); Plein (1966:17); Simon (1976:100-101); Wilson (1980:188); Würthwein (1973:166-72).

sign[F] YHWH[G] has decreed: behold, the altar shall be split and the fat which[H] is upon it will be poured out."

Notes

A) Reading with KM and KG. KS adds שׁמע דבר יהוה, which is probably an explicating plus. Although one cannot rule out the possibility of a haplography by *homoioteleuton* (from דבר יהוה to דבר יהוה), the Syriac reading is redundant.
B) KM, KG^{B}, read המזבח, whereas boc$_2$e$_2$ have the genitive *του θυσιαστηριου*. KG^{AN}, the Armenian, and the SyrH add *αυτου*. However, this addition is *sub obeliscus* in the SyrH. We read with KM and KG^{B} (*lectio brevior*).
C) Reading with KG^{B}. KM and KG^{A} add explicating ויאמר.
D) Reading the sing with KG and KS. KM has the pl ישׂרפו.
E) I am omitting most of 1 Kgs 13:3a (ונתן ביום ההוא מופת לאמר, "and he shall give on that day a sign, saying"). Although the *waw copulativum* occasionally occurs in preexilic narratives (Spieckermann 1982:130), its use in v 3 (ונתן) is problematic. Haupt proposes to repoint נתן as an infinitive absolute (quoted in Stade and Schwally [1904:131-32]; GKC #113z). But I favor excising almost all of v 3a (נתן ביום ההוא מופת לאמר) as a gloss, which attempts to harmonize the prophecy of vv 2-3 with the actions of Josiah in 2 Kgs 23:15, 17. The author of v 3a has the man of God explicitly predict Josiah's destruction of the Bethel altar. This interpolation (v 3a) only succeeds in confusing the text, because 1 Kgs 13:5 marks the fulfillment of the sign (v 3b). I follow many scholars (e.g., Noth 1968:292-93; Simon 1976:88; de Vaux 1971:109; Dozeman 1982:383; cf. Dietrich 1972:118), who see (at least) v 3a as a late insertion into the text. My

proposed emendation (וזה המופת אשר...) is informed by a passage depicting a similar prophecy/sign sequence: 2 Kgs 19:29, וזה-לך האות אכול השנה (cf. 2 Kgs 20:9).

F) KM reads המופת, whereas KG[BL] read *το ρημα* (= הדבר). We retain the reading of KM. KG[BL] may represent an assimilation toward the recurrence of דבר in this chapter.

G) Reading with KM and KG[L]. KG[B] explicates, λεγων (= לאמר).

H) Reading with KM and KG[B]. The plus of ms b, KL, Theodotion, and Lucifer (*ουσα*) may be an attempt to render the perceived sense of the Hebrew.

B. THE TEXT OF 1 KGS 13:31-34

> (31) And after he [the prophet from Bethel] had buried him[A], he said to his sons, "When I die, bury me in the grave[B] in which the man of God is buried. Next to his bones, rest my bones.[C] (32) Indeed, this word shall surely occur, which he [the man of God from Judah] proclaimed by the word of YHWH against the altar which is in Bethel and against[D] the shrines of the high places which are in[E] Samaria." (33) [F]After this event Jeroboam did not turn from his evil way, but again made priests of the high places from all sectors of the people; whosoever desired [G]he consecrated a priest of the high places. And this[H] thing became a sin to the house of Jeroboam to efface (it) and destroy (it) from the face of the earth.

Notes

A) I am following KM, קבר אתו. KG[B] and KV read *το κοψασθαι αυτον* (=ספדו לו).

B) I am following KM (בקבר). KGB adds specifying *τουτω*.

C) Reading with KM (*Lectio brevior praeferenda est*). KG adds, *ινα σωθωσι τα οστα μου μετα των οστων αυτου*, an explication modelled after 2 Kgs 23:18.
D) Reading with KG^B. KM adds explicative כל.
E) Reading with KG^B (maximum differentiation). KM assimilates to the full expression, בערי שמרון, in 2 Kgs 17:24, 26; 23:19.
F) I am following KM. Both KG and KS add the copula.
G) Reading with KM. KG and KS add the copula.
H) In 1 Kgs 13:34 I am reading הדבר הזה with KG and KS rather than KM's anomalous בדבר הזה (cf. 1 Kgs 12:30). KM may represent an assimilation toward the recurring בדבר in 1 Kgs 13:1, 2, 5, 9, 17, 18, 32.

II. THE COMPOSITION OF 1 KINGS 13

Even some of those scholars (e.g., McKenzie 1991:55) who see 1 Kings 13 as a late addition acknowledge that there is a long and complex history to the prophetic traditions preserved in 1 Kings 13. Not surprisingly, pundits have presented a wide range of reconstructions.[3] I will concentrate my attention upon the reuse of these older traditions in 1 Kings 13. Two related issues dominate the compositional debate about 1 Kings 13. First, scholars debate the date of the language used in 1 Kings 13. Second, commentators disagree whether the repetition between the final verses of 1 Kings 12 and 13 indicate that 1 Kings 13

---

[3] One issue centers on whether the two sections (vv 1-10 and vv 11-32) represent one or more originally distinct works. Another involves the nature and extent of the narrative underlying vv 1-10 (Eynikel 1990:229-37; Gross 1979:102-106; Jepsen 1971:171-82; Noth 1968:292; Würthwein 1973:168-72).

is an insertion by a Deuteronomist or by a later editor. Definitions of the intrusion vary. Some view 1 Kgs 13:33 as resuming 1 Kgs 12:31[4] or 1 Kgs 12:32.[5] Others view 1 Kgs 13:34 as a resumption of 1 Kgs 12:30[6] or 1 Kgs 12:31.[7]

A. 1 KINGS 13: A LATE INSERTION?

I view the arguments for dating 1 Kings 13 late on the basis of language as weak (*pace* Rofé 1974:163). The occurrence of a few words (e.g., מתת instead of מַשְׂאת, סעדה instead of סעד לב) allegedly characteristic of late biblical Hebrew is insufficient to prove that the narrative is late.[8] Some of the cited expressions (e.g., דבר יהוה as a source of prophetic inspiration) appear in a variety of biblical sources and do not comprise evidence for a late date.[9] More important, argu-

4 Plein (1966:17); Jones (1984:262). Eissfeldt (1965:290) equivocates, seeing 1 Kgs 13:33 (34) as resuming 1 Kgs 12:31.

5 Those scholars who contend that 1 Kgs 13:33 echoes 1 Kgs 12:32 include Campbell (1986:90-91), Debus (1967:36), Dietrich (1972:115-16, 138), McKenzie (1991:52), Noth (1968:295), and Seebass (1967/68:169).

6 Hölscher (1923:183); Jepsen (1956:6); Lemke (1976:305). Provan (1988:81) views all of 1 Kgs 12:31-13:34 as intrusive.

7 Crenshaw (1971:41); Lemke (1976:305, 326).

8 The use of the impv of סעד without the object לב is characteristic of rabbinic Hebrew (Rofé 1974:163), but 1 Kgs 13:7 is the only biblical example of this use. It therefore seems precarious to generalize that this form is typical of Late Biblical Hebrew.

9 2 Sam 7:4; 1 Kgs 16:1; 17:2, 8; 18:31; 19:9; 21:17, 28; Jer 1:2, 4, 11; 2:1, 13; 8:16; Ezek 3:16; 6:1, etc.

ments for late dating on the basis of a few words or phrases are simply inadequate to make the larger case.[10]

In my view, at least part of 1 Kgs 13:1-2[11] and part of 1 Kgs 13:32 (ועל כל-בתי הבמות אשר בשמרון) are deuteronomistic. More important, I would argue both that all of 1 Kgs 13:33-34 are editorial and that the editor responsible for these additions is the Deuteronomist. Three considerations lead to this conclusion. First, the literary technique of inverting a quotation (Zeidel's Law) is employed to frame the narrative of 1 Kings 13. The citation of Jeroboam's sacerdotal innovations (1 Kgs 12:31) in 1 Kgs 13:33 basically appears in reverse order.

<u>1 Kgs 12:31</u>	<u>1 Kgs 13:33</u>
ויעשׂ את-בית במות	וישׁב ויעשׂ מקצות העם
ויעשׂ כהנים מקצות העם	כהני במות

A comparison between the two readings suggests, however, that the author of 1 Kgs 13:33 does not simply duplicate his source. He also interprets it. The use of וישׁב initially signals that Jeroboam is repeating an earlier action. But the source (1 Kgs 12:31) does not

10 Such a hypothesis, to be convincing, would have to include a more extensive analysis of lexicon, orthography, morphology, and syntax (e.g., Kropat 1909, Polzin 1976, and Rooker 1990).

11 In 1 Kgs 13:1 the connections with 1 Kgs 12:26-33 (e.g., והנה, וירבעם עמד על-המזבח להקטיר) are most probably deuteronomistic. As Gross (1979:100-101) notes, the beginning of 1 Kings 13 presupposes grammatically (והנה) and thematically the events of 1 Kgs 12:28-33. Hence, the original beginning of the prophetic narratives can no longer be recovered. In 1 Kgs 13:2 the mention of Josiah and the references to the priests of the high places are obviously deuteronomistic.

explicitly state that Jeroboam appoints priests for the high places (כהני במות; 1 Kgs 13:33). Hence, even as the author cites 1 Kgs 12:31, he alters the force of his source. Moreover, 1 Kgs 12:31 has Jeroboam appointing non-Levitic priests, but the assertion of 1 Kgs 13:33 is more sweeping. There Jeroboam democratizes the priesthood, consecrating any interested parties as priests of the high places.[12] The Deuteronomist, as opposed to his source, faults Jeroboam for exercising no discrimination whatsoever in sacerdotal affairs.[13]

It is, therefore, highly unlikely that one author is responsible for both lemmata. Indeed, inverted quotations (Zeidel's Law) customarily indicate a writer quoting earlier tradition, rather than an author quoting his own composition.[14] Who, then, is this writer? The diction in 1 Kgs 13:33-34 provides a second indication of deutero-

---

12 The pro-Levitical stance of the deuteronomic writers (Nielsen 1959:267-71; von Rad 1953:66-67; Emerton 1962:129-38) should not be confused with the stance of the Deuteronomist. On the history of competition between priestly houses in ancient Israel, see Cross (1973:195-215) and Olyan (1982:177-93). Nelson points out that the Deuteronomist shows no real interest in priestly matters, except when he wishes to make a larger theological point (1989:132-47).

13 This is basically how the Chronicler, citing this deuteronomistic tradition, expounds Jeroboam's maneuver in King Abijah's speech to Jeroboam and Israel: "Have you not cast out the priests of YHWH, the sons of Aaron and the Levites, and appointed for yourselves priests like the peoples of the lands? Anyone who consecrates himself with a young bull and seven rams becomes a priest of no-gods" (2 Chr 13:9). Note, however, that the Chronicler has Jeroboam reject both Aaronids and the Levites, a claim that Dtr^1 never makes.

14 In addition to the standard treatment of Zeidel (1955-56), see the biblical examples supplied by Beentjes (1982:508-515, 521-23) and Levinson (1991). Beentjes (1982:523) points out that the very use of an inverted quotation calls attention to the content of the quotation.

nomistic editing. Unlike 1 Kgs 12:31-32, 1 Kgs 13:33-34 contain stock deuteronomistic clichés (Weinfeld 1972:347, 351).

1 Kgs 13:33:	שׁוב [אישׁ] מדרך הרעה
1 Kgs 13:34:	השׁמיד מעל פני האדמה / מעל הארץ

Third, as Lemke (1976:307-308) and Stipp (1987:403-407) observe, 1 Kings 13 includes three other expressions which are elsewhere only found in deuteronomistically authored passages.

כהני הבמות
(1 Kgs 13:2, 33; 2 Kgs 17:29, 32; 23:19).[15]
(ערי) שׁמרון
(1 Kgs 13:32; 2 Kgs 17:24, 26; 23:19).[16]
בתי הבמות
(1 Kgs 13:32; 2 Kgs 17:29, 32; 23:19).[17]

Given the deuteronomistic authorship of 2 Kgs 17:24-28 and 23:19, it seems likely that he has rewritten and supplemented 1 Kgs 13:2 and 1 Kgs 13:32. Conversely, if one contends that 1 Kings 13 is a post-deuteronomistic insertion, one has to concede that this text underwent at some stage deuteronomistic editing.[18] This is, however, a much

[15] Lemke and Stipp also cite כהני הבמות (1 Kgs 12:32), but 1 Kgs 12:32b is a probably a later addition (chap. 2).

[16] This idiom reflects a time after 722 BCE (Lemke 1976:320).

[17] Some commentators (e.g., Lemke 1976:308) would emend 1 Kgs 12:31 (from בית במות to בתי במות). De Vaux (1971:105) demurs, arguing for a translation of בית במות as "temple of the high places," that is, a sanctuary built to shelter the Bethel golden calf. I am interpreting בית במות as a composite pl (chap. 2).

[18] Or, one has to hold, as McKenzie (1991:55) does, that these verses were written by someone imitating deuteronomistic style.

more involved solution than simply admiting deuteronomistic authorship of part of 1 Kgs 13:32 and all of 1 Kgs 13:33-34.

B. THE REUSE OF PROPHETIC LEGENDS

Although I have argued that the Deuteronomist is responsible for the inclusion of 1 Kings 13 into the Jeroboam narrative, I do not believe that he has heavily edited the prophetic legends themselves (vv 1-10, 11-31).[19] There are clear indications of deuteronomistic editing at the beginning (vv 1-3) and end (vv 32-34) of 1 Kings 13, but there are few, if any, indubitable signs of deuteronomistic editing (e.g., stock expressions) in 1 Kgs 13:4-31.[20] The Deuteronomist seems to have largely integrated the prophetic legends into his narrative by rewriting their introduction (vv 1-3) and conclusion (v 32) and by adding his own commentary on their significance (vv 33-34).

---

[19] *Pace* Lemke (1976:307-309) and Halpern (1988:249-51). If the Deuteronomist did write 1 Kings 13, one would expect fewer incongruities between 1 Kgs 13:2 and 32 and between 1 Kings 13 and 2 Kgs 23:16-18. These tensions are sometimes resolved by attributing problematic verses to later editors, but I think it is more likely that most of these tensions result from the Deuteronomist's practice of editing, but not effacing, his sources (Wilson 1980:188).

[20] McKenzie (1991:53-54) observes that most of the deuteronomistic clichés which Lemke cites are found in the editorial ring around the prophetic narrative. Most of those idioms which Lemke cites within the narrative (e.g., למרות פי יהוה, לשמור את-המצוה) are found in a variety of sources and are not distinctly deuteronomistic.

Most critics agree that the present narrative, excepting some incongruities within vv 1-5, exhibits numerous indications of unity.[21] The phrase דבר יהוה recurs throughout 1 Kings 13 (vv 1, 2, 3, 5, 9, 18, 20, 32). Both the narrator and the Deuteronomist play on the roots שׁוב[22] and דרך[23]. The recitation of the divine directives to the man of God from Judah (vv 8-9, 16-17, 21-22) links major sections of the prophetic narratives. Finally, an *inclusio* (from v 2 to v 32; Van Winkle 1989:34) lends closure to the story.

III. A TALE OF TWO PROPHETS

The stories dealing with the Judahite and Bethel prophets both intrigue and confound scholars, eliciting a plethora of studies and almost as many opinions. The succession of miracles within 1 Kings 13 is unusual, even for a history which highlights the *magnalia Dei* (Halpern 1988:246). Some scholars praise the dramatic nature of 1 Kings 13. Barth, for instance, lauds 1 Kings 13 as "the richest and most comprehensive prophetic story in the Old Testament" (1957:409). Others find the story of the two prophets problematic. How one views 1 Kings 13 -- whether as profound or disturbing -- has much to do with one's view of its purpose (or lack thereof).

---

21 Some commentators would excise both the prophecy of the sign and its fulfillment (e.g., Noth 1968:292-93; Simon 1976:88; de Vaux 1971:109). I accept v 3a as a gloss, but I do not find these arguments compelling. See Dietrich (1972:117-18) and note E in the text-critical discussion of 1 Kgs 13:1-3.

22 1 Kgs 13:9, 10, 16, 17, 18, 19, 20, 22, 23, 26, 29, 33; Lemke (1976:311-12).

23 Vv 9, 10, 12, 17, 24, 25, 26, 28, 33; Dozeman (1982:382-83).

A. IS THERE A MORAL TO THE STORY?

Many scholars claim that 1 Kings 13 teaches single-minded obedience.[24] According to Dozeman (1982:392-93) and Van Winkle (1989:33), 1 Kings 13 helps a particular audience to distinguish between true and false prophecy.[25] For some the moral is quite specific. Hölscher (1923:183) and Noth (1968:300) see 1 Kings 13 as anti-northern, while Rofé sees 1 Kings 13 as anti-angelogical (1974:162-63). Finally, De Vries contends that 1 Kings 13 is a "prophetic-authorization legend" (1978:59-61).

A second group of scholars call attention to perplexing, if not contradictory, features of these narratives. Gressmann sees YHWH depicted in 1 Kings 13 as a magician, whose word is reduced to a formula (1921:248-49). Robinson states that the prophetic legends present both a mechanical sense of justice and a crude and insensitive view of God's nature (1972:162). Similarly, Würthwein asserts that the cynical nature of the present narrative leaves much to be desired (1973:185). Knierim (1971:232) and Crenshaw (1971:46) comment that 1 Kings 13 presents two equally inspired, yet conflicting oracles.

Both points of view -- to see the story as upholding a lofty moral or to critique the story as amoral -- assume that the narrative functions

---

24 Deboys (1991:210-212); Gross (1979:118-24); Lindblom (1962:64); Montgomery (1951:261); Van Winkle (1989:40); Wilson (1980:191). Deboys provides a survey of nineteeth century scholars who think likewise (1991:210-212). Lemke sees obedience as the theme of only vv 11-32 (1976:306).

25 The two options (obedience and true and false prophecy) are not mutually exclusive. Lindblom (1962:64), Wilson (1980:191), and Van Winkle (1989:33) hold to both views.

homiletically. I question this assumption. There is no doubt that 1 Kings 13 engages (dis)obedience, false prophecy, and retributive justice, but I do not see any clear evidence that the stories within 1 Kings 13 are written to advise readers on how they should distinguish between true and false prophecy or how they should lead moral lives. Nor does 1 Kings 13 seem concerned with defining justice. If there is an overarching theme in 1 Kings 13, I would agree with Simon (1976:86) and Long (1984:146-50) that it is the triumph of YHWH's word over both its subjects and its adversaries. Unlike Simon, however, I would argue that this word is intimately associated with the declamation against the Bethel altar by the man of God from Judah.[26] Whether in the foreground or in the background, this prophecy looms large in 1 Kings 13.

B. THE ENCOUNTER AT BETHEL

The Deuteronomist draws a close temporal connection between the visit of the man of God from Judah (1 Kgs 13:1-10) and the founding of the state cultus in 1 Kgs 12:25-33. There the pericope ends with Jeroboam ascending the altar he built at Bethel to burn incense (ויעל על -המזבח להקטיר). Immediately (1 Kgs 13:1), the anonymous "man of God" arrives in Bethel while Jeroboam is still standing by the altar (וירבעם עמד על-המזבח להקטיר). In a startling instance of *vaticinium ex eventu*, this seer predicts the reform of King Josiah three centuries later. As Cross (1973:279-80) observes, the prophecy reflects the

---

26 Both Simon (1976:85) and Gross (1979:107) believe that the man of God's prophecy against the Bethel altar fades from view after v 6.

hand of an overenthusiastic deuteronomistic editor, "preparing the reader for the coming climax" of the Deuteronomistic History.

As with some other prophetic oracles, a sign accompanies the prophecy, pointing toward a provisional fulfillment.[27] In this case, a sign is most felicitous, given that a span of three centuries separates the prophecy and its fulfillment. The sign is actualized when Jeroboam stretches out his hand to seize the Judahite prophet only to find his hand wither, the altar rent and desecrated (1 Kgs 13:4-5). At the hand of the Deuteronomist, the immediate fulfillment of this sign accentuates the oracle's validity and, hence, the surety of divine retribution through Josiah.

The subsequent narrative finds the king pleading with the man of God to restore his hand (1 Kgs 13:6). After being healed, the king offers the man of God both a gift and fellowship. Do the king's blandishments arise from gratitude (Dozeman 1982:384-85; Würthwein 1973:182) or from hostility (Simon 1976:88)? Or is the king attempting to disarm the prophetic threat against his altar (Noth 1968:298; Walsh 1989:360)? The king's motivations go unstated. The divine instructions the man of God recites are of some help, however, in understanding the relevance of the royal request. That the man of God is not to eat, drink, or travel by the same route by which he came (1 Kgs 13:8-9) underscores the gravity of the divine judgment against Bethel. To violate these directives would cast aspersions on the efficacy of the oracle itself. Hence, the southern prophet's rejection of the royal overture vouchsafes both his mission and his message. If the divine commands to the prophet from Judah

---

27 See, for instance, Deut 6:22; Judg 6:16-24; 2 Kgs 13:15-19; 19:29; 20:8-11; Jer 28:10-11; 51:61-64.

implicate the Bethel cultus (Simon 1976:91), the prophet's obedience to these directives punctuates his fidelity (1 Kgs 13:10).

C. THE MAN OF GOD AND THE PROPHET OF BETHEL

A summons to radical obedience does not seem to be the overall thrust of 1 Kings 13, even though the oracle and rebuff of the king (1 Kgs 13:1-10) evince the man of God's submission to his call. The old prophet from Bethel also claims to have a divine message, one that contravenes and supercedes the instructions given to the man of God from Judah.[28] Does the Bethel prophet lie to protect the Bethel altar (Jepsen 1971:178) or to protect Jeroboam (Noth 1968:300)? Is the northern prophet being hospitable (Gressmann 1921:248), or is he testing the man of God?[29] The text does not say.

In any case, the Bethel prophet's success in dissuading the man of God from fulfilling his divinely authorized mission seems to call into question the prophetic message itself.[30] From the perspective of the reader, who knows that the Bethel prophet is lying (1 Kgs 13:18), the word of the southern prophet has been undone. But the setback is only apparent. No sooner does the Judahite man of God sup with the Bethel prophet, then the disingenuous Bethel prophet receives a divine oracle reasserting the truth of the southern prophet's mission and

[28] To contend that the two do not exchange roles because the Bethel seer is an intermediary, rather than a receptor of the divine word, is to make a distinction without a difference (*contra* Gross 1979:118-19).

[29] So Dozeman (1982:392), Gray (1970:322), and Wilson (1980:190)

[30] See the discussions of Jepsen (1971:178), Klopfenstein (1966:657), and Simon (1976:92).

prophesying his death. The word of YHWH is indefatigable; the prediction is soon realized (vv 23-25*).[31]

As Barth (1957:395-96) points out, the surprising role reversals resist moralization. The southern prophet innocently disobeys one command and is consigned to death and burial in another's grave. The northern prophet lies, becomes the vehicle of divine revelation, continues to enjoy life, and secures rest for his bones by instructing his sons to bury him, when he dies, in the same grave as the Judahite prophet (1 Kgs 13:26-32). If the story offers lessons for distinguishing between true and false prophecy, they are not apparent.[32] Similarly, to claim that this story teaches the importance of following the (deuteronomic) law is unconvincing. First, there is no such deuteronomic command analogous to those the man of God receives.[33] Second, if the story counsels trenchant obedience, that

---

31 In 1 Kgs 13:23-25 I am following the reconstruction of Trebolle (1989b:293-94), who shows that 1 Kgs 13:25a is an interpolation by repetitive resumption (from והאריה עמד אצל הנבלה at the end of v 24 to ואת-האריה עמד אצל הנבלה).

32 Crenshaw (1971:47-48). Dozeman (1982:392) suggests the criteria of fulfillment, prophetic confirmation, and prophetic character, but it is unclear to me how the story communicates these values.

33 Van Winkle (1989:41) believes that מצוה can refer to the entire deuteronomic law. But, as Gross (1979:104) points out, the מצוה of 1 Kings unambiguously refers to the specific instructions the southern prophet receives from the deity. Citing the phrase למרות פי יהוה does not change the case (contra Van Winkle), because it, too, refers to the instructions the man of God abrogates (1 Kgs 13:21, 26). Van Winkle appeals to Deuteronomy 13, but this text prohibits incitement to apostasy, defined as the worship of other gods, and does not provide a criterion for dismissing the claims of the Bethel prophet.

obedience would be solipsistic, admitting no correction except, perhaps, from the celestial sphere.[34]

The role reversals manifest the triumph of the divine word. The southern prophet betrays his mission, yet bolsters it at the cost of his life (Simon 1976:112). The Bethel prophet perjures himself, yet sustains the word of YHWH by involuntarily becoming its mouthpiece. The lion, "God's obedient animal" (Gressmann 1921:243), contributes to the fulfillment of prophecy by killing the man of God and standing watch over his carcass. The fulfillment of the Bethel prophet's oracle, in turn, confirms the original message and mission of the man of God. Similarly, the Bethel prophet's desire to be buried in the same grave as the Judahite prophet (1 Kgs 12:32) evinces his confidence in the oracle the Judahite prophet proclaimed against the Bethel altar (Klopfenstein 1966:666-69). The present form and context of 1 Kings 13 therefore point toward the victory of the divine word three centuries later. Testifying to its inexorable nature, Josiah fulfills the prediction unconsciously. Josiah is initially unaware of the original prophecy and its implications (2 Kgs 23:17).

As if Josiah's actions are not remarkable enough, the Deuteronomist heightens their relevance. The Deuteronomist reworks the Bethel prophet's asseveration in his source, extending its force.[35]

1 Kgs 13:2:	ויקרא על-המזבח בדבר יהוה
1 Kgs 13:32:	כי היה יהיה הדבר אשר קרא בדבר יהוה

---

34 Rofé's argument (1974:161) that the story has an anti-angelogical force seems overly subtle. The reference to a divine messenger (מלאך) seems incidental to the larger concerns of the story.

35 In 1 Kgs 13:32 I am reading with KG (*lectio brevior*). KM expands to בערי שמרון (cf. 2 Kgs 17:26, בערי שמרון and 2 Kgs 23:19, בערי שמרון).

על-המזבח אשר בבית-אל ועל בתי הבמות
אשר בשמרון

By expanding the interdiction against the Bethel altar to include the high places, the Deuteronomist turns the original prophecy into a warrant for Josiah's desecration of every northern shrine. The deuteronomistic presentation of Josiah's reforms follows suit. Having been apprized of the prophecy against the Bethel altar, Josiah leaves the prophets' bones untouched but destroys all the northern high places (2 Kgs 23:19). Josiah realizes the prophecies of both prophets. In word and in action, in life and in death, the man of God from Judah and the prophet from Bethel ultimately testify to the same truth.

Conclusions

Whatever the original function of the prophetic traditions included in 1 Kings 13, the Deuteronomist reworks them as forewarnings to Jeroboam, accentuating the gravity of his transgressions and the certainty of divine reprisal. The Deuteronomist exploits the dramatic qualities of his source(s) to impugn both the Bethel altar and the northern high places. In deuteronomistic perspective, the highly unusual series of miracles and predictions should have made an impact on Jeroboam, yet Jeroboam responds to the judgment and sign of the man of God by first attempting to seize him (v 4) and subsequently by trying to placate him (v 7). In neither case does Jeroboam alter his policies. Nor does the death of the Judahite seer or the sober reflections of the prophet from Bethel impress Jeroboam. In this manner, Dtr^1 shapes his sources to underscore a long-range point. Whatever their shortcomings, the Judahite man of God and the northern prophet from Bethel finally concur in decrying the Bethel cultus. The demise of the man of God from Judah is a warning heeded by a scheming Bethel prophet, but not by a recalcitrant northern king.

IV. JEROBOAM, THE FALL OF ISRAEL, AND JOSIAH'S REFORM

The sequence of Jeroboam's sin (1 Kgs 12:26-33) and Jeroboam's obduracy (1 Kings 13) elucidates the deuteronomistic history of the northern kingdom. The Deuteronomist cites Jeroboam not only for refusing to return from his evil way (לא־שׁב ירבעם מדרכו הרעה), but also for compounding his transgression by continuing indiscriminately to appoint priests for the high places (וישב ויעשׂ מקצות העם כהני במות; 1 Kgs 13:33-34). Unlike Aaron and the people at Sinai who repent, Jeroboam perpetuates apostasy. Both Jeroboam's sin and his intractability become paradigmatic for the northern kingdom.[36] All

---

36 A writer who supplements Dtr^1's editorial on Israel's fall by adding 2 Kgs 17:7aβ-17 is indebted to this conception. The literary history of 2 Kings 17 is complex, as even Hoffmann (1980:137-39) concedes (cf. Albright 1964:66-67; Baena 1973:357-84; 1974a:5-29; 1974b:157-79; Brettler 1989:268-82; Cogan 1978:40-44; Gray 1970:638-50; MacDonald 1969-70:29-41; McKenzie 1991:140-42; Nelson 1981a:55-65; O'Brien 1989:210-212; Provan 1988:71; Talmon 1981:57-68; Viviano 1987:548-59). In seeing vv 7aβ-17, vv 19-20, and vv 34-40 as additions, I basically follow McKenzie (1991:140-42, 152). But I see all of v 18 and v 41 as stemming from Dtr^1 (note the operation of Zeidel's Law in v 34, הם עשׂים כמשפטים הראשׁנים and v 40, (כמשפטם הראשׁון הם עשׂים). The author of vv 7aβ-17 democratizes Jeroboam's sins, "and YHWH warned Israel and Judah by the hand of all his prophets, every seer, saying: 'Return from your evil ways (שׁובו מדרכיכם הרעים) and observe my commandments and decrees'" (2 Kgs 17:13), and applies for the first time some of Judah's sins to Israel (Tadmor and Cogan 1988:206-14).

of Jeroboam's successors perpetuate or exacerbate his influential malfeasance. The refrain, "he did evil in the sight of YHWH...he walked in the way of Jeroboam who caused Israel to sin," punctuates the deuteronomistic evaluations of most northern kings.[37] No king "turns from the sin(s) of the house of Jeroboam."[38] But what is the import of these repeated denunciations?

A. JEROBOAM'S SINS AND THE DEMISE OF ISRAEL

Following Noth, most scholars have taken the notices of royal Israelite recreancy as indicating the Deuteronomist's concern "to develop the theme of accelerating decline to the bitter end" (1981:80). Careful reading of the Deuteronomist's exposition reveals, however, that not only does the Deuteronomist document Israel's moral decline, he also laments the failure of Israelite royalty to redress the essential problems confronting their nation. Jeroboam's sin is a sufficient, but not a necessary cause of Israel's demise. Northern monarchs could have extirpated the Bethel cultus, but none did. Jeroboam's successors render Israelite history a miscarriage because of their allegiance to Jeroboam's influential sins. Commenting upon the use of the verb שוב in the Deuteronomistic History, Wolff observes that "It is not so much the total apostasy which makes judgment final as the contemptuous disregard of the call to repentance" (1975:91). The Deuteronomist's fulminations against Jeroboam culminate in his peroration on the fall of Israel.

---

[37] 1 Kgs 15:26, 34; 16:13, 19, 26, 31; 22:53; 2 Kgs 3:3; 10:31; 13:2, 11; 14:24; 15:9, 18, 24, 28.

[38] 2 Kgs 3:3; 10:29, 31; 12:4; 13:2, 6; 14:4; 15:4, 18, 35; 17:22.

> Indeed, he [YHWH] [39] tore Israel away from the house of David and they made Jeroboam son of Nebat king, but Jeroboam led Israel astray[40] from YHWH and caused them to commit a great sin. And the Israelites followed in all the sins of Jeroboam, which he committed, they did not turn away from it until YHWH turned Israel away from his presence as he said by the hand of all his servants the prophets. So he exiled Israel from his land to Assyria until this day.[41] (2 Kgs 17:21-23).

In spite of exile, there still is apparently no Israelite repentance or expurgation.[42] The Deuteronomist ends his independent coverage of the northern tribes with this long reflection; nevertheless, the severe and incessant nature of his criticism ironically reveals a continuing

---

39 I am interpreting the subject of כי־קרע ישראל in 2 Kgs 17:21 as YHWH. To see the verb as an otherwise unattested *Qal* middle voice of (מן) קרע is unnecessary (contra Brettler 1989:277-79). Whether seen from a diachronic standpoint (n. 36) or from a synchronic standpoint, the antecedent to קרע in 2 Kgs 17:21 is יהוה in 2 Kgs 17:18, 20. The discrepancy in number (the sing קרע as opposed to the pl וימליכו) also speaks against Brettler's interpretation. In 2 Kgs 17:21 the Deuteronomist conjoins his references to YHWH's sundering of the kingdom in 1 Kgs 11:11, 31 with his reference to the Israel's enthronement of Jeroboam in 1 Kgs 12:20 (וימלכיכו אתו על־כל־ישראל). See also chaps. 4-5 in vol. 1.

40 In 2 Kgs 17:21 the *Kethib* has וידא, while many Hebrew mss, KG, KS and the *Qere* have וידח. We read with the *Qere* (the verb נדח).

41 In 2 Kgs 17:23 I am reading with KM (*lectio brevior*). KG and KS explicate by adding יהוה after דבר.

42 In contrast, the Chronicler depicts northern awareness of guilt (2 Chr 28:9-15) and some northern repentance (2 Chr 30:6-11). See Japhet (1989;308-24), Williamson (1977:114-26), Dillard (1987:219-30), Throntveit (1987:113-20), and Knoppers (1989:74-88).

preoccupation with the fate of Israel. The immense literary effort involved in writing a history of the North, at least a century after the Assyrian exile, contradicts the very point Noth wishes to make. By detailing Israel's demise and tracing its cause to Jeroboam's investiture of the Bethel cultus, the Deuteronomist sustains the Bethel cultus as an object of divine concern.

B. THE PERSISTENCE OF JEROBOAM'S CULT

Paradoxically, the Assyrian exile does practically nothing to change the cultic state of affairs established by Jeroboam. The humiliation of Samaria and the deportation of Israelite leadership obviously causes profound upheaval in Israel. The Deuteronomist does not downplay the devastating effects of this defeat (2 Kgs 17:1-7a). Yet if the Assyrian exile finds the Deuteronomist stressing political discontinuity, it also finds him stressing religious continuity. Consistent with his distinction between cult and kingdom in 1 Kings 11, the Deuteronomist distinguishes between the fate of Israel's monarchy and the fate of its cult. Immediately after attributing Israel's exile to its stubborn allegiance to the sins of Jeroboam, the Deuteronomist announces that these sins prevail in radically altered circumstances (2 Kgs 17:24-33).[43]

The Assyrians effect the immigration of a number of peoples into the former northern kingdom. The worship practices of foreign settlers "in the cities of Samaria" occasion upheaval because these immigrants do not fear YHWH (2 Kgs 17:24-25). Attacks by lions,

---

[43] In assigning these verses to the Deuteronomist, I am largely following the arguments of McKenzie (1991:140-42). See n. 36.

to paraphrase Gressmann, "God's obedient animals," kill some of the new settlers (2 Kgs 17:25; cf. 1 Kgs 13:24). The king of Assyria responds to this problem by commissioning an exiled priest from Samaria "to teach them the ways of the deity of the land" (2 Kgs 17:27). But the results are at best ambiguous (2 Kgs 17:27). Like Jeroboam, the immigrants make shrines of the high places.

1 Kgs 12:31:	ויעשׂ את־בית במות
2 Kgs 17:32:	ויהיו עשׂים להם בבית הבמות

Parodying Jeroboam's heteropraxis, "each people continued making its own deities."

2 Kgs 17:29:	עשׂים גוי אלהיו
1 Kgs 12:28:	ויעשׂ שׁני עגלי זהב
1 Kgs 14:9:	ותעשׂה־לך אלהים אחרים ומסכות

The immigrants then settle their cult symbols in "the shrines of the high places which the Samarians had made." In so doing, they ensure that the widespread infidelity decried by the prophet from Bethel continues, albeit in revised form.[44]

2 Kgs 17:29:	וינחו בבית הבמות אשר עשׂו השׁמרנים גוי גוי בעריהם אשר הם ישׁבים שׁם
1 Kgs 13:32:	כי היה יהיה הדבר אשר קרא... על־המזבח אשר בבית־אל ועל כל־בתי הבמות אשר בשׁמרון

44 In 1 Kgs 13:32, I am reading with KG (*lectio brevior*), which lacks KM's ערי (in בערי שׁמרון).

The settlers learn to fear YHWH (2 Kgs 17:28). Yet, like Jeroboam, they appoint priests of the high places from their own ranks.

2 Kgs 17:32:	ויעשׂו להם מקצותם כהני במות
1 Kgs 12:31:	ויעשׂ כהנים מקצות העם
1 Kgs 13:33:	וישׁב ויעשׂ מקצות העם כהני במות

The behavior of the Assyrian-sponsored émigrés is not completely mysterious. The repatriated priest comes to reside in Bethel (2 Kgs 17:28). Whether consciously or unconsciously, the immigrants he instructs revive and perpetuate Jeroboam's sins.

The resemblances between the Samarian cult and Jeroboam's cult are too detailed and too many to be accidental. The Deuteronomist's point is clear. The Assyrian exile has no effect whatsoever on the prophecies of 1 Kings 13. In fact, the upheaval which attends the Assyrian conquest of the northern kingdom only reinvigorates the northern cultus Jeroboam founded. In the essential matters of sacerdocy, iconography, and sanctuaries, the cult which the immigrants establish is but a new version of Jeroboam's cult.

2 Kings 17 is therefore more than an epitaph for Israel (contra Noth 1981:6). The exile of Israel, as Halpern (1988:249) points out, does not bring the issue of Jeroboam's sin to a climax. Reform is no less necessary in the aftermath of the Assyrian exile than in the two preceding centuries. The cultic aftermath of Israel's fall renders the predictions of the man of God and the Bethel prophet about the Bethel cultus and the northern sanctuaries as likely as ever (1 Kgs 13:2, 32). 2 Kings 17 is not the Deuteronomist's last word on the future of the Israelite people (contra Noth 1981:80, 89). Already in narrating the reign of its first king the Deuteronomist proleptically sets the agenda both for Israel's ruin (2 Kings 17) and its salvation (2 Kings 23). In

this respect, von Rad (1966b:221) is right: the deuteronomistic presentation of cultic affairs in the northern monarchy is a triumph of the divine word. The Deuteronomist self-consciously describes Israel's religious decline as a tragedy which importunes redress.

C. JEROBOAM'S CULT AND JOSIAH'S CAMPAIGNS

In describing Jeroboam's recalcitrance, the Deuteronomist's long-range perspective is evident. Writing approximately a century after the fall of Israel, the Deuteronomist achieves two ends with his coverage of Jeroboam's obstinance. First, he distinguishes between the course of Judahite history and the course of Israelite history. The Deuteronomist composes a national history with the thesis that royal (and popular) fate is cultically derivative.[45] Assyria, much less Judah or Syria, has ultimately less to do with Israel's destiny than Jeroboam's royal sanctuaries. Given that a specific cultic issue, as opposed to a complex set of economic, political, cultural, and international factors, causes Israel's demise, those who remain are not left without any recourse. The Deuteronomistic History provides them with both a coherent explanation and a program. In the deuteronomistic schema, the Assyrian exile is, paradoxically, a manifestation of YHWH's power, exonerating his involvement in Israelite history and the standards he established for his people at disunion. The

45 Ironically, as Noth (1981:91-94) and Weinfeld (1972:190-243) point out, the Deuteronomist exhibits little interest in the details of cult: sacerdotal hierarchy, types and numbers of sacrifices, and cultic objects. Whether this amounts to "demythologization" or "secularization" is doubtful (Weinfeld 1972:190-243; 1973b:230-33; Nicholson 1991:191-203; cf. Milgrom 1973:156-61; Levinson 1991:230-33).

linkage between Jeroboam and Israel's demise therefore confirms, rather than discredits, central deuteronomistic tenets. The northern kingdom's problems were longstanding and endemic. The ill effects of Jeroboam's Bethel cultus upon the course of Israelite history absolve the Jerusalem cultus Jeroboam abandoned. Since, in fact, the destiny of Israel was contingent upon its stance toward the Jerusalem temple, the fall of Israel demonstrates the centrality of the Jerusalem temple to the destiny of all those who remain. For the descendants of Israelite émigrés in Judah and for the Judahites themselves, Israel's downfall becomes an argument for renewed commitment to YHWH and the central sanctuary he mandated and sanctioned in perpetuity.

Second, the prophecies against the Bethel cultus, the demise of the Israelite kingdom, and the persistence of Jeroboam's sins in Samaria (1 Kgs 13:1-3, 31-32; 2 Kgs 17:21-33) conspire toward a favorable assessment of Josiah's forays into the former northern kingdom. Josiah's northern crusade represents the resolution to the bane of northern existence. Considering the promising beginning which the deity afforded Jeroboam and the northern kingdom, his arch-crime mandates correction. The exclusive use of the deuteronomistic expressions "the cities of Samaria," "the shrines of the high places," and "the priests of the high places" in 1 Kings 13 and 2 Kings 17 establishes a continuing tradition of transgression. The deuteronomistic description of Josiah's reforms (2 Kgs 23:19), the only other use of these same expressions, announces the long-awaited solution. 1 Kings 13 ultimately functions as an *apologia* for the Josianic reform, elucidating his imperial program and marshalling historical support. Retribution only comes, as the man of God predicted, with the reforms of Josiah of Judah.

CHAPTER 4

THE FALL OF JEROBOAM

Ill fares the land, to hast'ning ills a prey,
Where wealth accumulates, and men decay;
Princes and lords may flourish, or may fade;
A breath can make them, as a breath has made.
(Oliver Goldsmith, *The Deserted Village*, 1.51).

Introduction

1 Kings 14 is intriguing. If the stories in 1 Kings 12 raise a variety of thematic issues and the prophetic legends in 1 Kings 13 raise a variety of ethical issues, the confrontation of Jeroboam's wife with Ahijah raises a variety of formal issues. What begins as a story dealing with a child's illness (vv 1-6), becomes a tirade against the house of Jeroboam (vv 7-11), a death sentence on Jeroboam's son (vv 12-13), a prediction of an imminent *coup d'État* (v 14), and finally a judgment of exile against the entire northern kingdom (vv 15-16).

Because of this diversity, scholars cannot agree on what 1 Kings 14 is. Debus (1967:51) and Long (1984:156) guardedly type this passage a prophetic legend. Long notes, however, that an echo of an oracular inquiry can also be discerned in 1 Kgs 14:1-18 (1984:156). De Vries (1985:177) terms the text a "succession-oracle subgenre" since Ahijah's oracle mandates the usurpation of Jeroboam's throne (1

Kgs 14:14). Cohn sees 1 Kgs 14:1-18 as an example of a pattern unique to Kings: a "deathly ill king commissions his royal messengers to seek out the prophet of Yhwh and through him to inquire whether or not he will recover from his illness" (1985a:603). Dietrich makes no attempt to type the whole (1972:10, 51-54). He sees 1 Kings 14 as a study in contrasts: an old prophetic story (1 Kgs 14:1-6, 12, 13a, 17, 18a), centering on the fate of a sick child, and a deuteronomistic threat (1 Kgs 14:7-11, 15f.) focusing on dynasty and nation. Each of these views contains an element of truth. 1 Kgs 14:1-18 incorporates legendary motifs, recounts a prophetic consultation, involves succession, and addresses the fate of dynasty and nation. One might add that 1 Kgs 14:1-18 includes three commissions (vv 2-3, 7, 12) and two judgment oracles (vv 7-11, 12-16). The narrative of 1 Kgs 14:1-18 is complex, resisting easy categorization.

In my judgment, the formal complexity of 1 Kgs 14:1-18 represents deliberate narrative strategy. I would argue that 1 Kgs 14:1-18 is a mixed genre and should be approached from several generic coordinates.[1] Although 1 Kgs 14:1-18 proceeds according to the form of a consultation story and so partially fulfills readers' expectations, the Deuteronomist challenges the assumptions of this genre. The deity intervenes through the mediation of a prophet, not to redress but to doom, confirming the bleak predicament of an individual. The complex interplay of forms yields startling results.

Formal complexity enhances thematic development. Transforming a tale about a sick child into the condemnation of an entire nation, the Deuteronomist dramatizes the sudden, but decisive reversal of political fortunes effected by the inauguration of Jeroboam's cult. The

---

[1] On mixed genres, see Lewalski (1986:2-4).

Deuteronomist's literary strategy in shaping the story of Jeroboam's sick son is therefore similar to his strategy in shaping the tale of the two prophets (1 Kings 13). In the deuteronomistic record, the remarkable reversals in the tale of two prophets adumbrate the reversal effected by Josiah's cultic reforms. In 1 Kings 14 the issue is not the upshot of Jeroboam's cult, but the consequences of this cult upon Jeroboam's lineage and realm. The Deuteronomist links Abijah's prospects to Jeroboam's dynasty and kingdom. In 1 Kings 14 the surprising death of Jeroboam's son prefigures the demise of Jeroboam's house and Israel itself.

The judgment oracles (1 Kgs 14:7-11, 12-16) embedded within this story (1 Kgs 14:1-18) are especially important. Heavily edited by the Deuteronomist, Ahijah's judgments play, in my view, an analogous role in northern history to the role 2 Samuel 7 plays in southern history. As the Deuteronomist links the fate of David, his seed, dynasty, temple, and people in 2 Sam 7:5-16, so he also links the fate of Jeroboam, his son, dynasty, cultus, and people in 1 Kgs 14:7-16.[2] The condemnation of Jeroboam and his kingdom is central to northern history in much the same way that the promises to David are central to southern history. Both promise and threat affect later kings -- for good or for ill. Like David, Jeroboam is an archetypal figure -- the benchmark for later monarchs in his realm. The story of Jeroboam is not the whole story of Israel. The northern monarchy is, of course, just beginning. Nevertheless, these prophetic speeches set the stage for the Deuteronomist's pessimistic coverage of northern

2 The passages are not completely parallel, because 2 Samuel 7 anticipates the construction of a temple, whereas 1 Kings 14 presupposes Jeroboam's establishment of state sanctuaries.

political history. The fate of the Israelite kingdom is anticipated by the fate of its first king and his kin.

Comparing the consultation stories of 3 Rgns 12:24g-nα and 1 Kings 14 with other consultation scenes, mostly in Samuel and Kings, will contextualize the KG and KM oracles denouncing Jeroboam. I will then examine what the interplay between the Davidic promises and the judgments against Jeroboam suggests about the nature and function of the Deuteronomist's program.

I. PROPHETIC CONSULTATION AND CONFRONTATION

An appreciation of the Deuteronomist's version of the consultation with Ahijah can be enhanced by comparisons with other consultation stories, including the consultation story of the supplement (3 Rgns 12:24g-nα). Olmstead observes that 3 Rgns 12:24g-nα shares affinities in style and phraseology with other prophetic legends (1913-14:30). Similarly, Trebolle compares this story with incidents in the Elijah/Elisha cycles depicting an audience with a prophet about a malady (1980:159-62). These observations merit further investigation, but neither the supplement nor KM make such a simple correlation. Long (1973:344) and Cohn (1985a:604) note that genre analysis establishes the lowest common denominator of a group of stories, but does not address dramatic variations. The narratives in the supplement and KM are highly complex, containing not only dramatic variations but also a variety of generic features. We will chart typical conventions of a consultation scene and then proceed to analyze the particular characteristics of 3 Rgns 12:24g-nα and 1 Kgs 14:1-18.[3]

---

[3] Long (1984:254-55), followed by De Vries (1985:433), speaks of an "oracular inquiry," and Long applies this term to 1 Kgs 14:1-18.

A. PROPHETIC CONSULTATIONS AS A TYPE-SCENE

Consultation stories in Kings typically center on a crisis: an illness (1 Kgs 14:1; 2 Kgs 5:1-3; 8:7; 20:1), a death (1 Kgs 17:17-18; 2 Kgs 4:18-20), abject poverty (2 Kgs 4:1), an injury (2 Kgs 1:2), a war (1 Kgs 22:1-37; 2 Kgs 3:9-27), or a siege (2 Kgs 6:24-7:20; 19:3-4).[4] The supplicant seeks an audience with a noted Yahwistic prophet whose mediation is critical: Ahijah (1 Kgs 14:1-18), Elijah (1 Kgs 17:17-24), Elisha (2 Kgs 3:11; 4:1-7, 8-37; 5:1-19; 8:7-15), or Isaiah (2 Kgs 19:1-7; 20:1-11).[5] In many prophetic consultation stories, messengers mediate between major characters (2 Kgs 1:2, 5; 4:25-26, 29, 31, 36; 5:10, 19-27; 8:8, 14; 19:2, 5).[6] Because prophets speak

---

Long (1984:156) and De Vries (1985:434) also discuss a related form: "report of an oracular inquiry." Such classifications are helpful but are too limited for my purposes. Oracular inquiries usually occur in the context of consultation narratives.

4 The story describing the discovery of the book of the law also belongs to this category of consultation stories (2 Kgs 22:8-20). The tradition history of this passage is, however, quite complex. See McKenzie (1991:111-12, 143-44) and the following chapter.

5 Ahaziah's injury (2 Kgs 1:2) is an exception which proves the rule. Because Ahaziah has recourse to the god of Ekron, rather than to the god of Israel, Elijah intervenes and condemns this monarch.

6 In some tales a prophet provides a sign (1 Sam 2:34; 1 Kgs 13:1-3; 2 Kgs 20:8-11; Isa 37:30; Westermann 1967:158-60). In others a prophet tells the supplicant to perform an action to effect or aid a resolution (1 Kgs 17:13; 2 Kgs 4:3-4; 5:10). Such signs or actions do not seem to be essential components of the consultation form.

for the deity, both divine and prophetic reputations are at stake.[7] Such stories hinge on the prophet's ability to resolve an altogether bleak situation through remedy (1 Kgs 17:20-23; 2 Kgs 4:17, 34-35; 5:14; 8:14-15!), amelioration (2 Kgs 20:6), or foretelling (1 Kgs 14:7-18; 2 Kgs 1:4, 6, 16-17; 5:10; 8:10; 19:6-7; 20:1).[8] However severe the predicament, the outcome is usually favorable to the afflicted.[9] These stories end by marking restoration (1 Kgs 17:22-23; 2 Kgs 4:35; 5:14) or fulfillment of the prophetic word (1 Kgs 14:17-18; 2 Kgs 1:17; 19:37; 20:11). An overall consistency, despite variation, establishes these consultation stories as a "type-scene."[10]

Virtually every consultation narrative includes this constellation of features, hence this genre as a frame of reference establishes a "horizon of expectations" on the part of a reader. Since 3 Rgns 12:24g-nα and 1 Kgs 14:1-18 both begin with typical conventions of consultation scenes but subsequently incorporate other forms, such as judgment oracles, I will first present an overview of each account and then discuss the significance of each prophecy.

---

7 Although this is implicit in all of these stories, it is explicit in 1 Kgs 17:17, 24; 2 Kgs 1:3, 10; 5:8, 15.

8 These are obviously not exclusive categories; a given tale can involve both a predicted cure (2 Kgs 8:10) and the fulfillment of the prophetic word (2 Kgs 8:14-15).

9 A notable exception is 2 Kgs 1:17 (see n. 5). The endings of a few other stories are complex. For instance, the story of 2 Kgs 8:7-15 ends with Ben-hadad's death and Hazael's accession.

10 The terminology stems from the work of Arend (1933), but has been popularized by Alter (1981:47-62). Cohn (1985a:605) also sees the presence of a type-scene in this narrative, but his definition (the prophetic inquiry of a dying monarch) is much more restricted than the one I am adopting here.

B. ADVISE AND CONFRONT: 3 RGNS 12:24g-nα

Strictly speaking, the story of Ahijah's confrontation with Jeroboam's wife as recorded in 1 Kgs 14:1-18 is not found in the Old Greek.[11] Instead the supplement contains a variant tradition of these events, 3 Rgns 12:24g-nα, which is considerably shorter than 1 Kgs 14:1-18. The story of 3 Rgns 12:24g-nα is an easily defined unit. Yet it, like the other pericopes in the supplement, is not set within the context of a larger unified whole. There is no evidence that an editor has attempted to integrate 3 Rgns 12:24g-nα with what precedes it (3 Rgns 12:24g-nα) or with what follows (the assembly of Shechem; 3 Rgns 12:24nβ).[12] If the supplement is read as a continuous narrative, Jeroboam's son and his dynasty are condemned to death before Jeroboam is even made king (3 Rgns 12:24t).[13] It seems best, then, to focus on the unit of 3 Rgns 12:24g-nα itself, recognizing that the supplement represents a collection of pericopes, rather than a unified and continuous narrative.[14]

3 Rgns 12:24g-nα begins much like other consultation narratives. Responding to the illness of their son, Jeroboam and his wife set out

---

[11] It has been reinserted in the Hexaplaric texts, but it is not found in KG[B]. Shenkel notes that the very omission of 1 Kgs 14:1-18 from the LXX* may help explain why the supplement survives (1968:32).

[12] McKenzie believes that 3 Rgns 12:24f and 12:24nβ form a kind of *Wiederaufnahme* (1991:35).

[13] None of the events in 1 Kings 13 are found in 3 Rgns 12:24a-z. The events which KM takes for granted in 1 Kings 14, such as the royal oracle to Jeroboam and the assembly at Shechem, obviously have not yet transpired in 3 Rgns 12:24a-f.

[14] See my earlier introduction to and commentary on the supplement in vol. 1 (chaps. 1 and 5).

to inquire of Ahijah about the prospects for their son. Kings in other consultation stories often employ intermediaries. Hence, it is not surprising that Jeroboam sends his wife to meet with Ahijah (3 Rgns 12:24g). The sending of gifts is also not uncommon in consultation stories. Naaman, for instance, brings along gifts on his visit to Elisha (2 Kgs 5:5, 15). Similarly, Ben-hadad sends along a gift with his intermediary, Hazael, for Elisha (2 Kgs 8:8). Jeroboam's wife, identified as Ano, bears assorted gifts for Ahijah and his children.[15]

Prophets sometimes employ intermediaries. In this case, Ahijah sends a servant to meet Ano upon her entry into Shiloh, invite her in, and inform her that Ahijah has "harsh" news for her (3 Rgns 12:24k). However many similarities exist between 3 Rgns 12:24g-nα and other consultation stories, the supplement departs from standard consultation form. Upon Ano's entry into his house, Ahijah does not deliver a brief oracle, offer words of solace, or impart a cure. Instead, he confronts Jeroboam's wife with an enigmatic question and two judgments (3 Rgns 12:24l-m).

C. ADVISE AND CONFRONT: 1 KGS 14:1-18

The narrative of 1 Kgs 14:1-18 is much longer than 3 Rgns 12:24g-nα and contains far more theological commentary.[16] Unlike the supplement, KM betrays the pervasive marks of deuteronomistic editing. Despite these variations in length and content, the basic storyline of the two texts is similar.

---

[15] 3 Rgns 12:24i (cf. 1 Sam 9:7-8, 1 Kgs 13:7, and 2 Kgs 20:12).

[16] I am not arguing that 3 Rgns 12:24g-nα is the most primitive version of this story. Since it incorporates several kinds -- a consultation and two judgments -- 3 Rgns 12:24g-nα could well be composite.

Comparative Outline:	14:1-18	12:24g-nα
Illness	14:1	g
Commissioning of Wife	14:2-3	g
Gifts	14:3	h
Journey	14:4	i-k
Ahijah's Messenger	---	k
Commissioning of Ahijah	14:5	---
Confrontation	14:6	l
Re-commissioning of Wife	14:7	---
First Oracle	14:7-11	l
Second Oracle	14:12-16	m
Fulfillment	14:17-18	n

As in the supplement, the crisis precipitating the desire to consult a prophet is the illness of Jeroboam's son, identified in KM as Abijah (1 Kgs 14:1). Ahijah, as Jeroboam points out, is the same prophet who earlier promised him kingship.[17] Hence, KM, unlike the supplement, provides a rationale for Jeroboam's seeking counsel with this particular prophet. Other typical conventions of a consultation scene follow. In both narratives, Jeroboam responds to the news of his boy's illness by dispatching his wife to inquire of the prophet Ahijah (3 Rgns 12:24g; 1 Kgs 14:2-3). Both accounts have Jeroboam sending along similar, although not identical, gifts for Ahijah (3 Rgns 12:24h-l; 1 Kgs 14:3-4).

Jeroboam commands his wife, however, to disguise herself so that "they will not know that you are the wife of Jeroboam" (1 Kgs 14:2). The disguise, not found in the supplement, comprises an integral component in the plot of KM, which mentions it three times (1 Kgs 14:2,

---

17 Reading the infin of the verb מלך with the preposition ל- (see KG^{o} and KS). KM has the preposition ל- and the noun מלך.

5, 6). Jeroboam wishes to find out "what will happen to the child" (1 Kgs 14:3) without Ahijah discovering the true identity of the boy's parents.[18] Jeroboam's subterfuge therefore paradoxically assumes the divinitory powers of the prophet, exclusive of an ability to discover the identity of the sender. This deception sets 1 Kgs 14:1-18 apart from 3 Rgns 12:24g-nα and from most other consultation stories because it impugns Jeroboam's integrity.[19] Moreover, the placement of this tale in KM, following the prophetic legends of 1 Kings 13, underscores Jeroboam's culpability. Jeroboam, whose only reaction to the Judahite prophet's death was to democratize the priesthood and appoint more priests to the high places (1 Kgs 13:33-34), now avoids direct contact with the very prophet who invested him.

The irony of Jeroboam's sending his disguised wife to inquire of a mantic is heightened by the observation that "Ahijah was not able to see, because his eyes had become dim with age" (1 Kgs 14:4b). Given Ahijah's blindness, a disguise is technically unnecessary.[20] YHWH's revelation to Ahijah, "the wife of Jeroboam is about to come to seek a word (לדרש דבר) from you..." (1 Kgs 14:5), is essential to Ahijah's discovering the ruse. Whereas, then, Jeroboam commissions his wife with a message, in KM the deity explicitly notifies his prophet and commissions him with a response: "such and such

[18] Cohn (1985a:607) believes that the peasant attire of Jeroboam's wife is meant to appeal to the prophet's sense of charity.

[19] Ahaziah's inquiry impugns his character (2 Kgs 1:2). Ahaziah does not, however, deceive Elijah; he simply has recourse to a foreign deity (Begg 1985b:75-86).

[20] 1 Kgs 14:4; 3 Rgns 12:24i. The motif is not superfluous in KM. There is no indication at the beginning of 1 Kings 14 that either Jeroboam or his wife knows that Ahijah is blind (cf. 1 Kgs 11:29-38).

shall you say to her."[21] Precisely because Ahijah receives this revelation, the fate of the boy is already sealed before Jeroboam's wife arrives. The disguise, embodying Jeroboam's deception, is cited by Ahijah when Jeroboam's wife enters his residence: "Come in wife of Jeroboam. What is this -- you have disguised yourself? I have been sent with harsh (news) to you" (1 Kgs 14:6). Whereas, then, in the supplement Ahijah questions Ano about her gifts (3 Rgns 12:24k), in KM Ahijah questions her about her deception.

In the context of a consultation narrative, an audience with a prophet usually leads either to a prophet's delivering a brief oracle or to his supplying the cure himself. Instead of the expected scenario, Ahijah delivers two judgment oracles (1 Kgs 14:7-11, 12-16) affecting the fate of Jeroboam's dynasty, child, and nation.[22] In the first instance (1 Kgs 14:7-11), Ahijah employs a typical commissioning formula (לכי אמרי), followed by a citation formula (כה אמר יהוה אלהי ישׂראל) to instruct Jeroboam's wife.[23] A concluding citation formula (כי יהוה דבר) marks the end of the judgment (1 Kgs 14:11). Hence, Ahijah commissions Jeroboam's wife as his emissary to bring the

21 1 Kgs 14:5. The sequence of a prophetic word formula, directions, and a message is standard in the commissioning of a messenger (Long 1984:246-47).

22 This point is obscured by commentators (except Long 1984:153), who treat 1 Kgs 14:7-16 as a single prophecy.

23 1 Kgs 14:7. On commissions and commissioned commissions, see Vater (1979:365-82) and Meier (1988:36-66). I am using the term citation formula, rather than messenger formula, in light of Meier's studies on the role of messengers in the ancient Semitic world (1988; 1992b:277-91).

judgment oracle he himself, as the deity's appointed emissary, received to rebuke Jeroboam.[24]

Whereas the supplement moves from the demise of the child to the demise of Jeroboam's dynasty (3 Rgns 12:24l-m), KM presents the opposite sequence. Ahijah directs this second judgment directly at Jeroboam's wife (1 Kgs 14:12-16). Introduced by a *casus pendens* construction (ואת) and a commission (קומי לכי), the second oracle predicts the death of Abijah, alludes to the overthrow of Jeroboam's dynasty, and forecasts YHWH's abandonment of Israel. The compliance of Jeroboam's wife to the instructions she receives from Jeroboam and Ahijah is couched in similar phraseology.[25]

1 Kgs 14:2-3:	קומי...והשתנית...והלכת...ולקחת...ובאת
1 Kgs 14:4:	תעשׂ...ותקם...ותלך...ותבא
1 Kgs 14:12:	קומי...לכי...בבאה...ומת
1 Kgs 14:17:	ותקם...ותלך...ותבא באה...מת

In each case the wife's obedience matches the precise commands given to her. Her actions are critical to both the progression and the conclusion of the narrative. The second set of parallels therefore balances the first, lending a sense of symmetry and closure to the whole. Two other literary devices unify the account: the double prophecy/fulfillment schema of vv 12-13, 17-18, involving both death

---

24 As Long points out, 1 Kgs 14:7-11 is therefore both a judgment oracle and the message Jeroboam's wife is commissioned to bring to her husband (1984:156).

25 Cohn aptly comments that Jeroboam's wife makes "symmetrical silent journeys" (1985a:606-607).

and mourning,[26] and the *inclusio* of vv 1 and 18. Beginning with Abijah's illness, the account ends with his burial.

Conclusions

The deuteronomistic version of the consultation with Ahijah is marked by ironic reversals. YHWH's disclosure to Ahijah negates Jeroboam's deception. Ahijah's commissioning of Jeroboam's wife counters Jeroboam's commissioning of his wife. Jeroboam avoids direct contact with Ahijah, but he eludes neither accountability nor punishment. Sending his wife on an oracular inquiry -- "he will tell you what will happen to the child" (1 Kgs 14:3) -- Jeroboam hears an oracle of judgment, not salvation. Moreover, the divine word he receives goes far beyond the scope of his inquiry; it foreordains the demise of his entire dynasty (1 Kgs 14:7-11).

Jeroboam's hapless wife is caught in the crossfire between Jeroboam and Ahijah. Commanded to speak to Ahijah concerning her ill child, she in turn is commanded by Ahijah to become the bearer of ill tidings to her own husband concerning all of his male heirs. Unlike her husband (1 Kgs 11:37-38), she is obedient to the prophetic commands she receives. Like the widow of Zarephath (1 Kgs 17:13), the prophet's widow (2 Kgs 4:3-4), and Naaman (2 Kgs 5:10), she follows prophetic instructions vital to the resolution of a crisis. Yet, in this instance, the resolution she effects is the death of the very child she and her husband sought to help (1 Kgs 14:17). Hence, Jeroboam's wife is finally more than a recipient of judgment and an envoy for opposing parties. She carries the action.

26 For greater detail, see Dietrich (1972:52).

Jeroboam, by contrast, becomes a helpless bystander. Having sent his wife on a mission, he is completely powerless to affect the results. The immediate fulfillment of the prophecy concerning his son's death and burial intensifies the force of the other judgments aimed at him, his royal house, and his kingdom (1 Kgs 14:7-11, 14-16). The *contaminatio* of an oracular inquiry, a divine revelation to Ahijah, and the (re)commissioning of Jeroboam's wife therefore draws attention to Jeroboam's sudden and complete shift in fortunes. The king who refused to "turn from his evil way" following the death of the Judahite man of God (1 Kgs 13:33) and subsequently sought to deceive his own prophet (1 Kgs 14:1-3), is now entirely unable to reverse the demise of the kingdom which began with such promise under his tutelage. By the time his wife returns from her mission, Jeroboam's son is dead and the death of his line and kingdom is assured.

II. CONDEMNATION AND REPROBATION

Ahijah's speech is considerably shorter and less expansive in its application in the supplement than in KM. The significant similarities and contrasts between the two prophecies can best be adduced by first examining each account separately.

A. THE TEXT OF 3 RGNS 12:24l-m

> (l) Why have you brought me bread, a cluster of grapes, cakes, and a pot of honey? Thus says the Lord, behold you shall depart from me and when you enter the gate[A] of Sareira,[B] your servant girls will come out to meet you[C] and they shall tell you, "The child is dead."

(m) [D]For thus says the Lord, I am destroying all those belonging to Jeroboam[E] who urinate[F] against a wall. The dead of Jeroboam in the city,[G] the dogs shall eat.[GH] The one dying in the field, the birds of the heavens shall eat.[I] And one[J] shall lament for the child,[J] "Alas, master!"[K] because there was found in him something good to his master. (3 Rgns 12:24lβ-m).

Notes

A) Reading with KE and KL (*lectio brevior*). The other Greek witnesses add *εις*.
B) So KG^{B}. Lucifer expands to *ciuitatis Arira*. KG conistently names the home of Jeroboam and his wife as Sareira (3 Rgns 12:24k, s). KM anachronistically names their home as Tirzah (1 Kgs 14:17).
C) Reading with KG^{B}. KG^{Nghn}, Lucifer, and KL omit *σοι*.
D) Reading with KL. KG's *οτι* is an explicating plus, influenced by the occurrence of *οτι ταδε λεγει Κυριος* in 3 Rgns 12:24l.
E) Following KG. KL expands to *Hieroboam regis*.
F) In the idiom *ουρουντα προς τοιχον* (= משתין בקיר), KL has the present sing acc part *metentem* for *ουρουντα*.
G-G) Reading with KG^{B}. Mss bioe_2 read *καταβρωμα τοις κυσι*.
H) Reading with KG^{B}. KL and Lucifer expand to *et comedant eos*.
I) KG^{N} (mss hnuva_2) read the pl *καταφαγωνται*, while KL and Lucifer again read *comedant eos*. The pl may be an assimilation toward the pl of the 1 Kgs 14:11; hence, we read with KG^{ABu}.
J-J) KG^{N}, *reliqui*, and KE all read the pl *κοψονται*. KL also reads the pl and expands *to pueri plangent dicentes*. The pl may be an assimilation to the use of the pl earlier in this verse and MT 14:11. We read the sing *κοψσεται* with KG^{Bu} (maximum variation). On the 3 masc sing verb used with an impersonal subject, see GKC #144b, d.

K) The retroversion for *Ουαι κυριε* is most likely הוי אדון, an expression also found in Jer 22:18 and 34:5, referring exclusively to royalty. As Gordon (1973-74:66) notes, the lamentation appropriate for a commoner would be הוי אחי (e.g., 1 Kgs 13:30; cf. Jer 22:18). Since Jer 22:18 and 34:5 refer to royalty -- Jehoiachim and Zedekiah -- I have translated 3 Rgns 12:24m accordingly.

B. THE COMPOSITION OF 3 RGNS 12:24l-m

The formulation of Ahijah's query is puzzling, even though the accusation (*Anklage*) in judgment oracles can take the form of a question (Westermann 1967:142-44). There does not seem anything inherent in the "bread, cluster of grapes, cakes, and pot of honey" (3 Rgns 12:24k) to warrant condemnation and, at any rate, no explicit reason is given for the judgment which follows. The first declaration is introduced by the citation formula, *ταδε λεγει Κυριος* (= כה אמר יהוה; Westermann 1967:151-2). The second declaration of punishment, introduced by the citation formula, *ταδε λεγει Κυριος* (= כה אמר יהוה) and the demonstrative particle *ιδου* (= הנני), unequivocally extends the verdict from the boy to all of Jeroboam's male progeny.

Trebolle thinks that an older version of this story limited the prophetic response to a verdict on the fate of the child (1980:152-53). He sees the bulk of 3 Rgns 12:24m (through *τα πετεινα του ουρανου*) as intrusive. McKenzie claims that excising most of 3 Rgns 12:24m leaves Ahijah's judgment against the boy unexplained.[27] But if the judgment against Jeroboam's house (3 Rgns 12:24m) justifies the

27 He (1991:30) understands the *οτι* of 3 Rgns 12:24m as a causal particle, but *οτι* (= כי) can, of course, serve other functions.

death of the boy (3 Rgns 12:24l), the verdict of 3 Rgns 12:24m does not justify the extirpation of Jeroboam's house. The text is abstruse.

In my view, one must recognize the interrelationship between literary criticism, form criticism, and redaction criticism to resolve this issue. Because 3 Rgns 12:24g-nα is mixed generically, it does not correspond to any one particular form. A rationale for an announcement of ill (*Unheilsankündigung*) is standard in a judgment speech, but the same is not true in a consultation story in which a prophet renders a verdict in response to a query. Because the prophet's sentence implicitly or explicitly responds to an inquiry, no rationale need be given.[28]

C. KIN AND KING

The supplement's version of the encounter with Ahijah is terse and much less complex than the tale in KM. Hence, it is surprising that many commentators view the supplement as an ideologically charged midrash on KM[29] or as a condensation of KM (McKenzie 1991:39-40). First, it hardly seems likely that most of the lacunae in the supplement, *vis-à-vis* KM, betray tendentious composition. If the authors or tradents of the supplement wished to vilify Jeroboam (Gooding 1967:187-88; Gordon 1975:392-93), why would they omit some of KM's most damning features, such as the disguise motif, Jeroboam's unmatched evil, and the exile of Israel? As Wallace observes, those

---

[28] *Pace* McKenzie (1991:31). See, for instance, 2 Kgs 20:1 (= Isa 38:1), Jer 22:10-12, 24-30; 37:17, and Westermann (1967:161-63).

[29] So, for instance, Stade and Schwally (1904:135), Montgomery (1951:265-66), de Vaux (1958:83), Gooding (1967:187-88; 1969a:28-29), and Gordon (1973-74:68-69; 1975:368-93).

"sections [in 1 Kgs 14:7-11] which are most savage in their attack on the king are omitted" in the supplement.[30] Conversely, if the authors or tradents of the supplement wished to compliment Jeroboam (Aberbach and Smolar 1969:69), why would they include such a gruesome declaration of punishment against all his male heirs?

Second, if the supplement is a midrash, why is it, as Debus points out (1967:80), considerably shorter than KM? Since by definition midrash explains puzzling or irregular features of a given text, in what way does 3 Rgns 12:24g-nα elucidate KM? How does 3 Rgns 12:24g-nα explicate, instruct, or edify? Third, if the supplement is an abbreviation of KM, why are there substantial variations in terminology and phraseology among those elements which the two traditions share? The supplement states that "she [Ano] arose from Sarira and journeyed. When she came into into the city, to Ahijah the Shilonite, Ahijah said..." (3 Rgns 12:24k). But KM states "and the wife of Jeroboam did so: she arose and went to Shiloh and came to the house of Ahijah" (1 Kgs 14:4). In the supplement Ano brings "bread, a cluster of grapes, cakes, and a pot of honey" (3 Rgns 12:24h, l), but in KM the wife of Jeroboam brings "ten loaves, cakes, and a pot of honey" (1 Kgs 14:3). In the supplement Ahijah uses the citation formula three times (3 Rgns 12:24k, l, m), but in KM only once (1 Kgs 14:7).[31] Only in KM (1 Kgs 14:11) does Ahijah use a concluding citation formula (כי יהוה דבר). It hardly seems likely, given the indiscriminate nature of these discrepancies, that the supplement is either reproducing or condensing a proto-rabbinic *Vorlage*.

---

30 1986:28. For similar comments, see Trebolle (1980:184-201).

31 These are random examples. Debus retroverts the LXX and provides a useful comparison of the similarities and differences between the two traditions (1967:55-92).

There is one final problem with the abridgement theory. It fails to explain why the supplement sometimes follows a different order from that of KM and includes a few motifs (e.g., Ahijah's servant) not found in KM. That a tradent reordered his *Vorlage* and added certain motifs to improve the story (McKenzie 1991:39) is unlikely because there is no clear indication that either the sequence of the supplement or its additions better KM. On the contrary, as most critics recognize, KM generally provides a more elaborate and coherent sequence than the supplement.

Although I have defended the supplement as an independent witness to the text, I would acknowledge that another explanation of the data is possible. The supplement of 3 Rgns 12:24g-nα could be an earlier version of KM. In other words, if the supplement is not dependent upon KM, is KM a development from or an elaboration of the supplement? I do not think so. There are too many incidental discrepancies in sequence, vocabulary, and themes to warrant such a conclusion. Instead, I would argue that KM and the supplement represent two distinct redactional traditions. Each has developed older materials in different ways (Trebolle 1980:184-85). 1 Kgs 14:1-18 may be more thoroughly and consistently developed than 3 Rgns 12:24g-nα, but the two are indirectly, and not directly, related.

III. KIN, KING, AND KINGDOM

I have argued that 1 Kgs 14:7-16, like 3 Rgns 12:24g-nα, contains two parts. Imparted to Jeroboam's wife, the first oracle is directed at Jeroboam and his house (1 Kgs 14:7-11). The second oracle, both delivered to and directed at Jeroboam's wife, forecasts the demise of her son, alludes to Baasha's *coup d'État*, and predicts Israel's exile (1

Kgs 14:12-16). For the sake of clarity, I have listed these two speeches separately.

A. THE TEXT OF 1 KGS 14:7-16

> (7) Thus says YHWH, God of Israel: "although I exalted you from the midst of the people and appointed you as commander over my people Israel (8) and tore away the kingdom from the house of David and gave it to you, yet you have not been like my servant David who observed my commandments and who followed me with all of his heart by doing only[A] that which is right in my sight. (9) You have done more evil than all who were before you and have made for yourself other gods and molten images[B] to provoke me; but me you have cast behind your back.[C] (10) Therefore, I am bringing[D] evil to[E] Jeroboam's house. [F]I will cut off everyone belonging to Jeroboam who urinates against a wall[GH] to the very last[H] in Israel! (11) And I will consume Jeroboam's house as one completely burns up dung. Those belonging to Jeroboam who die in the city, the dogs shall eat; the one[I] who dies[J] in the country, the birds of the air shall eat. For YHWH has spoken."
>
> (12) As for you, arise, go to your house. When your feet enter[K] the city,[L] the child will die. (13) [M]And all Israel will mourn for him[M] and they shall bury him, for he alone of Jeroboam's house will be buried, because there was found in him something good to YHWH, our God.[N] (14) [O]Today, at this very moment,[O] YHWH will establish for himself a king over Israel who will cut off the house of Jeroboam. (15) And YHWH will strike Israel like a reed swaying in the water and will pluck Israel from this good land, which he gave to their fathers,[P] (16) and he will give Israel up, on account of the sins Jeroboam has committed and has caused Israel to commit.

Notes

A) Reading with KM. A few mss, KS and KV lack the adv רק.

B) Reading with KG^A. KM, KS, and the Armenian add the copula.

C) Reading with KM. KG^A and mss xc_2 read *σωματος σου*, while KL^V reads *carnis tui*. The most common rendering of גו in KG is *σωμα* (Hatch and Redpath 1897:1330a).

D) Reading with KM. KG^A adds explicating *εγω*.

E) A few mss read instead of אל, the expected על. These prepositions are often confused in Samuel (Cross), Kings (Burney 1920:186) and late biblical Hebrew (Kropat 1909:41-42; Rooker 1990:127-31).

F) With KG^A we omit the copula of KM.

G) Reading with KM. Many Hebrew mss, KS, and a few mss of KT expand to ועצור.

H-H) Many scholars have tried to explain the unusual idiom עצור ועזוב (e.g., Talmon and Fields 1989:85-112). Holder surveys the theories (1988:31-32). Noth argues, probably rightly, that whatever the original connotations of this alliterative expression, those connotations were lost by the time of composition (1968:316). In its present usage the idiom comprises a *merismus* denoting totality.

I) Reading with KM. 3 Rgns 12:24m adds *και εσονται* (= והיו).

J) Reading with 3 Rgns 12:24m and KG^A (of 1 Kgs 14:11) *οι τεθνηκοτες* (= המתים). KM's reading of the sing המת assimilates toward the use of המת later in v 11 and in other oracles against the Israelite kings (e.g., 1 Kgs 16:4 and 21:24).

K) KG^A reads *εν τω εισερχεσθαι* (= בבוא). 3 Rgns 12:24l reads *εισελθουσης σου* (= בבואך). We read with KM as the *lectio dif-*

ficilior. The part occasionally occurs in the protasis of conditional sentences (Lambdin 1971:276-279).

L) 3 Rgns 12:24l presents a variant to KM, *την πυλην εις Σαρειρα* (= השערה אל-צרדה).

M-M) Again, 3 Rgns 12:24m presents an ancient variant to that of KM, *και το παιδαριον κοψεται Ουαι κυριε* (= וספד לילד הוי ארון).

N) Reading with KL^{V} *ad Dominum Deum nostrum* (maximum variation). KM assimilates toward the standard divine epithet in this oracle, יהוה אלהי ישׂראל.

O-O) The precise nuance of this expression is difficult to ascertain (Stade and Schwally 1904:137).

P) I am omitting 1 Kgs 14:15b as a late addition. See below.

B. THE COMPOSITION OF 1 KGS 14:7-16

Almost all scholars acknowledge that an older story underlies the deuteronomistic editing of 1 Kings 14. Scholars also generally agree that deuteronomistic additions to this older account are mostly confined to the oracles themselves.[32] Efforts to determine the nature and limits of these additions have not reached any consensus. Many commentators ascribe much, if not all, of 1 Kgs 14:7-16 to a single Deuteronomist.[33] Others see evidence of two or more redactions. For those who contend that deuteronomistic editing only partially affects the shape of these speeches, four main issues form the focus of

32 Some scholars do, however, believe that there are a few post-deuteronomistic insertions within the narrative itself.

33 Stade and Schwally (1904:135); Burney (1920:185-87); Holder (1988:27-38); Montgomery (1951:266); Trebolle (1980:184); Wallace (1986:23); McKenzie (1991:62-63).

discussion. First, does the condemnation of Jeroboam's line (1 Kgs 14:10-11) stem from the Deuteronomist or was it part of the prophetic materials available to him? Second, does the comparison with David (1 Kgs 14:8) belong to a pre-deuteronomistic, deuteronomistic, or late deuteronomistic stage of composition? Third, is the allusion to the usurpation of Jeroboam's throne (1 Kgs 14:14) pre-deuteronomistic, deuteronomistic, or post-deuteronomistic? Fourth, are the predictions of Israel's demise, due either to Israelite veneration of the *asherahs* (אשׁרים; 1 Kgs 14:15b) or to Jeroboam's apostasy (1 Kgs 14:16), pre-deuteronomistic, deuteronomistic, or post-deuteronomistic?[34]

Believing that this speech originally formed part of a cycle centering on Ahijah of Shiloh, Noth contends that the Deuteronomist expanded an older oracle by adding vv 7aβb-9 and vv 14-16 (1968:312). Debus, however, would limit deuteronomistic editing to vv 7aβ-10a (1967:51). Campbell contends that 1 Kgs 14:7-8a, 9bβ-13, 17-18 belong to the Prophetic Record, while vv 8b-9ba, 14-15, and 16 stem from deuteronomistic circles.[35] O'Brien largely follows Campbell's reconstruction, except that he ascribes vv 8b-9bα, 16 to deuteronomistic composition and vv 14-15 to late additions (1989:187-90). Hence, in this case Debus, Campbell, O'Brien, and Noth all see deuteronomistic editing in 1 Kgs 14:1-18 as light.

---

34 To the best of my knowledge, Seebass is the only scholar who argues that the most primitive layer (reconstructed as 1 Kgs 14:7-8a, 9bβ, 10aβ, 11a, 12, 13, 15aα) involves the punishment of Israel (1975:188-89). I would argue, however, that even the application of curse language to Israel (v 15aα) stems from the Deuteronomist.

35 Campbell discusses the individual verses within this passage in several places (1986:32-34, 103, 181, 185, 206, 212).

Arguing that the most primitive oracle did not contain any rejection of Jeroboam's descendants, Gray posits the Deuteronomist's contributions as vv 7-11 and vv 13-16 (1970:333-34). Similarly, Jones (1984:269) discerns deuteronomistic editing in vv 7-11 and vv 13a-16. Dietrich ascribes part of the historical retrospect (1 Kgs 14:7-8a), the fabrication of images, the extirpation of Jeroboam's house (1 Kgs 14:9b-11), and the reason for mourning (1 Kgs 14:13b) to DtrP. He assigns to DtrN the comparison with David (1 Kgs 14:8b-9a) and the extension of perdition to Israel (1 Kgs 14:15-16; 1972:53, 112-14).

Würthwein (1977:172-79) argues for at least three stages in the development of the text: 1) an old prophetic tradition about Ahijah of Shiloh (vv $2a\alpha^{*}\beta\gamma$, 3a, 5b, $6b\alpha$), a longer prophetic narrative (vv 1-6, 12, $13a\alpha^{*}$, 17, 18), and deuteronomistic additions, which extend the punishment to Jeroboam and the northern kingdom (vv 7-11, $13a^{*}b$-16). Hence, Dietrich and Würthwein disagree with Gray and Jones about the nature and extent of pre-deuteronomistic layers, but agree that the deuteronomistic editing of 1 Kgs 14:7-16 is heavy.

I also see the deuteronomistic editing of 1 Kgs 14:7-16 as substantial. I would diasgree, however, with those scholars who view 1 Kgs 14:7-16 as basically a deuteronomistic creation. Gray and Jones, for example, fail to distinguish between a hypothetical original oracle and the shape of that oracle as available to the Deuteronomist. One cannot deny the possibility of a long transmission and development of this oracle; however, the question should precisely concern the configuration of this oracle prior to deuteronomistic editing and expansion. Two considerations suggest that the condemnation of Jeroboam's house already formed part of the prophetic tradition to which the Deuteronomist had access. First, in the supplement Jeroboam's line is condemned to death in language which is not characteristically deuteronomistic.[36] Second, since scholars generally agree that 1 Kgs 11:29-39 contains a primitive account of a royal oracle to Jeroboam, it seems likely that, given the later extermination of Jeroboam's entire dynasty (1 Kgs 15:29), there also existed in prophetic tradition a condemnation of Jeroboam and his line. Whether such a prophetic tradition also alluded to the extirpation of Jeroboam's house by Baasha is unclear.[37]

Some sixteen deuteronomistic clichés permeate 1 Kgs 14:7-11, 15a, 16. The following summary is keyed to Weinfeld's list of deuteronomistic phraseology (1972:320-65).

---

[36] As even pundits (e.g., Montgomery 1951:266) who disparage the supplement admit, 3 Rgns 12:24lβ-m does not contain typically deuteronomistic language. A possible exception may be the curse in 3 Rgns 12:24m (// 1 Kgs 14:11) that reappears in other oracles against the northern royal houses (1 Kgs 16:4; 21:24; Weinfeld 1972:351; McKenzie 1991:61-62). Judging by ancient Near Eastern parallels to this curse (see below), the curse was probably a stock expression in the prophetic sources used by the Deuteronomist (Campbell 1986:24-25). It was taken up by Dtr[1] and, if 1 Kgs 16:1-4 is a deuteronomistic creation (Noth 1967:82; Campbell 1986:39-41; McKenzie 1991:64), reused by him. Its use in 1 Kgs 14:11 relates both to the extinction of Jeroboam's house and to the non-burial of his heirs, except Abijah (1 Kgs 14:13, 18).

[37] Noth (1968:317), Jones (1984:273-74), and O'Brien (1989:190) see this verse as a late attempt to legitimize Baasha. It seems doubtful, however, that a later scribe would have such an acute concern for Baasha. Stade and Schwally (1904:137), Würthwein (1977:174), and others would only excise problematic זה היום ומה גם־עתה in v 14b as a late gloss, but ascribing a difficult phrase to a late scribe only defers explanation. Given that the phrase connotes imminence, I would be inclined to assign this entire verse either to the Deuteronomist or to his source (so Debus 1967:53-54).

v 7	#4 (354),	#9 (355).		
v 8	#1 (332),	#9a (332),	#15 (332),	#16 (332).
	#10 (354).			
v 9	#5 (321),	#6 (339).		
v 10	#5 (350),	#8 (351),	#12 (352).	
v 11	#11 (351).			
v 15	#10 (343),	#10 (346-47).		
v 16	#5 (340).[38]			

None of these phrases is found in the supplement and each is clearly couched in formulaic deuteronomistic prose. In my view, most of the arguments for distinguishing between early and later Deuteronomists within these verses are overly optimistic. I see no compelling criteria to assign these rhetorical phrases to a succession of

[38] Campbell (1986:24-25, 33) and O'Brien (1989:191) contend that some of the foregoing expressions are not deuteronomistic. This may be true of the phrase in 1 Kgs 14:11, but I do not find most of their arguments convincing. Given the distribution and use of the locution הנני \ הנה אנכי מביא רעה על within the Deuteronomistic History (Weinfeld 1972:350), it seems forced to claim that this phrase with a sing object is not deuteronomistic as opposed to the same expression with a pl object (Campbell 1986:33). Similarly, to assert that the expression מעל פני האדמה (מעל הארץ) with the verb נתץ is late, because of the relative frequency of נתץ in Jeremiah and the infrequency of the same in the Deuteronomistic History (O'Brien 1989:191), is misleading. First, the expression הארץ \ האדמה הטובה is clearly deuteronomistic (Weinfeld 1972:343). Second, there is no regular verb or verbal form (e.g., נתץ, כלה, השמיד, האביד, אבד) with this locution in the Deuteronomistic History (Weinfeld 1972:346-47). Third, Jeremiah employs the verb נתץ in the collocation "to uproot and to plant," but never with מעל פני האדמה (מעל הארץ) as in Deuteronomy (29:27) and the Deuteronomistic History (1 Kgs 14:15).

Deuteronomists. Dietrich and Würthwein (1977:177) deem the comparison with David (1 Kgs 14:8b) nomistic, *ipso facto* late, and assign v 8b to DtrN. As we have seen, however, in dealing with 1 Kgs 11:37-38, there is no compelling literary reason to view the comparison with David as either early or late. On the contrary, the contrast between David and Jeroboam lies at the heart of the deuteronomistic exposition of Jeroboam's rise.

Similarly, there is simply no convincing evidence that the extension of Ahijah's judgment to Israel is intrusive. Shifts in person need not indicate shifts in redactors. The first speech, introduced and concluded with prophetic citation formulae, is YHWH's (first person) message for Jeroboam (second person), while the second speech, lacking any prophetic citation formulae, is Ahijah's speech to Jeroboam's wife (second person), informing her of YHWH's (third person) impending and future judgments against her son, Jeroboam's house, and Israel (third person).[39] Recognizing the existence and nature of the two orations (vv 7-11 and vv 12-16) elucidates the shifts in person. Hence, I assign much of vv 7-11 and most of vv 15-16 (except v 15b) to a single Deuteronomist.

O'Brien (1989:191) and McKenzie (1991:62) argue that 1 Kgs 14:15 is a post-deuteronomistic addition. Given the predominance of deuteronomistic phraseology in v 15a, I see no reason to excise the first part of v 15 (through לאבותיהם).[40] But I believe that their argu-

[39] Cf. 3 Rgns 12:24m, in which Ahijah does use a citation formula in his speech to Jeroboam's wife.

[40] Although McKenzie excises the entire verse, his arguments actually center on v 15b. O'Brien excises v 15a, because of what he asserts are the rarity of נוד and נתץ in the Deuteronomistic History (1989:191). In the first case (נוד), the Deuteronomist employs stereotypical curse formulae to underscore the grisly repercussions of

ments for excising v 15b are strong. The *asherahs*, first introduced in v 15b, play no role in either the descriptions of Jeroboam's cultus (1 Kgs 12:26-33) or in any of the condemnations of Jeroboam (1 Kgs 13:1-3, 31-33).[41] Moreover, as O'Brien observes, the assertion that "he [YHWH] will scatter (זרה) them beyond the River" is unparalleled in the Deuteronomistic History (1989:191).

Having isolated deuteronomistic elements in 1 Kgs 14:7-16, we are in a better position to analyze the author's compositional technique. In this regard, a comparison of 3 Rgns 12:24g-nα with 1 Kgs 14:7-16 is helpful. Deuteronomistic editing is evident in insertions, rearrangements, and comments. The Deuteronomist has elaborated upon each section of Ahijah's initial judgment oracle. First, he has (re)arranged the order of judgments: Ahijah pronounces judgment on Jeroboam's house (1 Kgs 14:10-11) and later pronounces judgment upon Abijah (1 Kgs 14:12).[42] Second, the Deuteronomist has added a historical retrospect (1 Kgs 14:7-8a) before the accusation. Third, unlike the terse question in the supplement, the accusation here takes

---

Jeroboam's abrogation of covenant. In the second case, O'Brien's analysis sidesteps the deuteronomistic character of the expressions occurring in v 15a (n. 36).

41 The first northern king who makes האשרה is Ahab (1 Kgs 16:33). Tolerance of *asherah(s)* is ascribed to subsequent kings (2 Kgs 13:6). In one of the additions to the Deuteronomist's editorial on Israel's ruin, Israel is accused of making *asherahs* (2 Kgs 17:10, 16).

42 Because the supplement and KM represent two distinct redactional traditions, it is unclear whether the Deuteronomist reordered older prophetic materials or simply followed the order of judgments in the prophetic sources bequeathed to him.

the form of rehearsing Jeroboam's election (1 Kgs 14:8b-9).[43] Fourth, he frames the announcement of punishment by formulating an introduction (1 Kgs 14:10a).

The Deuteronomist directs the second judgment at Jeroboam's wife: "as for you" (ואת; 1 Kgs 14:12-16). Hence, Dtr[1] associates the fate of her son with the usurpation of Jeroboam's throne and the demise of Israel itself. In both oracles, then, the Deuteronomist has evidently found himself sympathetic to the substance of his sources and has blended this older material with his own ample contributions. The result is a coherent, albeit prolix, narration.

C. THE PROMISES TO DAVID AND THE JUDGMENTS AGAINST JEROBOAM

A number of scholars point out that there are formal and thematic parallels between 1 Kgs 14:7-11 and the other judgment oracles against northern dynasties.[44] Like 1 Kgs 14:7-11, these oracles legitimate the transfer of the realm from one northern king or house to another and comment upon the fate of the deposed. Other scholars draw parallels between the rejection of Jeroboam and the judgment

43 Ahijah's question in KM involves her disguise (1 Kgs 14:6), not the gifts she brings. The question is preliminary to the judgment oracle of 1 Kgs 14:7-11. Only in v 12 does Ahijah deal with the original purpose of her visit.

44 1 Kgs 14:7-11, 16:1-4; 21:21-24; 2 Kgs 9:6-10. See Dietrich (1972:9-13), Weippert (1972:301-339), Wallace (1986:21-40), and McKenzie (1991:61-80).

oracles proclaimed against Saul (1 Sam 13:13-14; 15:22-29), David (2 Sam 12:7-12), and Solomon (1 Kgs 11:11-13).[45]

However helpful these comparisons may be, a fixation upon parallels between 1 Kgs 14:7-11 and other prophetic judgment speeches can obscure or even ignore the distinctive features of the second oracle (1 Kgs 14:12-15a, 16). The judgment speeches against the other northern houses are limited to forecasting the overthrow of these dynasties, but the judgment against Jeroboam's house is directly followed by a judgment against Israel, linking the sins of Jeroboam to exile. Hence, the second speech is foundational to understanding Dtr^1's long-term evaluation of the northern kingdom's prospects. The two orations have different foci. The first (1 Kgs 14:7-11) marks the beginning of the end for Jeroboam and his dynasty, while the second (1 Kgs 14:12-15a, 16) proleptically marks the end of his kingdom. Taken together, Ahijah's orations establish the Deuteronomist's criteria for evaluating all subsequent northern kings.

Given the content, context, and scope of the pronouncements in 1 Kgs 14:7-16, I would further argue that the most pertinent comparison for this passage has yet largely gone unexplored: the dynastic promises to David (2 Sam 7:5-16). The Davidic promises strikingly both complement and contrast with the judgments against Jeroboam. Both begin with historical retrospects. Both involve major issues -- dynasty, cult, and kingdom. Both are often alluded to in the respective histories of Judah and Israel. What the Davidic promises accomplish positively for Judah, the decrees against Jeroboam accomplish negatively for Israel. The Deuteronomist makes the con-

---

45 Weippert (1983:344-75); Campbell (1986:32-45); O'Brien (1989:186-208).

trast between David and Jeroboam explicit in 1 Kgs 14:8-9. Whereas the Davidic promises bring continuity of leadership and divine restraint in dealing with Judah's sins, the divine judgments against Jeroboam bring discontinuity of leadership and the actualization of divine wrath against Israel. Both texts are therefore critical to the deuteronomistic presentation of the dual monarchies.

In his treatment of judgment oracle form, Westermann emphasizes the juridical nature of these announcements of punishment: how they contrast the offense of the accused with prior divine beneficence on his behalf (1967:157). In effect, these oracles function as trial and verdict -- confronting the accused, exposing the crime, and proclaiming divine judgment.[46] In Ahijah's first oracle, YHWH indicts, tries, and convicts Jeroboam. No reference is given in this speech either to Jeroboam's wife or to their sick child. Rather, Jeroboam and his dynasty are at issue.

The Deuteronomist's historical retrospect in 1 Kgs 14:7-8a recounts YHWH's past favors, providing a clear rationale for the accusation which follows. The declaration that the deity exalted Jeroboam from the midst of the people in v 7 (הרימתיך מתוך העם) recalls Jeroboam's divine election as depicted both in the judgment oracle to Solomon (1 Kgs 11:11-13) and in the royal oracle to Jeroboam (1 Kgs 11:29-38). An almost identical expression occurs in the Deuteronomist's judgment oracle against Baasha, "I raised you from the dust" (הרימתיך מן-העפר; 1 Kgs 16:2). Like David before

46 Westermann's further observation, that judgment speeches in Kings are almost always addressed to individuals (1967:137-38), is insignificant because his base for understanding these oracles is a book about kings.

him (2 Sam 7:8) and Baasha after him, Jeroboam's ascent to power from relative obscurity was not his own achievement.

The phrase referring to the sundering of David's kingdom on Jeroboam's behalf in v 8 (ואקרע את-הממלכה מבית דוד ואתנה לך) explicitly reaffirms the divine indictment of Solomon in 1 Kgs 11:11 (קרע אקרע את-הממלכה מעליך ונתתיה לעבדך) and in 1 Kgs 11:29-31 (הנני קרע את-הממלכה מיד שלמה ונתתי לך), the implications of which, as we have seen, the Deuteronomist greatly develops.[47] As the kingdom was torn away from Saul to be given to David (1 Sam 15:28; 28:17), so it was also torn from Solomon and given to Jeroboam. Subsequently, in his reflection on the demise of the northern kingdom the Deuteronomist again reaffirms the divine initiative which led to the establishment of the northern kingdom (2 Kgs 17:21). Hence, the emphasis on divine beneficence to Jeroboam is a consistent motif throughout the deuteronomistic presentation of the divided monarchy.

Similarly, Ahijah's recollection that YHWH appointed Jeroboam a leader (נגיד) draws attention to Jeroboam's privilege and responsibility. Like Saul, David, and Solomon before him and Baasha and Hezekiah after him, Jeroboam commands his people at divine behest.[48] Perhaps the starkest, but most salient, comparison is with David. Like Jeroboam, David is designated a נגיד over Israel in the historical retrospect of 2 Sam 7:8-9. Recalling David's humble

---

[47] Cf. Samuel's accusation against Saul in 1 Sam 15:28, "YHWH is tearing the kingdom of Israel from you this day and has given it to your neighbor, who is better than you." Samuel's ghost repeats the charge almost verbatim in 1 Sam 28:17. On the deuteronomistic use of this expression, see our discussion in vol. 1 (chap. 5).

[48] 1 Sam 9:16; 13:14; 2 Sam 6:21; 7:8; 1 Kgs 1:35; 16:2; 2 Kgs 20:5. On the problems in translating נגיד, see Cross (1973:220-22), Ishida (1977b:35-51), and McCarter (1980b:178-79).

beginnings, YHWH declares that he will not withdraw his fidelity (חסד) from David as he withdrew it from Saul (2 Sam 7:15). Instead David's throne, kingdom, and dynasty will be established in perpetuity (2 Sam 7:16). YHWH also recalls Jeroboam's humble beginnings in the historical retrospect of 1 Kgs 14:8-9, but his message for Jeroboam is diametrically opposed to his message for David.

The rehearsal of the deity's establishment of the northern kingdom under Jeroboam casts a pall over Jeroboam's actions because Jeroboam's election justifies his indictment (1 Kgs 14:7-8). The disjunctive clause in v 8 (ולא היית) marks the beginning of the indictment. Consistent with the terms of Jeroboam's charge (1 Kgs 11:36-38), the deity evaluates Jeroboam's conduct by the Davidic standard (1 Kgs 14:8b-9). That Jeroboam is the only northern king whom the Deuteronomist compares with David highlights the pivotal nature of Jeroboam's reign.[49] Considering the predication of a David-like enduring dynasty based upon David-like fidelity, the unfavorable comparison of Jeroboam with David in v 8b is highly significant.

The prospect of Jeroboam attaining the Davidic standard of fidelity has proved to be an abysmal failure. Jeroboam is no David. Earlier YHWH had proclaimed to Jeroboam that Solomon's failure to observe the deity's commandments and statutes had led the deity to entrust the kingship of (northern) Israel to Jeroboam (1 Kgs 11:11, 33; 14:8). Now Jeroboam has done far worse. Because Jeroboam has not remained subject and loyal to his suzerain as David was, Jeroboam cannot expect the deity's protection and security. Quite the contrary, Jeroboam's misconduct is so egregious that he sets a new

---

49 The comparison with David is hereafter only applied to southern monarchs (e.g., 1 Kgs 15:11; 2 Kgs 14:3; 16:2; 18:3; 21:7).

standard for comparison. Jeroboam becomes the *Unheilsherrscher* of Israel (Evans 1983:97-125). As the fidelity of David comprises the deuteronomistic exemplar for Judah, so the infidelity of Jeroboam becomes the deuteronomistic paradigm for Israel. The reverberations between the two themes, originating here, unify the Deuteronomist's record of the divided monarchy (Cross 1973:284).

The claim that Jeroboam committed more evil than all who were before him (ותרע לעשות מכל אשר־היו לפניך; v 9) is therefore not, as most critics contend, anachronistic.[50] The negative incomparability formula is only applied to three northern kings: Jeroboam, Omri (1 Kgs 16:25), and Ahab (1 Kgs 16:30, 33) and to one southern king: Manasseh (2 Kgs 21:11).[51] The Deuteronomist decries each of these three northern kings for their unparalleled apostasy.

In the case of Jeroboam, the Deuteronomist pinpoints Jeroboam's unmatched evil: making "other gods and molten images" (1 Kgs 14:9). In the Deuteronomistic History both leaders and people are often denounced for following after, worshiping, or burning incense to other gods (Weinfeld 1972:320-22), but Jeroboam is criticized for

---

[50] A similar phrase in positive form is applied to four leaders: Moses (Deut 34:10), Solomon (1 Kgs 3:12), Hezekiah (2 Kgs 18:5), and Josiah (2 Kgs 23:25). Unlike the negative incomparability formulae, the positive incomparability formulae are unequivocal, applying to both past and future (Weinfeld 1972:358-59; Knoppers 1992:411-31).

[51] Along with Cross (1973) and Friedman (1981a:10-12), I regard the incomparability formula applied to Manasseh as the work of Dtr^2. There is more variation in the negative incomparability formulae than in the positive incomparability formulae. A negative formula also appears in the KG^L of 2 Kgs 17:2 (Hoshea). Trebolle (1989a:188-93) believes that the KG^L of 2 Kgs 17:2 is original.

actually making other gods.[52] Because his cultus is perpetuated by every subsequent northern king, it becomes the linchpin of the Deuteronomist's condemnations of the northern kingdom.[53] In so doing, the Deuteronomist concedes that Jeroboam's cultic initiatives enjoyed widespread success, exerting a lasting influence upon subsequent kings and upon the populace at large (cf. 1 Kgs 12:26-28). A northern king's "doing evil in the sight of YHWH" becomes virtually synonymous with his continuing "in the way(s) of Jeroboam."[54]

Whereas the Deuteronomist employed inversion, placing the pronominal object forward, in 1 Kgs 11:37 to emphasize Jeroboam's election: "But you I shall take and you shall rule over all that you desire" (ואתך אקח ומלכת בכל אשר-תאוה נפשך), in 1 Kgs 14:9 he again employs inversion to mark Jeroboam's rejection of his elector: "but me, you have cast behind your back" (ואתי השלכת אחרי גוך).[55]

---

[52] To excise 1 Kgs 14:9bα as a late gloss, because this is the only time a prophet attacks someone for making (עשׂה) foreign gods, is misguided (contra O'Brien 1989:189). First, it ignores the context and force of Ahijah's indictment. The accusation plays on Jeroboam's earlier actions in 1 Kgs 12:28 (ויעשׂ שׁני עגלי זהב ויאמר...הנה אלהיך ישׂראל). Second, 1 Kgs 14:9 is not the only example of this phrase within the Deuteronomistic History. The Deuteronomist also cites the foreign immigrants in 2 Kgs 17:29 for making gods for themselves (יהיו עשׂים גוי גוי אלהיו). These settlers emulate Jeroboam and perpetuate his sin (chaps. 3, 6).

[53] 1 Kgs 13:34; 14:16; 15:26, 30, 34; 16:2, 13, 19, 26, 31; 21:22; 22:53; 2 Kgs 3:3; 10:29, 31; 13:2, 6, 11; 14:24; 15:9, 18, 24, 28; 17:21-22; 23:15.

[54] On the deuteronomistic locution, "to do that which is evil in the sight of YHWH," see Weinfeld (1972:339).

[55] Campbell notes (1986:33) that the technique of inversion is also found in 1 Sam 15:1, 2 Sam 12:9b, and 1 Kgs 1:35b (KM). Cf. Jer 2:27; 32:33; Ezek 8:16.

The declaration of punishment follows in vv 10-11, introduced by the adverb לכן and the demonstrative particle הנני (1 Kgs 14:10a; cf. 1 Kgs 11:31; 21:21). As in other judgment oracles levied against northern monarchs, the judgment is couched as מביא על followed by a series of converted perfects.[56] The use of both metonymy (משתין בקיר) and a *merismus* (עצור ועזוב) underscore the exhaustive and absolute results of the deity's intervention.[57] As Holder observes, the verb בער suggests the removal and rejection of something abhorrent to YHWH.[58] The finality of the deity's judgment against Jeroboam's house is dramatized through a prodigious simile (ובערתי אחרי בית-ירבעם כאשר יבער הגלל עד-תמו).[59]

D. CONDEMNATION AND REPROBATION EXTENDED AND AMPLIFIED

Ahijah's second oracle, addressed to Jeroboam's wife (1 Kgs 14:12-15a, 16), implements and extends the doom against Jeroboam's house. In KM Ahijah only addresses the fate of the child, the original reason for consultation, after he has doomed all of Jeroboam's male heirs. In 3 Rgns 12:24l the proclamation of the child's death becomes the occasion for the demise of Jeroboam's line, but in 1 Kings 14 the

---

56 1 Kgs 14:10; 21:21 (29); 2 Kgs 21:12; 22:16, (20). A similar phrase occurs in the addition of 1 Kgs 9:9. The expression is also common in Jer C (Weinfeld 1972:350).

57 Again, these stereotypical phrases recur in the Deuteronomist's judgments against other northern kings (1 Kgs 21:21; 2 Kgs 9:8; cf. 1 Kgs 16:11; 2 Kgs 14:26; Weinfeld 1972:352).

58 Deut 13:5; 17:7, 12; 19:13, 19; 21:19, 22; 2 Kgs 23:24; Holder (1988:32-33).

59 The phrase בערתי אחרי is also found in 1 Kgs 16:3; 21:21.

child's death sentence (vv 12-13) is an immediate consequence of the destruction declared against Jeroboam's dynasty (vv 10-11). Similarly, the judgment against Jeroboam's house is no longer future (1 Kgs 14:10-11), but imminent; YHWH "this day" will raise up a usurper (1 Kgs 14:14). The burial of Abijah paradoxically represents a mark of divine favor, because of the gruesome fate that awaits the rest of Jeroboam's male line (1 Kgs 14:13).

The contrast between 1 Kgs 14:7-16 and 2 Sam 7:5-16 is striking. In both cases the Deuteronomist ties the establishment of a cultus to the fate of offspring and dynasty. In 2 Sam 7:11-12 the promise of an offspring who will build YHWH a house (בית) is critical to YHWH's establishment of David's house (בית; 2 Sam 7:13-16). In 1 Kings 14 Jeroboam's creation of a (counter)cultus is critical to YHWH's destruction of Jeroboam's house (בית), with the death of Jeroboam's offspring its guarantee. Solomon's construction of the temple is associated with the deity's establishment of an enduring Davidic dynasty (2 Sam 7:11-16). Conversely, Jeroboam's fashioning of "other gods and molten images" at Bethel and Dan leads YHWH to doom Jeroboam's prospects for attaining an enduring dynasty.

Before narrating the actual death of the child (1 Kgs 14:17-18), the Deuteronomist extends Ahijah's judgment to include all of Israel (1 Kgs 14:15a, 16). Ahijah associates the death of Abijah with the political fate of Israel itself. The Deuteronomist telescopes and frames the entire course of northern history, linking its demise to the fall of Jeroboam.[60] Abijah's sudden death is the first realization of

60 1 Kgs 14:12-13, 17-18; 2 Kgs 17:21-23. See Hoffmann (1980:59-73), Mullen (1987:213), and below.

the judgment rendered against both Jeroboam's line (1 Kgs 14:10-11, 14; 15:29) and Israel itself (1 Kgs 14:15a, 16; 2 Kgs 17:23).

I would further argue that this renunciation of Israel (1 Kgs 14:15a, 16) serves as a counterpoint to blessings of peace and rest for Israel in the Davidic promises (2 Sam 7:10). Consistent with the Deuteronomist's presentation of the monarchy, the people's fate is inextricably bound up with that of their king. The dependence of popular fate upon royal fate is, of course, also evident in other deuteronomistically edited discourses, such as Samuel's farewell speech (1 Sam 12:14-15), Solomon's temple dedication (1 Kgs 8:28-30), and the editorial on Israel's demise (2 Kgs 17:21-23). The link between nation and king bodes well for the people in 2 Samuel 7, but the opposite is true here. Jeroboam not only sins, but as the Deuteronomist repeatedly laments, also "caused Israel to sin."[61]

The Deuteronomist's association of kin with kingdom draws attention to his (re)use of curse formulae in vv 11 and 15 (cf. 3 Rgns 12:24m). Weinfeld (1972:129-33) and Wallace (1986:34-36) show that these curses resemble imprecations in Deuteronomy, Jeremiah, the vassal treaties of Esarhaddon, the annals of Assurbanipal, and the judgment oracles against the other northern houses.

<u>1 Kgs 14:11</u> .

"those belonging to Jeroboam who die in the city, the dogs shall eat; the one who dies in the country, the birds of the air shall eat" (cf. Deut 28:16, 26; 1 Kgs 16:14; 21:24; Jer 34:20).

"the one dying in the city the dogs shall eat" (cf. 1 Kgs 16:4; 21:24; Wiseman 1958:63 [VTE #451]).

61 1 Kgs 14:16; 15:26, 30, 34; 16:13, 19, 26; 22:53; 2 Kgs 3:3; 10:29, 31; 13:2, 6, 11; 14:24; 15:9, 18, 24, 28; 17:21; 23:15.

"the one dying in the field the birds of heaven shall eat" (cf. Streck 1916:38 [Assurbanipal II, IV:74-76]; Wiseman 1958: 62 [VTE #426-27]).

1 Kgs 14:15

"YHWH will strike Israel as a reed sways in the water" (cf. Wiseman 1958:77 [VTE #630]).[62]

"and he will uproot Israel from this good land, which he gave to their fathers" (cf. Wiseman 1958:69 [VTE #538-39; 543-44]).

Beyond recognizing parallels, however, it is pertinent to pursue their relevance for understanding the penalties meted out against Jeroboam and the kingdom he leads. The deuteronomic curses graphically depict the consequences of breaching the covenant: "if you do not listen to the voice of YHWH your God, observing to do all his commandments and statutes which I am commanding you this day, all these curses shall overtake you" (Deut 28:15). Similarly, as Weinfeld points out, Assurbanipal's scribes employ stereotypical imprecations to accent the actualization of divine curses (1972:133). In 1 Kings 14, then, the verdict in the deity's lawsuit has been rendered and the covenant curses are coming into effect. The curse formulae in 1 Kgs 14:11 signify the divine reprobation of Jeroboam's house, while the curse formulae in 1 Kgs 14:15 announce the divine reprobation of Israel itself (1 Kgs 14:16).

The linkage between the curses in 1 Kgs 14:11, 15 and Jeroboam's countercultus, specifically his fabrication of molten images and other gods, is critical to the deuteronomistic presentation of the northern

62 VTE #630: ki-i GI.AMBAR i-na A.MEŠ lu-ni-šu-u-ku-nu. I am reading with the *CAD* 1 (A II) 181-2, GI.AMBAR = qan appari and not GI.BUNIN = buginnu (so Wiseman 1958:77, 89).

monarchy. In both deuteronomic (Deut 6:18; 8:10; 9:6; 11:17) and deuteronomistic (Deut 1:35; 3:25; 4:21, 22; Josh 23:13, 15, 16) contexts, Moses and Joshua speak of "the good land" that YHWH is giving to his people. Moses (Deut 4:12; 6:15; 11:17; 28:21, 36, 63; 29:27) and Joshua (Josh 23:13, 15, 16) also threaten Israel with exile from this land if Israel makes molten images or worships other gods.[63] In fact, virtually every curse of exile in Deuteronomy and the Deuteronomistic History involves other gods.[64] Although Israel is repeatedly warned about or chastised for following after foreign deities in Deuteronomy, Joshua, Judges, and Samuel, only with the demise of Jeroboam does the threat of exile become verdict. 1 Kgs 14:7-16 therefore occupies a critical place in the deuteronomistic coverage of the northern monarchy.

Conclusions: After the Fall -- Jeroboam, David, and the Josianic Reforms

In his concluding formulae to Jeroboam's reign, the Deuteronomist acknowledges that Jeroboam actually ruled Israel for 22 years (1 Kgs 14:19-20). Jeroboam does not die an unnatural death. His reign shows no ill effects of the cultus he established. Jeroboam's

---

63 The threat of exile has parallels both in ancient Near Eastern treaties (e.g., Reiner 1969:532-33 [Mat'ilu IV:6]; Fitzmyer 1967:16-17 [Sefîre I. A:42]; Hillers 1964:34ff.) and in the Code of Hammurapi (Meek 1969:179 [xxvii:22-23, 74]). Exile is also tied to worship of other gods in the addition of 1 Kgs 9:7 (vol. 1: chap. 3).

64 Deut 4:25-28; 6:14-15; 11:16-17; 28:36, 63-64; 29:17-27; Josh 23:15-16. Deut 7:3-4 and Josh 23:13-16 link exile to exogamy and the ensuing worship of other gods. See my forthcoming study (in *HAR*) on intermarriage in the Deuteronomistic History.

house is only overturned during the reign of his son, Nadab (1 Kgs 15:29).[65] The Deuteronomist wishes to leave his readers with a different impression of Jeroboam's tenure. He chooses not to discuss how "Jeroboam fought and ruled" (1 Kgs 14:19). Instead, he transforms and supplements his sources to use the reign of the first northern king as a metonym for the northern kingdom. Jeroboam's commitment to the state cult he founded, despite prophetic warnings, entails a precipitous reversal in the prospects for his dynasty and kingdom (1 Kgs 14:15a, 16). YHWH will raise up a series of dynasties after the demise of Jeroboam's dynasty (e.g., 1 Kgs 14:14), but Israel's fate has been anticipated in the life of her first king. Ironically, Jeroboam gains notoriety rather than a lineage. The illness of one child has become an occasion of national significance.

The Deuteronomist's linkage between Jeroboam and the fall of Israel clarifies, in turn, his linkage between the Davidic promises and Judah's prospects. Although he recognizes a fundamental affinity between Israel's twelve tribes, his history both exploits and negotiates the differences between North and South. The two realms are related, sharing common origins and the same stringent obligations.[66] Their histories are rehearsed synchronistically. But the two nations are also

---

65 It is thus misleading to group Jeroboam and Nadab with David and Solomon, and Solomon and Rehoboam as instances of a prophecy, delay, fulfillment typology (contra Mullen 1987:219-220). Although he cites Baasha's coup as the fulfillment of Ahijah's prophecy, the Deuteronomist does not mention any delay in 1 Kings 14. Instead, he links Jeroboam's house to the fate of Abijah.

66 By stringent obligations, I mean the complete abrogation of all rival cults (including Yahwistic sanctuaries) to the Jerusalem temple.

different.[67] Dtr[1] freely attributes dynastic potential to Benjaminite Saul and to Ephraimite Jeroboam. That Judah's history is spared the ravages of northern history results not simply from divine favoritism toward David and Jerusalem (*pace* Weinfeld 1985:86-87), but also from Jeroboam's failure to fulfill his dynastic charge.

The Deuteronomist responds to the catastrophe of the Assyrian exile by establishing distinctions between Judah and Israel, but he does not disassociate the two altogether (contra Wallace 1986:40). To begin with, the Deuteronomist asserts that cultic impropriety characterized both Israel and Judah. Judah under Rehoboam is also tainted with cultic malfeasance.[68] A number of other southern kings are assailed for abrogating deuteronomistic norms (Hoffmann 1980:35-46). Even the commendation of six Judahite kings, who do "what is right in the the sight of YHWH" is qualified, because they tolerate the high places.[69] Judah fares better than Israel, but is clearly not immune to the same problems which afflict its northern neighbor. Infidelity is common to both.

---

67 I therefore disagree with Mullen's blanket assessment that "the literary and theological patterns established for one kingdom can be applied to the other" (1987:215).

68 The textual history of 1 Kgs 14:22-24 is complex. In contrast with the terse evaluation in 3 Rgns 12:24a: "and Rehoboam did evil in the sight of YHWH," the evaluation in KM 1 Kgs 14:22-24 is considerably protracted and bears clear marks of expansion. Not only is Judah(!) impugned for having done evil in the sight of YHWH, but also for having provoked the deity more than all their fathers. The Chronicler's evaluation of Rehoboam may reflect a somewhat different *Vorlage* than the MT of Kings (Knoppers 1990:424).

69 Asa (1 Kgs 15:11-15); Jehoshaphat (1 Kgs 22:43-44); Jehoash (2 Kgs 12:3-4); Amaziah (2 Kgs 14:3-4); Azariah (2 Kgs 15:3-4); Jotham (2 Kgs 15:34-35).

Close analysis of 1 Kings 14 and the larger deuteronomistic presentation of Jeroboam's reign therefore furnishes insight into the development of the deuteronomistic movement. Those scholars who have pointed to the evidence for a northern origin of the deuteronomistic movement have had difficulty explaining how this movement came to embrace a royal Judahite theologoumenon of kingship. My work sheds light on this issue by revealing the deuteronomistic movement as having a more complex and nuanced point of view. Understanding the transformation of deuteronomic ideals in the deuteronomistic movement involves appreciating the impact of the Assyrian conquests of Israel upon Judah.[70] But it also involves understanding how the Assyrian campaigns stymied a long process of growth in Judah, causing tremendous political and demographic upheaval.

Perhaps because of the rich and varied literature dealing with the Babylonian exile and its aftermath -- 2 Kings 24-25, Jeremiah, 2 Isaiah, Ezekiel, Habakkuk, Zephaniah, Obadiah, Lamentations, Psalm 137 -- biblical scholars have privileged the events of 586 BCE as the critical turning point in the history of ancient Judah. The Babylonian exile marks the transition from ancient Israelite religion to early Judaism. Even though the biblical literature dealing with the Assyrian campaigns is much less extensive, both the material and the written remains from ancient Judah suggest a much more complex picture of decisive developments in the history of Jerusalem and its environs.[71] The eighth century witnessed an impressive increase in

---

70 See Becking (1992), Ahlström (1993:665-707), and the references listed in these works.

71 2 Kgs 18:1-20:21; Mic 1:8-16, Isa 1:4-9, 10:5-34, 11:12-16, 18:1-4, 22:1-14, 30:1-17, 27-33, 31:1-9, 36:1-39:8, 2 Chr 29:1-32:33. Note the comprehensive treatments of Stohlmann (1983:168-74), Gonçalves (1986:137-527), Seitz (1991), and Japhet (1993:910-

the settlement of Judah.[72] Eighth century Judah was also characterized by a significant number of public works projects, such as walls, water systems, and fortifications.[73] The number of towns and fortifications in the Judean Hills and the Shephelah was unprecedented (Shiloh 1989:97-103; Mazar 1990:455).

Sennacherib's campaign effected immense transformations, however, in the demography of Judah.[74] He claims to have decimated "46 of his [Hezekiah's] strong-walled cities, as well as the small cities in their environs, which were without number."[75] Similarly, the author of 2 Kgs 18:13 soberly admits that "Sennacherib, king of Assyria, came up against all of the fortified cities of Judah and cap-

98). On the major changes in the social structure of Judah, see Halpern's forthcoming "Sybil, or the Two Nations?: Archaism, Alienation and the Elite Redefinition of Traditional Culture in Judah in the 8th-7th Centuries B.C.E." I wish to thank the author for making a copy of this paper available to me.

72 Mazar (1990:438-62); Halpern (1991:19-34); Jamieson-Drake (1991:48-73).

73 See, for instance, KAI 189 and the discussions of Mazar (1982:87-109), Na'aman (1986:5-21), Shiloh (1987:203-44), King (1988:29-87), and Jamieson-Drake (1991:81-106).

74 2 Kgs 18:13-16; Luckenbill (1924:32-34 [.18-49], 68-70 [.18-32], 77 [.20-21], 86 [.15] // 1927:119-21 [#240], 142-43 [#311], 148 [#327], 154 [#347]); Gonçalves (1986:102-36); Miller and Hayes (1986:353-63); Tadmor and Cogan (1988:223-51); Halpern (1991:34-41); Ahlström (1993:680-740).

75 Luckenbill 1924:32-33 [.18-23]; see also the analyses of Dion (1988:3-25) and Halpern (1991:34-49).

tured them."[76] Given this picture of systematic devastation, it is not surprising that Stohlmann (1983:147-75) speaks of a "Judaean exile after 701 B.C.E."

In this case, there seems to be a general correlation between the written remains and the material remains. Sennacherib's invasion is associated with the systematic destruction of Judahite border fortresses.[77] Mazar credits Sennacherib with taking Lachish (III), Ramat Rahel (VB), Timnah (Tell el-Baṭash [III]) and perhaps also Beer-Sheba (II), Gezer (IIB),[78] and Tell Beit Mirsim (A2).[79] The

---

76 Na'aman (1974:25-39) calls attention to a "letter to god" by an Assyrian king, whom Na'aman identifies as Sennacherib. This letter asserts that the Assyrian king took Azekah and the royal Philistine city (of Gath?), formerly captured and fortified by H[ezek]iah.

77 See Aharoni (1982:253-69) and Fargo (1987:157-64), although the evidence from Tell el-Ḥesi is ambiguous (Doermann 1987:129-56). As Halpern points out, one need not expect that the Assyrians levelled every town to demonstrate the impact of Sennacherib's invasion. A number of towns may have "surrendered to threats and blandishments, others to shortages; still others (Batashi III) suffered local breaches, not general destructions" (Halpern 1991:34).

78 But Lance (1967:43-44), Seger (1987:122-28), and Becking (1992:114-18) attribute the destruction of Gezer (IIB), to the campaign of Tiglath-pileser III through Philistia. It is possible, as Na'aman (1979:76) asserts, that Hezekiah later annexed Gezer (IIC).

79 Mazar (1990:416-38); cf. Aharoni (1979:387-94). Mazar (1990:439-40) and Ahlström (1993:698) believe that Arad (X-VIII) may have been destroyed by the Edomites following Sennacherib's conquest of Judah. Seger's excavations (1983:10-16) at Tell Halif also reveal an Iron II (VIB) destruction layer, which Seger attributes to the invasions of Sennacherib or those of his successors after 701 BCE. Aharoni (1982:266) attributes the destruction of Bet Shemesh (IIC) at the end of the eighth century to Sennacherib, but Ahlström (1993:698) is unsure about who bears responsibility for this ruin.

Assyrian king was apparently also responsible for the marked depopulation of many parts of Judah at the end of the eighth century. Many critics have understandably reacted to Sennacherib's claim that he took away 200,150 people (Luckenbill 1924:33 [.24-26]) with incredulity, but he does seem to have annihilated or deported many Judahites.[80] Ofer's recent archaeological surveys suggest, for instance, that Sennacherib killed or exiled most of the inhabitants of the Shephelah and about 50-70% of the inland residents. Only Jerusalem withstood the Assyrian onslaught.[81]

Given the turbulent history of late eighth-century Judah, it is understandable that the Deuteronomist interprets the survival of Jerusalem in the Assyrian crisis as historical confirmation of Zion's inviolability and YHWH's promises to David (2 Kgs 18:34; 19:34; 20:6). To abandon Jerusalem or to overthrow the Davidids would be tantamount to ignoring the past, especially David and Solomon's

---

80 On this Aharoni (1979:387-94; 1982:253-66), Bright (1981:285-86), Mazar (1990:544-47), Halpern (1991:30-34), and Ahlström (1993:715, 719-20) all agree.

81 Tadmor and Cogan (1988:250-51) argue that the oft-quoted passage in *The History* of Herodotus (Greene 1987:192-93 [2.141]; cf. Josephus *Ant*. x.19), referring to hordes of mice knawing the weapons of the Assyrian soldiers during their war against the Egyptians, has nothing to do with the endurance of Jerusalem in the Assyrian crisis. The reason why Jerusalem survives varies in the biblical sources identified by Stade (1886:172-83). In the B^1 narrative (2 Kgs 19:7, 36-37), YHWH causes Sennacherib to hear a rumor and return to his own land, where he is assassinated. In the B^2 narrative (2 Kgs 19:35), a מלאך יהוה kills 185,000 Assyrian troops. This matter need not detain us. In either case, Sennacherib's failure to conquer Jerusalem is understood as divine deliverance (see also Isa 37:36-37, 2 Chr 32:21, and the detailed comments of Japhet 1993:988-92).

accomplishments, and threatening the present by jeopardizing a verified source of security. However much Judahite kings stray from their obligations to their deity, the Davidic promises remain valid and, concomitantly, Davidic kingship remains an asset to Judah.

The Deuteronomist does not, however, highlight the Davidic promises as *the* crux to revitalizing either the former northern kingdom or what was left of the southern kingdom. The continuation of Jeroboam's sins brings destruction to Israel, but continuation of the promises to David does not *ipso facto* bring renascence to Judah. In Kings the Davidic promises only qualify the demise of the united kingdom, ensuring that the Davidids retain one tribe.[82] Similarly, throughout Judah's tumultuous history, the divine assurances to David only mean that a fief (ניר) continues in Jerusalem (1 Kgs 11:36; 15:4; 2 Kgs 8:19). Jerusalem may be inviolable, but Judah is clearly not. The deuteronomistic application of the Davidic promises is primarily defensive, legitimating Davidic kingship and ameliorating the operation of divine wrath in Judah. Comparing the deuteronomistic comment on the secession, "none remained to the house of David, except the tribe of Judah alone" (לא היה אחרי בית-דוד זולתי שׂבט-יהודה לבדו; 1 Kgs 12:20), with the deuteronomistic comment on the Assyrian exile, "none remained, except the tribe of Judah alone" (לא נשאר רק שׂבט יהודה לבדו; 2 Kgs 17:18), reveals a tempered view of the past.

However much, then, he cites the Davidic promises as warrant for continuing Davidic rule, the Deuteronomist does not tout them as sufficient to solve Judah's problems. The promises to David and the judgments against Jeroboam are not opposites. In the age of the monarchy, the people's welfare depends upon their dedication to the

---

82 1 Kgs 11:12, 13, 34, 36; 15:4; 2 Kgs 8:19; 19:34; 20:6.

temple and royal suppression of all rival cults. The Deuteronomist presents David as the paradigm of this concern for centralization and Jeroboam as the antithesis of this concern.[83] History becomes an argument for the imposition of *Kultusreinheit* and *Kultuseinheit* throughout the land. Hence, whether positively (David) or negatively (Jeroboam), the Deuteronomist promotes similar standards for both northern and southern realms. In both cases, the movement of history is geared toward the need for restoration and thoroughgoing reform.

---

[83] 1 Kgs 15:3, 11; 2 Kgs 14:3; 16:2; 18:3; 22:2.

CHAPTER 5

INNOVATION AS RENOVATION: JOSIAH AND "THE SCROLL OF THE TORAH"

> Royalty is a government in which the attention of the nation is concentrated upon one person doing interesting actions. A Republic is a government in which that attention is divided among many, who are all doing uninteresting actions.
> (Walter Bagehot, *The English Constitution*, chapter 1: *The Cabinet*.)

Introduction: Josiah's Reign and the Provenance of Deuteronomy

In the past two centuries of critical research, more attention has been lavished on 2 Kings 22-23 than on any other chapters in the Former Prophets.[1] Among the reasons for this avid interest three stand out. First, the events of 2 Kings 22-23 appear momentous for the history of ancient Israelite religion: Josiah centralizes the Yahwistic cult (*Kultuseinheit*) and extirpates alien cults (*Kultusreinheit*). Second, most modern scholars regard the reign of Josiah as the Archimedean point for dating the major Pentateuchal sources, be-

---

[1] Nicholson (1967:1-17), Preuss (1982:1-12), Lohfink (1985:24-48), and Graham (1990:9-42, 117-50) provide overviews.

cause they associate "the scroll of the torah" (2 Kgs 22:8, 11) with the old deuteronomic law code (*Urdeuteronomium*). The eighteenth year of Josiah (2 Kgs 22:1; 23:23) is the *terminus ad quem* for the composition of *Urdeuteronomium*. Third, critics agree that Josiah is one of the most revered figures in the Deuteronomistic History. Hence, 2 Kings 22-23 is of great interest to historians of religion, Pentateuchal scholars, and scholars who study the Deuteronomistic History.

Not surprisingly, the conclusions of the three groups often converge.[2] Because of Josiah's unparalleled zeal for executing the old deuteronomic law code, his reign attempts a revolution in ancient Israelite religion: "the Deuteronomic law fell like a thunderclap of conscience" (Bright 1981:321). The acceptance and promulgation of *Urdeuteronomium*, whatever its precise origins, is associated with the Jerusalem authorities (2 Kgs 23:2; Nicholson 1967:16-17). The Deuteronomist extols Josiah's reforms, hence his history is properly deuteronomic (Weinfeld 1991:53-55).

My agenda in this chapter is concerned with the last two claims. There can be little doubt that the Deuteronomist wishes to project an image of Josiah as scrupulously upholding the deuteronomic law. Yet I question whether Josiah's reign represents the triumph of Deuter-

---

2 I do not claim that there is a consensus about what Josiah did. There have been, in fact, a great variety of views expressed in the last two centuries on the historicity, nature, and extent of Josiah's reforms (e.g., Ahlström 1982:68-74; 1993:770-81; Gramberg 1829:xxvi-xxvii, 305-308; Hölscher 1922:161-255; Horn 1988:137-41; Nowack 1925:221-31; Oded 1977:458-69; Suzuki 1987:22-58; Weinfeld 1991:37-44; Welch 1924:9-23). My point is simply the interdependence of literary and historical reconstructions of Josiah's reign and the close relationship between these theories and the critical analysis of ancient Israelite law, cult, and politics.

onomy not because Josiah implements some other legal code or text (Lundbom 1976:293-302), but precisely because Josiah implements Deuteronomy. The very notion of a king applying massive force to impose a document which radically curtails royal powers, is, from a deuteronomic point of view, highly problematic.

In contrast with the authors of Deuteronomy, who severely qualify royal prerogative, the Deuteronomist applauds Josiah's intervention in, and supervision of, cultic affairs. The Deuteronomist neither minimizes nor hides Josiah's revolutionary initiatives. Quite the contrary, he promotes them. As Lohfink (1963:267-71; 1985:39-40) demonstrates, Josiah is the subject of every major initiative (2 Kgs 22:3, 12; 23:1, 4, 21). The divergence between Deuteronomy and the Deuteronomistic History raises the question of their relationship. What is the Deuteronomist's agenda, given his indebtedness to *Urdeuteronomium* in language, style, and theology?[3] If the Deuteronomist esteems the institution of kingship, particularly Davidic kingship, why does he link Josiah so closely to the "the scroll of the

3 The shape of the Deuteronomist's deuteronomic *Vorlage* is much-debated (Preuss 1982:20-45). I am assuming, along with most scholars (e.g., Wellhausen 1963:191-95; Driver 1895:lxv-lxvii; Carpenter 1902:166-71; Fohrer 1968:169-72) that *Urdeuteronomium* contained at least a core of laws within Deuteronomy 12-26. Some (e.g., Lohfink 1971; Rüterswörden 1987) propose that part or all of Deut 16:18-18:22 represent a later stage in the composition of Deuteronomy, whether preexilic (Lohfink) or preexilic and exilic (Rüterswörden). I hesitate to call this material deuteronomistic, because I see significant disparities between the royal ideology of the Deuteronomist and the careful (re)configuration of powers in Deut 16:18-18:22. It seems more likely that most of this material is an integral part of a preexilic deuteronomic program (Milgrom 1983; Suzuki 1987; cf. Levinson 1991:325-465).

torah?" In so doing, why does the Deuteronomist endorse Deuteronomy's own assertions of antiquity and divine authority?

In my judgment, the Deuteronomist marshals the force of Deuteronomy behind Josiah's reforms, even as Josiah undercuts certain deuteronomic standards, to advance his royalist agenda. The Deuteronomist knows and endorses key elements of the deuteronomic program -- the unity of Israel, the abolition of foreign cults, and the centralization of the Yahwistic cult. But if the authors of Deuteronomy innovate by demanding centralization, Dtr^1 innovates beyond Deuteronomy by commending royal authority and supervision of the cult. Given the tremendous upheaval Josiah creates with his cultic revolution, the Deuteronomist downplays, even obfuscates, his differences with Deuteronomy. The spotlight on Deuteronomy enables the Deuteronomist to portray Josiah's innovations as renovations, his revolution in religion as a restoration of an ancient ideal. The Deuteronomist's very promulgation of *Urdeuteronomium* in the Josiah narrative involves its transformation.

The Deuteronomist presents Josiah's reign in two major movements, each of which contains three sections.

22:3-10	Discovery of the Torah	23:4-14	Southern Reforms
22:11-20	Counsel with Huldah	23:15-20	Northern Reforms
23:1-3	National Covenant	23:21-23	National Passover

Each movement climaxes in a national convocation that consolidates and celebrates a reorientation toward torah. In the first movement (the subject of this chapter), the Deuteronomist orchestrates the early portion of Josiah's eighteenth year to establish the need for thorough reforms. The discovery and recitation of the torah scroll dramatizes Judah's plight. Huldah's counsel, in turn, confirms

Josiah's interpretation of the newly discovered torah scroll -- Judah is in the throes of a national crisis. Josiah responds to this predicament by hosting a national assembly. At this national convocation the people of Judah and Jerusalem enact a pact. In the deuteronomistic movement of history, drastic conditions warrant drastic measures. The ratification of a covenant between deity, king, and people galvanizes popular support for Josiah's massive intervention in cultic affairs.

Beginning with an overview of source criticism, I will analyze the Deuteronomist's portrayal of Josiah's response to the torah scroll, his consultation with Huldah, and his renewal of covenant. In each of these sections, the Deuteronomist promotes Josiah's initiative and leadership as exemplary.

I. THE CRISIS PRECIPITATED BY THE TORAH SCROLL

The deuteronomistic presentation of Josiah covers one year in Josiah's thirty-one year reign (2 Kgs 22:1; 23:23). All of the major events in 2 Kings 22-23 -- the discovery of the law book, the consultation with Huldah, the covenant renewal, the southern reforms, the northern reforms, and the Passover -- occur in this eighteenth year of Josiah's rule. In the Deuteronomistic History, as opposed to the Chronicler's History (Eslinger 1986:47-61), the chance find of a "scroll of the torah" drives the plot of Josiah's reign.

A. THE COMPOSITION OF 2 KINGS 22-23: AN OVERVIEW

Two issues dominate the literary-critical discussion of Josiah's reign -- the question of sources and the question of dating. By dating I am referring to the provenance of deuteronomistic editing -- is it preexilic, exilic, or postexilic, or some combination of the three? The controversy over sources has intensified in recent years. A useful comparison can be made with the critical study of Hezekiah's reign. Critics almost unanimously agree that the Deuteronomist draws heavily upon sources in his construction of Hezekiah's tenure.[4] This unanimity persists even as new approaches are applied to the text.[5] The opposite is true, however, with regard to 2 Kings 22-23. It will be useful to inquire why. Given the voluminous secondary literature on 2 Kings 22-23, I will focus on two figures who have helped to define the current debate: Oestreicher and Lohfink.

Numerous scholars have followed Oestreicher[6] in believing that the Deuteronomist integrates two major sources in his description of Josiah: the *Erzählung von der Gesetzesauffindung* or, as it is more commonly called, the *Auffindungsbericht* (2 Kgs 22:2-23:3, [16-18, 20-24]),[7] and a *Reformbericht* (2 Kgs 23:4-14, [15-20]). Oestreicher

---

4 Critics have long recognized that the Deuteronomist has included multiple accounts of Sennacherib's invasion within his narration of Hezekiah's reign: A (2 Kgs 18:13-16), B^1 (2 Kgs 18:17-19:9a, 36-37), and B^2 (2 Kgs 19:9b-35). See the foundational work of Stade (1886:172-83).

5 Cp. Gonçalves (1986:73-136) with Hobbs (1985:246-74). Camp provides a helpful summary of recent scholarly views on the sources embedded in 2 Kings 18-20 (1990:38-52).

6 Oestreicher (1923:12-55); Baltzer (1971:52); Cross and Freedman (1953:56-58); Gray (1970:715, 728); Noth (1966:42; 1981:80); Provan (1988:147-51).

7 Oestreicher (1923:16-29). Many recent scholars define and term the *Auffindungsbericht* somewhat differently, attributing, on the one hand, 2 Kgs 22:2; 23:24 to deuteronomistic composition, while, on the other hand, including 2 Kgs 23:16-18 (or 2 Kgs 22:15-20) in the *Reformbericht*. Würthwein defines the two sources as 2 Kgs 22:3-23:3 and 23:4-15 (1976:395-423). Gray (1970:715) ascribes 2 Kgs

contrasts the terse, abrupt style of the *Reformbericht* with the narrative style of the *Auffindungsbericht* (1923:30). That 2 Kgs 23:4-20 includes a series of *waw* perfects (2 Kgs 23:4, 5, 10, 12, 14, 15) confirms to some scholars that the editor of 2 Kings 22-23 drew upon archival materials.[8] Another contrast between the two lies in terminology: 2 Kgs 22:2-23:3, 21-23 mention "the scroll of the torah" (2 Kgs 22:8, 11) and "the scroll of the covenant" (2 Kgs 23:2, 21), but 2 Kgs 23:4-20 never mention either.

Lohfink extends and modifies Oestreicher's observations, pointing out that the *Auffindungsbericht* highlights a series of royal initiatives (1963:269-71). Each of the five sections within this narrative begins, "the king sent" (2 Kgs 22:3, 23:1) or "the king commanded" (22:12; 23:4[!], 21). Hence, Lohfink sees the celebration of the Passover as an essential component of the *Auffindungsbericht* (1963:269-75). Form-critically, Lohfink (1978:320-42) tries to link the *Auffindungsbericht* to a genre of propagandistic historical narratives, which he reconstructs in Jeremiah 26, 36, 37-38, and 40-43.[9] Loh-

---

22:3-23:3, 21-25 to the Deuteronomist or to one of his circle among the temple personnel. Lohfink surveys current opinion (1985:24-48).

8 E.g., Montgomery (1951:534). On the *waw* perfect, see Joüon (1923:#119z) and Spieckermann (1982:120-30). Others (e.g., Hölscher 1922:209) point to this same feature as reason to date these verses late. To complicate matters, the *perfectum copulativum* in the MT can sometimes be taken as an infinitive absolute. Epigraphic remains have shown wide use of infinitives absolute in a sequence of verbs, precisely in the seventh-sixth centuries (Cross 1983:150-51).

9 The later *Reformbericht* was reshaped to accommodate the *Auffindungsbericht* (Lohfink 1987:465). Isbell sees both similarities and contrasts between 2 Kings 22-23 and Jeremiah 36. He contends that Jeremiah 36 was composed in the light of the Josianic edition of 2 Kings 22-23 to contrast Jehoiakim with Josiah (1978:41-43).

fink attributes the combination and editing of these two documents to a Josianic Deuteronomist.[10]

Scholars challenge this reconstruction from basically three perspectives -- unity, diversity, and deuteronomistic editing.[11] Burney sees 2 Kgs 22:3-23:25 (minus deuteronomistic additions in 2 Kgs 22:16-17; 23:3, 19, 25, 26, 27) as a continuous narrative originating in temple archives (1920:355-56). Weinfeld maintains that what Lohfink terms the *Auffindungsbericht* is a deuteronomistic composition.[12] Hoffmann (1980:264-70), followed by Van Seters (1983:317-19) and Hobbs (1985:317-21), also maintains that the depiction of Josiah's reign is a highly unified account, but attributes this integrity to deuteronomistic composition.[13] Tagliacarne unstintingly defends the unity of 2 Kings 22-23 from the perspective of linguistic (morphosyntactic and semantic) analysis (1989:45-332).

A second group of scholars sees much greater diversity within 2 Kings 22-23 than can be accounted for through the citation of *Vorlagen*. They reconstruct multiple editorial layers within these chap-

---

[10] 1987:462. Lohfink's views on the growth of the Deuteronomistic History are complex (1981:87-100). See vol. 1: chap. 1.

[11] In their assessments of scholars who criticize the reconstruction of Oestreicher, Spieckermann (1982:20-22) and Gerbrandt (1986:195-200) demonstrate that the positions of unity and deuteronomistic editing are not mutually exclusive.

[12] 1991:70-71. Weinfeld's view of deuteronomistic editing is thus diametrically opposed to that of Lohfink, because Weinfeld believes that most of 2 Kgs 23:4-20 is drawn from Josiah's court archives.

[13] Hoffmann argues, for instance, that the narrative depicting the discovery of the law book is a deuteronomistic creation (1980:192-97). Tadmor and Cogan (1988:293) believe that the story of temple repairs is a free deuteronomistic composition.

ters. Dietrich (1977b:18-27) ascribes only scattered portions of 2 Kings 22 to pre-deuteronomistic material (vv 3, 8, 10, 12, 13*, 14, 15aαb, 16aα, 18bβ, 20b). Würthwein also sees substantial deuteronomistic editing in 2 Kings 22-23 (1976:395-423; 1984:445-466). Levin's analysis is the most radical; he assigns only 2 Kgs 22:1-2 to an exilic Deuteronomist (DtrH) (1984:363). The rest of 2 Kings 22 stems from the postexilic period (1984:354-71). Spieckermann (1982:46-71), like Dietrich, Würthwein, and Levin, discerns a variety of levels in 2 Kings 22: a *Vorlage* (vv 1, 3-5, 7-13aα, 13bα, 14-15aβ, 15b-16aβ, 17b-18, 19aα-aγ, 20aγb) expanded by DtrH (vv 2, 6) and later again by DtrN (vv 13αbβ-bg, 16b-17aβ, 19aα-aβ, 19a$\delta\varepsilon$-b, 20a$\alpha\beta$, 20a$\delta\gamma$-aε). He therefore assigns substantially more material to the Deuteronomist's sources than do Dietrich, Würthwein, and Levin.

A third group of scholars does not deny the possibility of sources but focuses on distinguishing between preexilic and later deuteronomistic composition. These scholars ascribe most of 2 Kings 22-23 to a preexilic Deuteronomist (Dtr^1) whose work has been retouched by an exilic Deuteronomist (Dtr^2). Cross (1973:286), Friedman (1981a:25-26), and Nelson (1981a:76-79) seem to assign all of 2 Kings 22, except for part of Huldah's oracle, to Dtr^1.[14] Similarly, Isbell assigns almost all of 2 Kings 22 (except v 20a) to the Josianic Deuteronomist (1978:42). Other scholars comment more directly on the question of sources. O'Brien thinks that the Josianic Deuter-

[14] Nelson sees Dtr^2 as adding portions of vv 16-17 and 20b, and retouching the rest (1981a:78-79). My caution in summarizing this position stems from the fact that none of these scholars presents a comprehensive exegesis of 2 Kings 22-23.

onomist is responsible for 2 Kgs 22:3-10, 15aαb, 18b, 20aα.[15] He also contends that two post-Josianic additions were made to Huldah's oracle: vv 19, 20aβ and vv 16-17, 18a.[16] McKenzie ascribes vv 8-10, 14(?) to sources, vv 2-7, 11-13, 15-20* to Dtr[1] and glosses in vv 15-20 to post-deuteronomistic composition (1991:110-112).

This brief overview of recent criticism reveals that the disagreement about the Deuteronomist's *Vorlage* cuts across various schools of thought. O'Brien and Spieckermann attribute substantial portions of 2 Kings 22 to sources, while McKenzie and Dietrich attribute most of 2 Kings 22-23 to deuteronomistic composition. What scholars in all three groups hold in common is a disbelief that an *Auffindungsbericht* can be reconstructed from the text of 2 Kings 22-23. I share this skepticism. First, one is struck by the differences in style, sequence, and content between 2 Kings 22-23 and the stories Lohfink posits as parallels.[17] Based on the analogy of Exodus 34, the direct movement from Huldah's oracles and the covenant renewal to the Paschal feast, without any intervening reforms, is surprising.[18] One

---

15 He (1989:247) believes that 2 Kgs 22:11-14 may be either predeuteronomistic or deuteronomistic.

16 O'Brien sees this third addition as reflecting the style and vocabulary of Jeremiah (1989:247-48).

17 The Jeremiah narratives seem to share more elements with each other than any of them shares with 2 Kings 22-23*.

18 Paul (1990:269-76) observes that the oracle should precede repentance, not vice versa (cf. the covenant renewal of Exodus 34). Paul's explanation -- that the covenant is not actually broken -- is not compelling. First, the sins which Josiah corrects seem at least as heinous as, and certainly more numerous than, the sin of Aaron's calf. Second, even if the covenant was simply threatened, there still would be ample need for a salvation oracle.

expects that, as in Exodus 32-34, the offense has to be removed before harmony in divine-human relations can be restored.[19]

Second, there are signs of heavy deuteronomistic editing in 2 Kings 22-23. The very term, for instance, used to describe the discovered document, "(the) scroll of the torah" (2 Kgs 22:8, 11) is characteristic of Deuteronomy and the Deuteronomistic History (Weinfeld 1972:339).[20] The descriptions of Josiah's covenant (2 Kgs 23:1-3), and especially his Passover (2 Kgs 23:21-23), are so resonate with the prescriptions or language of Deuteronomy that one is pressed to posit deuteronomistic authorship for these two pericopes.[21] Hence, I do not find the model of an *Auffindungsbericht* particularly productive for approaching the composition of 2 Kings 22-23.

If the Deuteronomist employed a source for the non-reform portions of Josiah's reign, it was probably more limited in scope than Oestreicher and Lohfink allow. In my view, 2 Kgs 22:3-20 exhibits the essential conventions of a consultation narrative.[22] The crisis in 2 Kings 22 centers on the accidental discovery of "the scroll of the torah" in the temple (v 3). Josiah's abject reaction upon hearing the words of this scroll underlines the impression of an emergency.[23] He

---

19 A connection with reform is also evident in Gen 35:2-4, Exod 19:3-8, Josh 24:23, Judg 10:6-16, 1 Sam 7:3-4, and 2 Kgs 11:17-18.

20 *Pace* Lohfink (1963:267-71). That 2 Kgs 23:2, 21 refer to "the scroll of the covenant" reflects Dtr^1's attempt to link Josiah's covenant and Passover with the Sinaitic covenant.

21 The author of these texts displays a thorough familiarity with the prescriptions of Deuteronomy, yet obviously lauds Josiah's involvement in covenant-making and Passover observance. The simplest explanation for these factors is deuteronomistic authorship.

22 On consultation scenes, see chap. 4.

23 Rending one's garments is a sign of contrition and distress (e.g., Gen 37:34; 2 Sam 3:31; 13:31; 2 Kgs 5:7; 6:30; 11:14; 18:37; 19:1).

immediately seeks counsel from a Yahwistic prophetess, Huldah (2 Kgs 22:12-14). As in many other prophetic consultation stories, messengers (Hilkiah, Ahikam, Achbor, and Shaphan) relay messages between the two parties (2 Kgs 22:12).

I do not think, however, that the Deuteronomist simply inserted a consultation story into his narrative. He seems to have edited his source according to his own agenda. The account of temple repairs in 2 Kgs 22:3-7, for instance, resembles the account of temple repairs in 2 Kgs 12:5-17. Josiah, like Joash before him (2 Kgs 12:5-6), orders temple renovations (2 Kgs 22:3-7). Whether 2 Kgs 22:3-7 is modelled after 2 Kgs 12:5-17 (Dietrich 1977b:18-21; Hoffmann 1980:192-97; O'Brien 1989:241) or vice versa (Spieckermann 1982:48-53, 179-82), there seems to be a conscious patterning at work.

An examination of the two temple repair stories reveals that they play different roles within their respective contexts. Joash's temple refurbishments are a major subject of discussion in their own right (2 Kgs 12:7-17), but the briefer account of temple repairs (2 Kgs 22:3-7) in Josiah's reign sets the stage for a longer account describing the momentous discovery of "the scroll of the torah" (2 Kgs 22:8-14). It seems that the Deuteronomist has included only an abbreviated version of temple repairs to introduce his prime interest -- Josiah's reaction to the discovery of the torah scroll. It therefore becomes difficult to deny the presence of an active deuteronomistic hand in the composition of this narrative. Apart from the speeches of Huldah in 2 Kgs 22:15-20 (see below), I do not see any conclusive evidence for a series of systematic deuteronomistic redactions in 2 Kings 22.[24] I

---

24 As O'Brien (1989:241-43) demonstrates, there is no need to assign major portions of 2 Kgs 22:3-10 to the postexilic age (*pace* Levin 1984:354-56 and Würthwein 1984:357-58).

agree with the majority of scholars who maintain that only one Deuteronomist edited 2 Kgs 22:1-14.[25]

B. THE IMPETUS TO REFORM

The Deuteronomist depicts the early portion of Josiah's reign in very positive terms. His superlative estimate of Josiah has two parts.

1) He did what was right in the eyes of YHWH and
2) he followed in all the ways of his forefather David: he did not turn to the right or to the left. (2 Kgs 22:2).

The second element distinguishes Josiah as an excellent king. Only Hezekiah (2 Kgs 18:3) and Josiah are compared so favorably with David. The expression "to turn to the left or to the right" occurs infrequently in Deuteronomy and in the Deuteronomistic History, almost always as a command.[26] Friedman (1981b:171-73) calls attention to the use of this phrase in the law of the king (Deut 17:20), but Josiah is the only person in the entire Deuteronomistic History whom

---

25 Dietrich (1977b:18-27), followed by Mayes (1983:128), argues that the story of the lawbook's discovery (2 Kgs 22:3*, 8, 10) should be disentangled from the story of temple repair (2 Kgs 22:4-7, 9). But as Hoffmann (1980:192), O'Brien (1989:238-40), and McKenzie (1991:110) point out, the tensions Dietrich posits in 2 Kgs 22:3-10 can be satisfactorily explained without recourse to multiple redactions. For example, the story of temple repairs could stem from the Deuteronomist himself. See also Spieckermann (1982:46-58, 423-24), who ascribes most of 2 Kgs 22:3-14 to a source and sees DtrH and DtrN as making only limited additions.

26 Deut 2:27; 5:32; 17:11, 20; 28:14; Josh 1:7; 23:26; 1 Sam 6:12.

the Deuteronomist upholds as having fulfilled this mandate. Josiah is completely obedient.

The story of temple renovations in 2 Kgs 22:3-10 also compliments Josiah. Like other pious ancient Near Eastern kings, Josiah provides for and exhibits a keen interest in the upkeep of the cult. Even before the scroll is found, Josiah arranges major repairs to the only shrine the Deuteronomist approves of, the temple in Jerusalem (2 Kgs 22:3-7).[27] According to the standards set forth in Deuteronomy, the community is to read the torah every seven years (31:11), and the king is supposed to read it daily (17:19). As Friedman (1981b:172) observes, Josiah is the only king in the Deuteronomistic History who reads it at all.

Josiah's commission to his messengers, "go, inquire of YHWH (לכו דרשו את־יהוה) on behalf of me, on behalf of the people, and on behalf of Judah about the words of this scroll," demonstrates his concern for not only his own future, but also that of his people.[28] Friedman maintains that Josiah's manner of seeking (דרש) a judgment is consonant with the stipulations of Deuteronomy (17:8-12), in which people are to journey to "the place YHWH your God will choose" and present their problem to the proper personnel (Friedman 1981b:171-72). It is interesting to observe, however, that Josiah does not consult a levitical priest, a magistrate, or Hilkiah, but a prophetess. Josiah's actions therefore comport with the actions of other kings seeking advice in the consultation narratives of Kings, but do not accord with the specific instructions of Deuteronomy. In any event, Josiah's

[27] Hence, Hoffmann views Josiah's reform activity as beginning before the discovery of the torah scroll (1980:192-97).

[28] Josiah's commission in 2 Kgs 22:13 accords with regular form (Long 1984:246).

profound respect for "the scroll of the torah" is evident in his rationale for consulting Huldah.

> Indeed, great is the wrath of YHWH, which has been kindled against us, because our fathers have not heeded the words of this scroll to do all that has been written concerning us.[29]

Covenant abrogration can lead to covenant curse. Baltzer observes that in Hittite treaties two offenses constitute violation: disobedience and loss of the treaty document (1971:41-42). 2 Kings 22 presupposes the latter and explicitly mentions the former as the source of Josiah's agitation (2 Kgs 22:11-13). Josiah's comment does not imply, however, that previous kings have been entirely recalcitrant (contra Provan 1988:116). Instead, Josiah's apprehension stems from his ancestors' unwillingness to obey all that the torah scroll prescribes. Even before Huldah speaks, Josiah's own interpretation of the torah scroll anticipates his later reforms.

C. JOSIAH, THE DEUTERONOMIST, AND DEUTERONOMY

A number of historians doubt the Deuteronomist's version of the discovery of the torah scroll. Oestreicher argues that the story functions as a literary camouflage for a historical compromise between adherents of the deuteronomic movement and Josiah. Oestreicher (1923:60-65) believes that the Chronicler's account (2 Chronicles 34-35), in which Josiah is already busily reforming when the scroll is found, is historically more probable than the litany of events found in

---

[29] Reading with KM 2 Kgs 22:13 (עלינו). A few mss read עליו. KG^B reads *καθ΄ ημων*, but KG^L has *εν αυτω*.

Kings.[30] In Oestreicher's theory, Josiah was already long engaged in anti-Assyrian maneuvers when he was able to extend his reforms through the support of the deuteronomic movement.[31]

Other scholars, while giving more credence to what I term the consultation narrative, agree that Josiah must have been engaged in reform activity before his eighteenth regnal year.[32] Some of these critics trace the composition of *Urdeuteronomium* to the time of Hezekiah.[33] In this hypothesis the discovery and recitation of Deuteronomy caused a sensation, because the curses contained in this book (e.g., Deut 28:37) threatened the future of king and people. Hence, the conclusions of this second group differ little from the first. In

---

30 The historical value of the Chronicler's reconstruction is debated (Ahlström 1993:770-74; Dillard 1987:276-82; Eslinger 1986:37-62; Lowery 1990:190-209; Mosis 1973:194-200; Weinfeld 1991:69-74; Welten 1973:180-83). See the judicious overviews by Japhet (1985:83-107; 1989:444), Graham (1990), and Wright (1992:20-42). Disputing the reliability of the Chronicler's History does not in itself disprove, however, the basic features of Oestreicher's theory. Williamson (1982b:396-403) remarks that the Chronicler's version of Josiah's reign exhibits its own problems. Huldah's prophecy of doom becomes a response to Josiah's reforms.

31 Josiah purportedly won the allegiance of this group by implementing the cultic demands of *Urdeuteronomium* (Oestreicher 1923:43-49; Nicholson 1967:13).

32 Cross and Freedman (1953:56-58); Gressmann (1924:313-27); Noth (1966:43-49); Nicholson (1967:9-14); von Rad (1962:75-77); Weinfeld (1991:53-57). Different reconstructions of royal Assyrian chronology may affect the timing of Josiah's campaign for independence, but they do not refute the probability that Josiah was engaged in nationalistic reforms prior to his eighteenth regnal year.

33 E.g., Freedman (1976:227); Gray (1970:716-20), Miller and Hayes (1986:394), Sellin (1910:40-41), and Weinfeld (1991:44-53).

both theories the goals of Josiah's domestic policy and foreign policy coalesced. By abolishing foreign cults and centralizing the Yahwistic cult, Josiah intensified his campaign for independence.

A third group of scholars contends that the scroll discovery narrative is an exilic or postexilic creation with little or no connection to the historical events of Josiah's reign.[34] Josiah's reaction to the scroll reveals how the Deuteronomist wishes a godly king would, rather than did, behave. This third hypothesis provides, however, little explanation for the problems associated with this story. The absence of law in a history, which holds kings accountable to a legal standard, is self-referentially problematic.[35] The Deuteronomist could simply have been content to claim that Josiah, like Hezekiah (2 Kgs 18:3) "did what was right in the sight of YHWH, according to all what his father David did" (cf. 2 Kgs 22:2). Paton observes that the later one ascribes the composition of this story, the more difficult the story becomes (1928:337-338). For an exilic or postexilic editor to concoct the torah scroll story makes far less sense than a preexilic

[34] E.g., Kennett (1920:2-3); Hölscher (1922:231; 1923:206-213); Horst (1923:226); Würthwein (1976:421); Rose (1977:50-62); Levin (1984:354-56); Davies (1992:94-112).

[35] A comparison between 2 Kgs 22:3-10 and a postexilic treatment of torah is pertinent. In the Chronicler's treatment of the monarchy, references to torah are many (1 Chr 16:40; 22:12; 2 Chr 12:1; 14:3, 14; 15:1-7; 17:9; 23:18; 25:4 30:16; 31:3, 4, 21; 33:8; 34:14, 15, 16, 19, 21, 24; 35:12, 26; von Rad 1930:41-63; Willi 1972:48-52; Japhet 1989:234-47; Shaver 1989:73-86). One king, Jehoshaphat, even mandates the dissemination of "the scroll of YHWH's torah" (2 Chr 17:9). But the Chronicler does not attribute the lack of such dissemination to the loss of this scroll. Instead, the problem is royal and popular reluctance to follow what is presumed to be the constitution of the community (Knoppers 1991:508-509).

author wishing to undergird the authority of a relatively new system of laws. Hence, this third theory strikes me as implausible.[36]

Either of the first two theories therefore better explains the literary issues in the depiction of Josiah's rule than the third. The Deuteronomist's portrait of Josiah is highly stylized, presenting an extraordinary amount of activity in a very brief period. This portrait, however idealized, is best seen as engaging actual events: Josiah's campaign for centralization and his concomitant campaign against foreign cults.[37] Given Dtr^1's great interest in composing a literary defense of Josiah's activities, one must inquire why he employs the torah

---

36 Perhaps the Deuteronomist meant that the lawbook was lost or forgotten for some time, but not for centuries (Driver 1914:86-87). Nevertheless, the paucity of references to the lawbook in his history suggests a different and more complex historical development.

37 There are obvious problems with the deuteronomistic construction of the past (sources, use of sources, redactions, *Tendenz*, etc.). Yet the archaeological evidence pointing to the destruction of certain cult sites and cult objects in Judah during the eighth and seventh centuries should not be ignored (Stern 1975:26-54; Halpern 1991). Aharoni's dating of the destruction of the Arad temple (1968:25-27; 1973:1-8) to the late seventh century is no longer accepted (see Cross [1979:75-77] and Mazar [1990:497-98] on the inscriptions and altar at Arad). Elitzur (1969:92-97) dates the construction of *regamim* in west Jerusalem, excavated by Amiran (1958:206-227), to the time of Josiah. Yadin dates the destruction of the Beer-Sheba sanctuary to the time of Josiah (1976:5-17). But, as Tadmor and Cogan (1988:287) point out, the excavators date the destruction of this high place to the time of Hezekiah. Similarly, Kenyon dates the deposit of destroyed cult objects on the eastern slope of the Ophel to a time closer to the reign of Hezekiah than to the reign of Josiah (1974:137-44). However one dates and explains the material evidence, the destruction of cult places and cultic objects was clearly a preexilic issue.

story within his history. Why does he present Josiah's major reforms as postdating, rather than antedating, the discovery of the scroll?

In my judgment, the Deuteronomist employs the story of the torah scroll to justify and explain Josiah's unprecedented intrusion into the religious affairs of his people. Even by deuteronomistic standards Josiah's reforms are radical. None among the three kings of the united monarchy, none among the eighteen kings of Israel, and none among the thirteen previous kings of Judah attempt the wholesale revolution in cultic practice attempted by Josiah. The appeal to Deuteronomy's mandate for centralization of the Yahwistic cult and the elimination of alien cults serves the deuteronomistic agenda well. Josiah's reforms are severe but necessary, unprecedented but legitimate -- the appropriate response to a national crisis. The discovery of "the scroll of the torah" provides Dtr[1] with the necessary justification for Josiah's upheaval of religious practice.

But the Deuteronomist's consultation narrative reveals more than he perhaps intended. By using Proto-Deuteronomy to defend and promote Josiah's implementation of certain deuteronomic standards, the Deuteronomist deconstructs his own history. He tacitly acknowledges that a primary criterion for his critique of previous leaders and kings -- Deuteronomy's mandate for centralization -- is anachronistic. Dtr[1] upholds Josiah's response to the torah scroll as evidence for Josiah's greatness. The failures and partial successes of all previous kings point toward his reign (chap. 6).[38] Yet the Deuteronomist himself

---

38 The Deuteronomist holds kings accountable for overseeing the cult. Hence, if there was a compromise between Josiah and this deuteronomic group, it must have been more complex than Oestreicher allows. Such a compromise would also likely have involved scribal circles (Weinfeld 1972:298-306; 1991:53-57) and the Jerusalem temple priests.

concedes, both in his depiction of Josiah's stunned reaction to the torah scroll discovery and in his very infrequent references to "the scroll of the torah" (Josh 1:8; 8:31-32; 1 Kgs 2:3; 2 Kgs 14:6), that generations of previous leaders did not have access to this text. Hence, Dtr^1 implicitly admits that Josiah's achievement was partially attributable to the unique circumstances of his reign.

II. THE ORACLES OF HULDAH

The much-debated oracle of Huldah is actually two oracles. Her first speech announces the doom of "this place" (2 Kgs 22:16-17), while her second delays this catastrophe until after Josiah's peaceful death (2 Kgs 22:18-20). Because Huldah's speeches are complex, I will begin by examining their formal and thematic characteristics in some detail. I will then summarize the major approaches to 2 Kgs 22:15-20 as a prelude to presenting my own reconstruction.

A. FORMAL AND THEMATIC ISSUES

Each of Huldah's utterances is prefaced by an address and by at least one citation formula.[39]

2 Kgs 22:15:	אמרו לאיש אשר־שלח אתכם אלי
2 Kgs 22:18:	ואל־מלך יהודה השלח אתכם לדרש את־יהוה כה תאמרו אליו

39 Meier (1992:32-22) describes these features in vv 15-16 as "multiple embedding of direct discourse."

2 Kgs 22:15: כה אמר יהוה אלהי ישׂראל
2 Kgs 22:16: כה אמר יהוה
2 Kgs 22:18: כה אמר יהוה אלהי ישׂראל

The first oracle includes two announcements of punishment (vv 16, 17b) that frame an accusation (v 17a). The second oracle contains an implicit condition (יען רך-לבבך ותכנע...לכן הנני אספך על-אבתיך...). Because this second speech merely postpones judgment, it is better viewed as an oracle of reprieve (Long 1984:244) than as an oracle of salvation (Westermann 1991:28). Both of the speeches recall earlier elements within the torah scroll narrative. Each of Huldah's announcements of punishment, for example, allude to earlier events. That YHWH is effecting "all the words of the scroll which the king of Judah recited" (2 Kgs 22:16) recalls Josiah's request for consultation concerning "the words of this scroll which has been found" (2 Kgs 22:13).[40] Huldah's second announcement of punishment recapitulates and extends Josiah's cause for worry.

<u>2 Kgs 22:13</u>
כי-גדולה חמת יהוה אשר-היא נצתה בנו
"Great is the wrath of YHWH which is kindled against us."

<u>2 Kgs 22:17</u>
ונצתה חמתי במקום הזה ולא תכבה
"My wrath is kindled against this place and it cannot be quenched."

The disparity between the two statements is critical. Josiah seeks advice based on his tentative interpretation of the torah scroll. But

40 Not Josiah, but Shaphan (vv 8, 10) actually reads the scroll.

Huldah confirms Josiah's assessment, brooking no retraction of the deity's judgment. The phrase תחת אשר introduces the reason for the deity's insatiable fury: "they abandoned me and burned incense to other deities, by which they provoked me according to all the works of their hands" (2 Kgs 22:17). There is no clear antecedent to "they abandoned me." Presumably, this refers to the inhabitants of this place (המקום הזה ועל-ישביו) in 2 Kgs 22:16.

The address in v 18, "and to the king of Judah who sent you to seek YHWH," introduces the second speech. It alludes to the command of Josiah in v 13, "Go, seek YHWH on account of me, on account of the people, and account of all of Judah." The second oracle cites Josiah's obeisance -- his tender heart (רך לבבך), his humility (ותכנע מפני יהוה), his rending of his clothes (ותקרע את-בגדך), and his weeping (ותבכה לפני; 2 Kgs 22:19) -- as grounds for a reprieve (2 Kgs 22:20). The previous story mentions, however, only Josiah's rending of his clothes (2 Kgs 22:11). In response to Josiah's repentance Huldah provides three assurances: that YHWH will gather him to his fathers, that Josiah will be gathered to his grave in peace, and that YHWH will make sure that Josiah will not see the evil which YHWH is going to inflict against this place (2 Kgs 22:20).[41]

There are both parallels and contrasts between the two speeches. The first oracle begins with an assertion of judgment, "Behold, I am about to bring evil against this place and its inhabitants" (2 Kgs 22:16), while the second ends with an assurance, "But your eyes shall not see all the evil which I am about to bring against this place" (2 Kgs 22:20). The two assertions form an *inclusio* around the oracles.

---

41 The two phrases אספך על-אבתיך (cf. Judg 2:10) and נאספת אל-קברתיך are unusual in the Deuteronomistic History, but both imply peaceful death (Halpern and Vanderhooft 1991:226-27).

הנני מביא רעה אל-המקום הזה ועל-ישביו
לא-תראינה עיניך בכל הרעה אשר-אני מביא על-המקום הזה

There are three references to "hearing" in the second speech. The third responds to the second.

2 Kgs 22:18bβ	הדברים אשר שמעת
2 Kgs 22:19aβ	בשמעך אשר דברתי על המקום הזה ועל-ישביו
2 Kgs 22:19b	וגם אנכי שמעתי נאם-יהוה

The second oracle begins by noting Josiah's hearing YHWH's message, "the words which you heard" (2 Kgs 22:18bβ). This clause may be alluding to Josiah's listening (ויהי כשמע המלך את-דברי ספר התורה) to Shaphan's recital of the torah scroll (2 Kgs 22:10-11). But the precise referent is unclear.[42] In any case, the second oracle alludes to the first oracle in v 19aβ, "when you heard what I decreed about this place and its inhabitants" (בשמעך אשר דברתי על-המקום הזה ועל-ישביו). Citations of Josiah's servility (2 Kgs 22:19aα and 2 Kgs 22:19aδε) frame this second reference to hearing. Some argue that the antecedent to this phrase is the reading of the torah scroll in v 11, but Hoffmann (1980:176) is likely right in claiming that the antecedent is

42 It could also refer to Huldah's first oracle. In any case, הדברים אשר שמעת is a dangling clause, often translated as a *nomen pendens* construction (Keil 1877:481; Nelson 1981a:77; NJPS; NRSV). Nicholson believes that אל or על has been lost through haplography after ישראל (1963:96-98). Rose argues that this clause is a corruption of a clause in v 19 (בשמעך אשר דברתי; 1977:60). Tagliacarne thinks that a number of explanations are possible (1989:135-36).

the first oracle (2 Kgs 22:16-17). Huldah's assertion resonates with the first declaration of punishment in her first speech.

2 Kgs 22:16	הנני מביא רעה אל־המקום הזה ועל־ישביו
2 Kgs 22:19	בשמעך אשר דברתי על המקום הזה ועל־ישביו

2 Kgs 22:19 also describes this place "becoming a desolation and a curse."[43] The second oracle thus recalls Josiah's obsequious response to Huldah's word of doom in her first oracle, even though Josiah has not yet heard that oracle! The deity's assertion in 2 Kgs 22:19b, "so also have I heard, oracle of YHWH," reveals that Josiah's humility has not gone unnoticed. YHWH's recognition of Josiah's predicament, in turn, calls attention to the divine promises to Josiah (2 Kgs 22:20). The present form of the second oracle is therefore written with a view to the content and import of the first oracle.

B. THE COMPOSITION OF 2 KGS 22:15-20

There are at least four ways of explaining the puzzling features of Huldah's oracles.[44]

1) There are no contradictions; both oracles stem from one author (an exilic or postexilic Deuteronomist).[45]

---

43 No like comment occurs in vv 11-13 (*pace* O'Brien 1989:244-49).

44 The views of a few scholars do not match any of these categories. For Mayes (1983:131) 2 Kgs 22:10-20 stem from an exilic (nomistic) Deuteronomist. Würthwein (1984:450-52) sees vv 12-17* as redacted by DtrP. DtrN adds v 13b and a later editor adds vv 18-20a.

45 Hoffmann (1980:170-87); Provan (1988:148-49); Tagliacarne (1989:420-21); Van Seters (1983:318-19).

2) The first oracle was supplemented by a second oracle which, by underscoring Josiah's repentance, explained the postponement of punishment upon Judah.[46]
3) Both oracles have preexilic and exilic elements and both have been supplemented by later writers.[47]
4) A preexilic form of the second oracle was updated and the first oracle was created or substantially changed to explain the exile.[48]

The third and fourth reconstructions differ in that the third postulates a process of gradual growth in both oracles, whereas the fourth posits fewer but more consequential changes in the content of Huldah's message. The first theory is untenable, given the formal and thematic diversity of 2 Kgs 22:15-20. As we have seen, the present form of the second oracle refers to Josiah's response to the first oracle. I agree with proponents of the second reconstruction that the second oracle is largely written with a view to the first oracle, but because the second oracle clearly contains preexilic components, this hypothesis is too simplistic. Incongruities in form, content, and phraseology speak in favor of the last two theories. Of these two, I advocate the latter (the fourth), because I see no evidence that the first oracle contains any preexilic elements.

My own view is actually a modified form of the fourth theory. The first oracle was created and the second oracle was substantially recast during the exile. An exilic Deuteronomist reinterprets Josiah's

---

46 Jepsen (1956:26-29); Weinfeld (1972:25-26).

47 Dietrich (1972:55-58; 1977b:25-35); Spieckermann (1982:58-71).

48 Cross (1973:286); Friedman (1981:25); Gray (1970:727-28); Halpern and Vanderhooft (1991:221-30); Lohfink (1987:471); McKenzie (1991:110-112); Nelson (1981a:78-79); O'Brien (1989:244-45); Tadmor and Cogan (1988:295).

reign in light of the catastrophe of 587/6 BCE to rehabilitate the reputation of Josiah. In so doing, this exilic Deuteronomist refashions both Josiah's merit and his reward. I will begin with matters of phraseology and then engage issues of form and content. A number of expressions in the first speech of 2 Kgs 22:16-17 stressing the dire consequences of popular impiety are characteristic of the Book of Jeremiah, as Driver (1914:203) pointed out over a half-century ago. Driver's observations may be modified and extended.

מביא רעה אל/על-המקום הזה (2 Kgs 22:16, 20; Jer 19:3; cf. 2 Kgs 21:16; Jer 5:15; 6:19; 11:11).

הכעיס את-יהוה במעשׂה ידיהם (2 Kgs 22:17; Deut 31:29; Jer 7:19; 25:7 [*Qere*]; 32:20).[49]

קטר לאלהים אחרים (2 Kgs 22:17; Jer 1:16; 19:4; 44:5, 8, 15).[50]

That virtually every one of these expressions is only found in Jeremiah and the Deuteronomistic History is remarkable. I should also point out that many of the parallels stem from Jeremiah C.[51]

One locution in 2 Kgs 22:17 is unparalleled in biblical literature. But those phrases which come closest are again found in Jeremiah.

---

49 Nelson convincingly argues on the basis of Deut 4:28, 27:15 and Jer 25:6-7, 44:8 that "all the works of their hands" refers to idolatry (1981a:78-79). A similar phrase occurs in 1 Kgs 16:7 (ידיו: Baasha).

50 Weinfeld lists this expression as deuteronomistic (1972:321). The evidence permits a more precise definition: an exilic Deuteronomist, who exhibits some linguistic affinities with Jer C.

51 Bright (1951:15-35); Nicholson (1970:30ff.); Stulman (1986:7-39, 56-118); Weinfeld (1972:6-9, 359-61).

ונצתה חמתי במקום הזה ולא תכבה (2 Kgs 22:17).[52]
וחמתי נתכת אל־המקום הזה...ובערה ולא תכבה (Jer 7:20).
פן־תצא כאש חמתי ובערה ואין מכבה (Jer 4:4; 21:12).

There is also one expression in Huldah's second oracle that is elsewhere found only in Jeremiah.

לשמה (ו)לקללה (2 Kgs 22:19; Jer 42:18; 44:12, 22).[53]

Two other expressions in Huldah's second speech are found once elsewhere in the Deuteronomistic History, but are otherwise found only in Chronicles and P.

רך לבב (2 Kgs 22:19; Deut 20:8; 2 Chr 13:7; [34:27]; cf. 1 Chr 22:5; 29:1).

כנע *Niphal*, with a reflexive sense.[54] (2 Kgs 22:19; 1 Kgs 21:29;[55] 2 Chr 12:6, 7, 12; 13:18; 30:11; 33:19, 23; [34:27]; 36:12).

The aforementioned parallels in phraseology reinforce the argument that 2 Kgs 22:15-20 evince different levels of composition,

---

52 Cf. Josiah's comment in 2 Kgs 22:13: כי גדולה חמת יהוה אשר־היא נצתה בנו. Since חמת נצתה is only found in vv 13 and 17, it does not *ipso facto* qualify as deuteronomistic (contra Weinfeld 1972:348).

53 See also לשמה לשרקה ולקללה (Jer 25:18) and לשמה לחרפה לחרב ולקללה (Jer 49:13).

54 On the specialized use of כנע in the *Niphal*, see Curtis and Madsen (1910:31) and Jepsen (1956:27-28).

55 Jepsen (1970:150-53) and McKenzie (1991:68-69) contend, I think persuasively, that 1 Kgs 21:27-29 are a later addition to Elijah's oracle against Ahab, qualifying the timing of divine retribution.

levels which, given the affinities with Jeremiah C, P, and the Chronicler, cannot be convincingly assigned to one (Dtr^1) or more preexilic writers. The parallels instead suggest that elements within Huldah's oracles are exilic or, less likely, postexilic.[56] The overlap in vocabulary cannot in and of itself be decisive, because Jeremiah contains material from different periods.[57] Moreover, there are other phrases in 2 Kings 22-23, which overlap with the phraseology of Jeremiah.[58] Nevertheless, the frequency of parallels between Huldah's oracles and Jeremiah (especially Jeremiah C) point to a reworking of Huldah's message that was substantial and not merely glossing.

A study of the discrepancy between the form of Huldah's speeches and the normal forms of prophetic oracles in consultation narratives supports the theory of at least two stages of composition. We saw in chap. 4 that virtually every consultation narrative, which includes a prophetic speech predicts a positive outcome or provides instructions to the supplicant to ameliorate his or her problem. But Huldah's oracles provide neither salvation nor any constructive advice to Josiah on how to reverse or avert the doom decreed against "this place and its inhabitants." The form of Huldah's oracles is anomalous.

One might be tempted to surmise that Dtr^1 rewrote his *Vorlage*, incorporating oracles of judgment and personal reprieve in much the same way he integrated judgment oracles against Jeroboam's dynasty

56 I see postexilic composition as less likely, because the destruction of "this place" is a predominantly exilic concern.

57 It is rather unlikely that Huldah was alluding to or drawing upon Deut 32:15-22 (contra Lundbom 1976:295-99). The closest parallels between the diction in Huldah's oracles and the diction of another text are between Huldah's oracles and the C portions of Jeremiah.

58 Tagliacarne (1989:404-407) provides a helpful list. The largest concentration of parallels to Jeremiah occurs in 2 Kgs 22:15-20.

and Israel in the consultation narrative of 1 Kings 14 (chap. 4). Yet there is a decisive difference. The type-scene or story pattern in 1 Kings 14 both presupposes (1 Kgs 12:26-33; 13:1-34) and condemns (1 Kgs 14:7-16) Jeroboam's gross misconduct.[59] Ahijah's judgment oracles therefore exploit the crisis within Jeroboam's family to condemn both his male heirs and Israel itself. The only other case I am aware of in which a prophet condemns a king in a consultation narrative is 2 Kings 1.[60] There Elijah intervenes against Ahaziah, because Ahaziah inquires of the god of Ekron, rather than of YHWH, about his injury (2 Kgs 1:2). Again, the judgment oracle is occasioned by the monarch's own perfidy. Formal parallels to the consultation narrative in 2 Kings 22 therefore suggest that an originally positive message has been overwritten with a decidedly more negative slant.

Finally, analysis of the content of 2 Kgs 22:15-20 evinces the work of at least two different writers, the first of whom must be pre-exilic. If Huldah told Josiah that the situation was hopeless, it would hardly motivate him to institute a covenant renewal and undertake risky and pioneering reforms. The inconsistency between this insistence upon perdition and Josiah's subsequent actions (2 Kgs 23:1-23) cannot be satisfactorily explained synchronically. On the contrary, the scope and extent of Josiah's reforms suggest the existence of an original oracle that offered Josiah an alternative to destruction.

---

59 A point Holder (1988:27-38) repeatedly stresses.

60 In 2 Kgs 8:7-15, Elisha makes two different predictions: a cure for Ben-hadad of Syria (2 Kgs 8:10) and the usurpation of Ben-hadad's throne by Hazael. Although this story includes a fulfillment notice marking Ben-hadad's death and Hazael's accession (2 Kgs 8:14-15), the first of Elisha's predictions goes unfulfilled.

Arguments for interpreting Josiah's burial as fulfilling all three parts of Huldah's promise in 2 Kgs 22:20 cannot be sustained.[61] Josiah, killed by Necho at Megiddo, is not gathered to his grave in peace (2 Kgs 22:20aβ).[62] Nor does the writer of 2 Kgs 23:29-30 make this claim. In contrast with the deuteronomistic pattern of accenting the fulfillment of prophecy, the author of 2 Kgs 23:29-30 does not explicitly mark the death of Josiah as fulfilling Huldah's prediction.[63] The curt note of 2 Kgs 23:30 merely states that "they buried him in his grave."[64] Even the claim, based on 2 Kgs 22:20aα and 2 Kgs 22:30a, that YHWH gathers Josiah to his fathers is highly problematic. The expression, "to be gathered to one's kin" in P con-

61 Contra Dietrich (1972:57-58), Hoffmann (1980:185), and Provan (1988:149). Josiah's unpeaceful end comes at the hands of Necho (2 Kgs 23:29). As Rose (1977:55-59) and, much more extensively, Halpern and Vanderhooft (1991:83-97, 223-230) show, Josiah's burial (2 Kgs 23:30) is not tantamount to dying in peace. That the Chronicler depicts Josiah as only wounded and not killed at Megiddo (2 Chr 35:20-24) indicates that he saw his *Vorlage* as problematic (Rose 1977:59-63; O'Brien 1989:246). But a caveat must be added here. It is not entirely clear what the Chronicler's *Vorlage* was for the death of Josiah (McKenzie 1985:18-22; Williamson 1982a:242-47; 1987:9-15; cf. Begg 1987a:1-8).

62 2 Kgs 23:29. Cross (1973:286); Lohfink (1978:340); McKenzie (1991:111); Priest (1977:367-68); Rose (1977:59).

63 Cf. 1 Kgs 12:15; 15:29; 16:12, 34; 17:16; 2 Kgs 1:17; 2:22; 4:44; 9:36-37.

64 Frost deems the terse notice of Josiah's death a "conspiracy of silence" (1968:369). Williamson describes 2 Kgs 23:28-30 as "an embarrassed appendix" (1982a:243).

notes a peaceful death as does the expression "to lie with one's fathers" in J and earlier portions of the Deuteronomistic History.[65]

Of the three promises afforded him in 2 Kgs 22:20, only one is explicitly realized: Josiah does not live to see the evil which YHWH inflicts against "this place and its inhabitants." The second promise, and probably also the first, predate Josiah's death in 609 BCE. The theory that one (exilic or postexilic) author is responsible for 2 Kgs 22:15-20 is untenable. If one author wrote the entire Josiah account (2 Kings 22-23) to show how a given person can absolve himself from a divine judgment rendered against an entire people (Tagliacarne 1989:411-21), his literary product contradicts his intentions. Josiah may escape national calamity, but he experiences an unkind death. Moreover, in the present arrangement of the text, Huldah's orations actually speak against Josiah's reforms. After receiving assurances of a peaceful death, based on his obeisance, Josiah implements massive reforms and then suffers an ignominious death. The incongruities between Huldah's oracles and the rest of the depiction of Josiah's reign therefore beg for diachronic analysis and reconstruction.

---

[65] Gen 25:8-9; 17; 35:29; 49:29, 33; Num 20:24, 26; 27:13; 31:2; Deut 32:50; Judg 2:10. Halpern and Vanderhooft (1991:224) comment that the P phrase "denotes a phase between expiration and burial." In their discussion of the deuteronomistic texts (1991:183-90), they note that the death of Ahab (1 Kgs 22:37) is the only counter-example (1991:230-35). See also the treatments of Alfrink (1943:106-18), Priest (1980:367-68), and O'Brien (1989:245-48).

C. HULDAH IN PREEXILIC AND EXILIC PERSPECTIVE

The exilic additions to Huldah's speeches are pervasive. In fact, I would argue that the present bipartite structure of Huldah's message reflects a second writer's reworking and supplementation of an older (Josianic) oracle. I believe that the entire first oracle is an exilic Deuteronomist's creation, inserted through Zeidel's Law from 2 Kgs 22:16aα through 2 Kgs 22:18bα.[66]

22:15aβ:	a) כה-אמר יהוה אלהי ישׂראל
22:15b:	b) אמרו לאישׁ אשׁר-שׁלח אתכם אלי
22:18aα:	b[1]) ואל-מלך יהודה השׁלח אתכם לדרשׁ את- יהוה כה תאמרו אליו
22:18bα:	a[1]) כה-אמר יהוה אלהי ישׂראל

The use of Zeidel's Law to interpolate the first speech explains both the distinctive terminology in this first oracle and the surprising repetition of instructions to the messengers following the end of the first oracle (2 Kgs 22:18aα-bα).[67] Having inserted a second speech in 2 Kgs 22:16aα-17b, this later writer reintroduces the older speech

---

66 That is, 2 Kgs 22:15aβ-15b were part of the original text that the exilic Deuteronomist partially duplicated to frame his interpolation.

67 Another possibility is a *Wiederaufnahme* from 2 Kgs 22:15aα, כה-אמר יהוה אלהי ישׂראל to 2 Kgs 22:18bα, כה-אמר יהוה אלהי ישׂראל (Dietrich 1972:56; cf. Levin 1984:364-66). This would leave, however, no address to Josiah. Dietrich (1977b:27) believes that the skeleton of the original oracles remains, even as the content has been altered to respond to later conditions. I would argue that the skeleton itself is partially editorial and that only lineaments of Huldah's preexilic oracle remain.

by recasting the address of 2 Kgs 22:15b in 2 Kgs 22:18aα and then repeating its citation formula in 2 Kgs 22:18bα. That is, he does not simply replicate the vague address of 2 Kgs 22:15b, but rewords it to bring it into line with Josiah's exclamation (2 Kgs 22:13).

This later editor also partially reworks the older (deuteronomistic) oracle of 2 Kgs 22:18-20*. There are ample grounds, given the disparity between Huldah's promises and Josiah's demise, for viewing at least part of the second oracle (2 Kgs 22:20aα and 2 Kgs 22:20aβ) as predating Josiah's death.[68] This older speech probably included the reference to Josiah's tearing his clothes (2 Kgs 22:19a$\delta\varepsilon$) and the deity's positive reaction to this gesture (2 Kgs 22:19b*). In its original context, the reference to Josiah's "being gathered" to his grave(s) in peace (2 Kgs 22:20aβ) likely provided Josiah with a personal assurance that there was still time to instigate major reforms. YHWH would gather Josiah to his fathers (2 Kgs 22:20aα). Such a link between royal actions and popular fate is, of course, a constituent feature of the deuteronomistic presentation of the monarchy. The bond between king and people is also evident in the other portions of Josiah's reign: the discovery of the law (2 Kgs 22:11-13), the ratification of a covenant (2 Kgs 23:1-3), and the celebration of a national Passover (2 Kgs 23:21-24).[69]

The preexilic, deuteronomistic version of Huldah's oracle thus confirmed Judah's danger, but encouraged Josiah to make amends. Consistent with the actions of prophets in other consultation scenes,

---

68 Burney (1920:356); Isbell (1978:42); Jones (1984:614); Kittel (1900:299); Lohfink (1978:340); Priest (1980:366-68); Rose (1977:55). See also those scholars listed under theory #4 above.

69 An oracle addressing the condition of the people would also be commensurate with the national focus of *Urdeuteronomium*.

Huldah instructed Josiah and predicted weal should he comply with her instructions.[70] In the deuteronomistic presentation, history, prophecy, and law converge in underscoring the need for drastic changes in Judah. Huldah's advice functions as a bridge between Josiah's inquiry and his decision to renew covenant (2 Kgs 23:1-3).

The exilic editor prefaces this older oracle (2 Kgs 22:18-20*) with his own (2 Kgs 22:16aα-17b), reinterpreting the reign of Josiah in the light of exile. The present account of the people's sins in vv 16aβ-17 stems from this writer. The author of these verses confirms Josiah's premonition of trouble in unequivocal terms (2 Kgs 22:13). From this tempered exilic perspective, Josiah did not and could not reverse the sins of the past. The ill fate of Judah had already been settled before the time of Judah's great reformer king. Since this writer uses language which resembles Jeremiah and traces Judah's demise solely to the perfidy of the people, one cannot be certain that he is Dtr^2.[71]

This second writer also rewrote the oracle bequeathed to him by the Josianic Deuteronomist (2 Kgs 22:18-20*) to redefine Josiah's distinction, as well as the divine stance toward this king.[72] If he did not rework the original prophetic speech, he risked two undesirable implications about Josiah's life and death. First, the addition of 2 Kgs 22:16aα-17b chanced the impression that Josiah's unparalleled obedi-

---

70 In 2 Kgs 20:8-11 Isaiah gives Hezekiah a sign, providing him with an initial verification of the prophetic word. In a few other stories, a prophet tells the supplicant to perform a certain action to achieve or aid a resolution (e.g., 1 Kgs 17:13; 2 Kgs 4:3-4; 5:10).

71 Cf. 2 Kgs 25:26-27, which blame Manasseh for Judah's demise. My identification of this writer as Dtr^2 is therefore tentative.

72 It is also possible, that two hands are at work, one adding (at least) the second oracle and another glossing (at least) the first oracle (Dietrich 1972:58; cf. Würthwein 1984:448-52).

ence was ineffectual or simply irrelevant. YHWH ominously declares that exile is unavoidable (2 Kgs 22:16-17); yet, YHWH proclaims this doom to Judah's most accomplished reformer king, a king who had already demonstrated his piety in his response to the discovery of the torah scroll. Second, the addition of the first oracle risked the implication that Josiah's death made a mockery of Huldah's prophecy.

The exilic editor tries to circumvent these difficulties with his additions to the original oracle. He boldly proclaims that Josiah realized that his people were doomed. He speaks of Josiah's consternation when Josiah heard that "this place and its inhabitants" were to become "a desolation and a curse" (2 Kgs 22:19).[73] By adding references to Josiah's tender heart, his humbling himself, and his weeping when he heard Huldah's oracle of doom (vv 19aα, 19aβ, and 19aγ), this exilic Deuteronomist underlines Josiah's shock and despair over what was to befall his people. In so doing, he redefines Josiah's plight and turns Josiah into a model of repentance.[74]

He shifts the focus of the earlier two promises from a peaceful death to a peaceful reign by adding Huldah's third promise (2 Kgs 22:20aγ, aδ, aε). The third assurance subtlely reinterprets the first two, creating an *inclusio* around the two oracles. From the perspective of this exilic Deuteronomist, Huldah's promises of a peaceful demise meant that Josiah would not have to witness the deity's fury against Jerusalem and its inhabitants. The author's stance is apologetic. He asserts that God took due notice of Josiah's servility (2 Kgs 22:19b) and rewarded him with a reprieve. I therefore cannot

73 The preceding narrative nowhere mentions, however, that Josiah believed that his people's fate was hopeless.

74 The emphasis upon Josiah's turning back (שׁוב) to YHWH is also found in the exilic addition of 2 Kgs 23:25 (Knoppers 1992:425-30).

agree with the view that the second oracle is mainly concerned with the postponement of exile (contra Jepsen 1956:27-28; Weinfeld 1972:26). The writer knows that the first Babylonian exile did not begin until at least a decade after Josiah's death. Rather than addressing a delay of exile, the editor creates a postponement motif to vindicate Josiah. The populace enjoys a respite as long as Josiah lives.

Although the changes and additions that the exilic Deuteronomist made to Huldah's oracle were substantial, he apparently did not rewrite the accounts of Josiah's covenant, reforms, or Passover. This partial editing creates two images of Josiah: penitent and iconoclast. From the perspective of the Josianic Deuteronomist, Josiah's reforms distinguish him from all preceding monarchs. From the perspective of the second editor, Josiah's obsequiousness defines his merit. The later image prefaced to the earlier image renders, however, the earlier image of Josiah superfluous. Josiah's reforms are anti-climactic, because they have no bearing upon either Josiah or Judah's fate. I therefore cannot agree that in the (final) exilic revision of Josiah's reign, the benefit of his reforms accrue to him rather than to the nation (contra Mayes 1983:131). In the present form of the text the benefits of Josiah's reforms ironically accrue to no one.

III. RENEWING THE NATIONAL COVENANT

Josiah's concern for his people's fate is patent in his reaction to the scroll's reading (2 Kgs 22:13). He calls a national convocation and leads his people in a public pact with the deity (2 Kgs 23:1-3). As Lohfink observes, the Josianic Deuteronomist strategically situates this covenant renewal in his presentation of Josiah's reign (1987:460). Josiah's covenant recalls the discovery of the law (2 Kgs 22:3-10), responds to Huldah's admonition (2 Kgs 22:18-20*), and lays the foundation for his reforms (2 Kgs 23:4-20).

A. THE COMPOSITION OF 2 KGS 23:1-3

A number of factors suggest that the account of Josiah's covenant (2 Kgs 23:1-3) is the Deuteronomist's own composition. First, the content of the covenant pledge (2 Kgs 23:3) is characterized by deuteronomistic clichés.[75] Second, identifying the scroll "which was found in the temple of YHWH" as "the scroll of the covenant" is best explained as a deuteronomistic trope, because it associates Deuteronomy, "the scroll of the torah," with the (Sinaitic or Mosaic) covenant between Israel and its deity. Third, some of the terminology used to describe the ratification of the covenant seems to be deliberately archaic. For instance, the reference to "all the elders of Judah" (2 Kgs 23:1) recalls the presence of elders in national assemblies during the eras of Sinai, conquest, league, and united monarchy.[76] Given both the deuteronomistic expressions in 2 Kgs 23:3 and the implication that the scroll is Deuteronomy, I would identify this writer as the Deuteronomist (Dtr^{1}).

---

75 Weinfeld (1972:332 [#1], 334 [#9], 336 [#16], 338 [#21d]) and see below.

76 Deut 27:1; 29:9; 31:9, 28; Josh 7:6; 8:33; 23:2; 24:1; 1 Sam 8:4; 2 Sam 5:3; 1 Kgs 8:1-2. In contrast, 2 Kgs 23:2 mentions "all the men of Judah and (all [KM]) the inhabitants of Jerusalem," an expression common in Jer C (Jer 11:2, 9; 17:25; 18:11; 32:32; 35:13). Tadmor and Cogan (1988:285) view the use of "all the men of Judah" (כל-איש יהודה; 2 Kgs 23:2) as anachronistic.

B. KING, PEOPLE, AND COVENANT

Josiah's covenant was undoubtedly a unique, epoch making venture in the history of Israelite religion (Wellhausen 1885:418-19; Tadmor and Cogan 1988:296-97). At first glance, the common assertion that 2 Kgs 23:1-3 also represents a milestone in Israelite polity seems well-taken because of the unanimous oath to "establish" (להקים) the words of "this covenant as written upon the scroll" (2 Kgs 23:3). In the time of Judah's nadir (the reign of Manasseh), Judah's monarchy was tied to a vassal treaty (i.e., a loyalty oath) with the Assyrian monarchy; yet, during Josiah's tenure the people entered a vassal treaty with YHWH (Frankena 1965:152-54).[77] Josiah's covenant makes the rediscovered law book the law of the state.[78] Or, to rephrase the Babylonian Talmud, Moses wrote the torah, but Josiah restored it.[79]

However valid these claims may be, I will argue for Josiah's uniqueness on somewhat different grounds. I question whether Josiah truly enshrines *Urdeuteronomium*, in spite of the Deuteronomist's assertion that he does so. It is important to recognize that Dtr[1] does

---

[77] As Lowery points out (1990:202-209), one cannot disassociate culture from religion in the Deuteronomist's depiction of Josiah (*pace* Cogan 1974:5, 113). Even if one were to concede, for the sake of argument, that Josiah's covenant is purely a cultic exercise, this compact clearly has political and economic repercussions for all those affected by its stipulations (2 Kgs 23:4-20).

[78] So, for instance, Ahlström (1982:73), Tadmor and Cogan (1988:296-97), and most recently, Weinfeld (1991:65-66, 81-84).

[79] The Talmud bestows, of course, this honor upon Ezra (*b. Sukk.* 20a; cf. *j. Meg* 1:9; *b. Sanh.* 21b; *t. Sanh.* 4:7; Blenkinsopp 1988:54-59).

not promote the covenant of Josiah as unique or unprecedented. The pact ratified under Josiah, like the pact of Jehoiada, is not a new covenant but a renewal of the Sinaitic covenant.[80] As such, the covenant between the people and God, in which Josiah acts as an intermediary, recalls the enactments of similar pacts in earlier Israelite traditions.[81] Upon critical examination of these compacts, the distinct features of Josiah's covenant become apparent. I will limit my comparison to a few passages which explicitly refer to the (re)making of a public covenant between YHWH and Israel: Exodus 34, Deuteronomy 29-31, Joshua 24, and 2 Kings 11.[82]

Three of these references to covenants -- Deuteronomy 29-31, Joshua 24, and 2 Kings 11 -- accompany the passing of leadership. Violation of covenantal stipulations and the loss of the covenant document form the background to the covenant renewals of Exodus 34 and 2 Kings 23.[83] 2 Kings 11 seems to involve two covenants: between

---

[80] In this manner, the Deuteronomist depicts Josiah as reviving institutions of the league (Lohfink 1963:272-73; Noth 1966:45).

[81] Baltzer (1971:52-54); Lohfink (1963:272-73); McCarthy (1978:216-21, 239-42, 259-60); Noth (1966:44-46).

[82] I speak of references to covenant, because some of these texts (e.g., Exodus 34 and Deuteronomy 29-31) are cast as speeches referring to the ratification of a covenant. In these passages the actual covenant is not described. Baltzer (1971:39-62) discusses a number of other preexilic passages as covenant renewals (e.g., 1 Kings 8; 2 Kings 18-19). But the authors of these texts do not overtly present these events as covenant renewals.

[83] Weinfeld aptly notes the Babylonian phrase for annulling a contract, *ṭuppam ḫepû*, "to break a tablet" (1973a:265).

people and king and between God, people, and king.[84] Assuming regression, the covenants of both 2 Kings 11 and 2 Kings 23 lead to cultic reform (2 Kgs 11:18; 23:4-20; Van Seters 1983:319). Like the covenant of Jehoiada, the covenant of Josiah bears clear marks of being a covenant renewal. The pacts of Exod 34:11-28 and Josh 24:25-26 include the composition of stipulations, but the pacts of Jehoiada and Josiah do not mention any new stipulations. The terminology used in describing Josiah's compact, "he cut the covenant" (ויכרת את-הברית), also points toward the Mosaic covenant.[85] So do the particular deuteronomistic clichés in 2 Kgs 23:3: "to follow after YHWH," "to observe his commandments, decrees, and statutes," "with a whole heart and soul."[86] These are not new commandments, but the terms of the Sinaitic covenant according to Deuteronomy.

All five of these pacts, whatever their differences, share common motifs. In each case, a leader functions as a covenant mediator: Moses, Joshua, Jehoiada, and Josiah. In each case, the covenant is a communal venture, involving a *mise en scène* (Deut 29:9; 31:9-28, Josh 24:1; 2 Kgs 11:17-18; 23:1-2). Hoffmann (1980:201) observes

---

84 There are some important differences between Kings and Chronicles in the ratification of these two compacts (McCarthy 1972:77-80). Weinfeld contends that the subject in the covenant between king and people in Kings is Jehoiada (2 Kgs 11:17; cf. 2 Chr 23:3), because Joash was still a minor (1973a:264).

85 In the Hebrew Bible references to "the covenant," as opposed to the Noachic, Abrahammic, or Davidic covenants, almost always signify the Mosaic covenant (Deut 4:23; 5:2-3; 7:12; 9:9, 11; Josh 7:15; 23:16; 1 Kgs 8:21; Hos 6:7; Ps 74:20; 78:10).

86 Weinfeld (1972:332, 336, 338, and 334). Lohfink's objection (1987:272), that בכל-לב ובכל-נפש is not deuteronomistic because there are no suffixes on לב and נפש, is overly subtle.

that 2 Kgs 23:2 presents an ideal gathering, attended by Josiah, "all the men of Judah and[87] the inhabitants of Jerusalem [who were] with him, the priests and the prophets,[88] all of the people, from small to great." In fact, the very terminology which the Deuteronomist uses to describe the basis of this compact underscores its corporate nature. Because 2 Kgs 23:2 identifies the scroll "which was found in the temple of YHWH" as "the scroll of the covenant," that is, the scroll dealing with the foundational pact between YHWH and his people, the Deuteronomist implies that obedience to the terms of this scroll is vital to the well-being of the nation.

Given popular participation in each of these compacts, it is not surprising to find some commentators (e.g., Baltzer 1971:52; Mayes 1979:95) claiming that the author of 2 Kgs 23:1-3 accentuates the role of the people. Noth even alleges that the Deuteronomist's real interest is in the people and not in Josiah (1981:82-83). To Noth's credit he recognizes a tension: a king enforces what Noth thinks was never meant to be a state law-code.[89] Josiah purportedly represents the auspices under which the community (re)establishes its covenant with the deity. The Deuteronomist clearly highlights the participation of all sectors of the community in Josiah's pact, but I completely disagree with Noth about the true interest of the Deuteronomist. What is the upshot of the Deuteronomist's presentation of popular participation? Are Josiah and the people co-determinate, or is one the sus-

87 Reading with KG. KM adds explicative "all."

88 Reading with KM and KG (*lectio difficilior*). KT omits והנביאים, "and the prophets." 2 Chr 34:30 reads "and the Levites."

89 1966:45-48. Noth contends that Deuteronomy was made operative by a sacral ceremony, not by an act of state. But 2 Kgs 23:1-3 is clearly both.

tained focus of attention? Is the role of the people, or the role of the priests and prophets, as significant a feature in the Deuteronomist's coverage as the role of Josiah?

The Deuteronomist does not present the collective participation in Josiah's pact as an end in itself. The king does not disappear from view. In fact, because "all the people solemnize the covenant" (ויעמד כל-העם בברית; 2 Kgs 23:3), Josiah enjoys a united front behind his radical reforms (2 Kgs 23:4-20). Even as the author celebrates the commitment of people and leaders alike, he accentuates Josiah's role in generating public interest, defining the terms of the covenant, and supervising its confirmation. Josiah gives the order to Hilkiah (2 Kgs 23:1), presides over the covenant ceremonies (2 Kgs 23:2), "cuts the covenant" (2 Kgs 23:3), and carries out the ensuing reforms (2 Kgs 23:4-20).[90] Such actions comport well with the Deuteronomist's royalist agenda, but ill-suit the prescriptions of Deuteronomy.

Josiah's behavior also manifests an explicitly sacral dimension (Widengren 1957:3-4). He journeys to the temple to ratify the covenant (2 Kgs 23:2) and stands "by the pillar" (2 Kgs 23:3).[91] He ratifies the pact "before YHWH."[92] Over against Deut 31:9-13, which mandates that priests read "this torah" publically to instruct the

[90] In contrast, Chronicles accentuates the people's participation in Josiah's major activities (2 Chr 34:3, 9, 30, 32, 33; 35:17, 18; Williamson 1977:127-30; Knoppers 1988:456-63).

[91] Reading with KM and KG. KT has "on the platform" (= על-העמוד). 2 Chr 34:31 (CM) reads "on his platform" or "by his place" (על-עמדו). A similar expression occurs in the description of Jehoiada's covenant, "the king was standing by the pillar" (המלך עמד על-העמוד; 2 Kgs 11:14; cf. 2 Chr 23:13 על-עמודו).

[92] 2 Kgs 23:3. Cf. Josh 24:1 ("before God") and Deut 29:9 ("before YHWH your God").

people, Josiah reads the covenant scroll to all assembled, including priests and prophets (2 Kgs 23:2)![93] Josiah's priestly functions may not comply with deuteronomic injunctions, but they do conform to the sacral deportment of other leaders in the Deuteronomistic History: Joshua (Josh 8:30-35), David (2 Sam 6:12-19) and Solomon (1 Kings 8).[94] Josiah is clearly more than a *membrum praecipuum* of the community (contra Baltzer 1971:52). The people take the covenant oath (2 Kgs 23:3), but Josiah initiates, leads, and completes the action. The involvement of the people, which Noth sees as the primary goal of the narrative, results from and supports Josiah's leadership.

C. JOSIANIC POWER AND DEUTERONOMIC POLITY

In advancing the interpretation of 2 Kgs 23:1-3 as establishing *Urdeuteronomium* as Israel's constitution, critics have largely duplicated how the Deuteronomist wants Josiah's actions to be understood. Yet if Josiah's pact was a singular achievement, why does Dtr^1 not present it as such? Why does the Deuteronomist portray Josiah's convocation as a revival of previous national assemblies? The Deuteronomist, in my view, wishes to undersore the links between Josiah and the (re)established constitution of the community to bolster the

---

93 Josiah's actions (ויקרא באזניהם את-כל-דברי ספר הברית) clearly replicate those of Moses in Deut 31:11 (תקרא את התורה הזאת נגד כל ישׂראל באזניהם), as Friedman claims (1981a:8), but they defy Moses' own instructions about who should recite the torah (Deut 31:9-11).

94 Cf. Samuel's censure of Saul in 1 Sam 13:13-24.

community's support for Josiah's reforms.[95] Writing in the ancient world was "the technology of the intellect," a medium that enabled the organization of dispersed parties, sects, and kin (Goody 1968:1-7). For the literate, the written word could provide a unifying cultural heritage (Goody and Watt 1968:55).

But as much as the Deuteronomist appeals to supporters of the deuteronomic movement by presenting Josiah as reviving, implementing, and conforming to the prescriptions of Deuteronomy, he also implicitly revises Deuteronomy. A comparison between Josiah's prerogatives and the deuteronomic program for a balance of powers (Deut 16:18-18:22) elucidates the program of Dtr^1. The deuteronomic authors posit the relationship between YHWH and his people as primary. The deuteronomic laws are primarily addressed to the community and the community, in turn, obliges itself to obey them.[96] Israel is to internalize this legislation (Deut 6:4-25; 13:2-6, 8-11, 16-17) and discipline itself. Even the hallmark legislation of Deuteronomy -- centralization -- paradoxically does not entail the ascent of royal authority. Quite the contrary, as Lohfink observes (1982:58-64), those stipulations which reapportion power in the light of a centralized cult partition leadership duties among a variety of office

---

[95] In my judgment, the Deuteronomist deliberately appeals to a number of constituencies within this community (chap. 6). His use of Proto-Deuteronomy is, for instance, clearly couched to appeal to the supporters of the deuteronomic movement.

[96] The personal address fluctuates, however, between 2 masc pl and 2 masc sing (Cazelles 1967:207-19). I assume that the copy of Proto-Deuteronomy in the Deuteronomist's employ had both. For a detailed comparison between the deuteronomic distribution of powers, especially the limitations on royal prerogative (Deut 17:14-20), and Dtr^1's royal ideology, see my forthcoming study in *ZAW*.

holders -- local courts (Deut 16:18; 17:2-7), a central court staffed by magistrates and levitical priests (Deut 17:8-13), a king (Deut 17:14-20), a levitical priesthood (Deut 18:1-8), and prophets (18:15-22).

The powers of the monarchy dominate the civilizations of the ancient Near East, but these powers are carefully circumscribed in Deut 17:14-17. The belief in sacral kingship is absent from Deuteronomy. The notion that a king should oversee and sustain the cult -- caring for its buildings, appurtenances, and personnel -- is absent from Deuteronomy (Nicholson 1991:195-97). Nor does the king define the assignments of other officials or appoint them. The community provides its own leadership (Deut 16:18). Except for the duty to read the torah scroll, the law of the king contains only constraints on kingly power, disqualifying non-Israelites from holding this post and limiting the quantity of a king's horses, the number of his wives, and the amount of his wealth (Deut 17:16-17).

Since the king's only positive duty is to read the torah scroll daily, he has no authority either to teach the torah or to interpret it (Deut 17:18-19). Teaching the torah is a function of the priesthood, which has custody of the torah (Deut 31:9-13), while speaking on behalf of God (Deut 18:1-8) is a prophetic function (Deut 18:19-22).[97] Nor is the king able to amend the torah's own regulations on the distribution of powers. The divine voice in Deuteronomy proclaims the torah scroll absolute, prohibiting any alteration of its content (Deut 13:1; 17:20). The carefully contrived balance of powers provides a king

[97] Mayes (1979:374-75) regards Deut 31:9-13 as stemming from a second phase in the composition of Deuteronomy. This is quite possible, but I disagree with Friedman (1981a:13-16) that Deut 31:1-13 is Josianic. There is a clear discrepancy between what Deut 31:9-13 mandates and what happens in 2 Kgs 23:1-3.

with no warrant to enlarge his authority at the expense of others. It is only by honoring these directives and restrictions that a king and his descendants can expect to reign for a long time (Deut 17:20).

We have seen that the Deuteronomist associates Josiah's covenant renewal with Deuteronomy. The use of the citation formula, הכתבים על-הספר הזה (2 Kgs 23:3), presents Josiah's actions as explicitly complying with the covenant scroll.[98] Ostensibly, Josiah also complies with the law of the king (Deut 17:20), because he follows Deuteronomy's decrees and does not formally modify the scroll of the torah in any way. Rather, he makes the basis and content of the Mosaic covenant -- the covenant scroll -- the constitution of the community. Josiah's cultic innovations (2 Kgs 23:4-20) appear as renovations, undertaken as the natural consequence of the community's renewed pledge to its ancient charter. Gray recognizes a problem: Josiah's implementation of Deuteronomy is selective, involving centralization and the elimination of alien cults (1970:715). Yet identifying this issue is not tantamount to resolving it. I would maintain that 2 Kgs 23:1-3 represents a transformation of Deuteronomy, a metamorphosis, which bolsters the Deuteronomist's royalist program.

Josiah's covenant renewal recalls not only the divine dispensation of law, but also the divine election of David and Zion. In fact, the

---

98 Lohfink (1990a:34-42) insightfully draws attention to the links between the command of Deut 6:17, שמור תשמרון את-מצות יהוה אלהיכם ועדתיו וחקיו אשר צוך, and the oath of 2 Kgs 23:3. I agree that the Deuteronomist wishes to tie Josiah's covenant to the (deuteronomic) scroll of the torah. Yet I would argue that this tie is mediated by the institutions of the monarchy (Davidic kingship and the Solomonic temple). Hence, I also see strong links between Solomon's second temple dedication blessing in 1 Kgs 8:57-61 and the community's commitment in 2 Kgs 23:3 (see below).

deuteronomistic linkage between Sinai and Zion in Josiah's covenant renewal reflects the same linkage between Sinai and Zion, which we saw in Solomon's temple dedication (vol. 1: chap. 3). Both the dedication and the covenant occur in the context of national assemblies at Zion (1 Kgs 8:1-2, 62-64; 2 Kgs 23:1-2) and both recall the national convocation on the Plains of Moab.[99] In fact, I would argue that the Deuteronomist couches the people's commitment in 2 Kgs 23:3 to resonate with the final blessing in King Solomon's dedication of the temple (1 Kgs 8:54-61).

Solomon requests that his prayer might always be before YHWH so that YHWH might provide for king and people (1 Kgs 8:59). Solomon also asks that YHWH would "incline" the people's heart "to follow in all of his ways" (ללכת בכל-דרכיו; 1 Kgs 8:57-58). The king instructs the people to be "wholehearted toward YHWH our God, to follow in his statutes and to keep his commandments, as at this day" (והיה לבבכם שלם עם יהוה אלהינו ללכת בחקיו ולשמר מצותיו כיום הזה; 1 Kgs 8:61). In Josiah's covenant Solomon's wishes are fulfilled. The people pledge with "a whole heart and soul" (בכל-לב ובכל-נפש) to honor the covenant (2 Kgs 23:3). Whereas Solomon hopes that YHWH might enable the people "to observe his commandments, his decrees, and his stipulations" (ולשמר מצותיו וחקיו ומשפטיו; 1 Kgs 8:58), the people confirm Solomon's request by pledging "to observe his commandments, his statutes, and his decrees (ולשמר מצותיו ואת-עדותיו ואת-חקיו; 2 Kgs 23:3). As we have repeatedly

---

99 This is not the only allusion to Solomon's temple dedication. As Pratt (1987:74-89) and Balentine (1993:61-64, 91-97) show, Hezekiah's prayers in 2 Kgs 19:15-19 and 20:2-3 are deuteronomistic compositions, which recall specific Davidic (2 Sam 7:18-29) and Solomonic (1 Kgs 8:22-53) petitions.

observed, keeping royal fidelity is bound up with honoring the temple and abolishing all competing shrines.

Validating Solomon's blessing, Josiah and the people set out to accomplish what Solomon himself fails to do. Solomon spoils his chance to follow through on his people's enthusiasm, because he worships alien gods at the high places he builds for his alien wives. He succeeds only in building a central shrine, not in centralizing the practice of cult in his state. The unanimous oath to implement the law in the time of Josiah echoes Israel's pristine commitment to YHWH at the temple (1 Kgs 8:1-2, 62-66), yet advances beyond it. Solomon's sanctuary has at last become the sole channel of popular and royal allegiance to YHWH.

Conclusions

Josiah's covenant is a renewal of a redefined Sinaitic covenant, a covenant which has been transformed in the deuteronomistic depiction of the monarchy. For the Deuteronomist, Sinai and Zion are not in opposition. Sinai points toward Zion as its goal (1 Kgs 8:56). The successful establishment of a central sanctuary, in turn, contributes to popular observance of the Sinaitic covenant (1 Kgs 8:58-59; 2 Kgs 23:3). Zion actually enhances Sinai by complementing it. Josiah's importance therefore transcends the monarchic period. He returns his people to its most sacred mores. But the Deuteronomist's very understanding of these mores reflects his transformation of them. The discovery of the scroll does not occur until the eighteenth year of Josiah's tenure (2 Kgs 22:3). This relatively late disclosure, along with the consultation with Huldah, and the covenant ratification coalesce in pointing toward the urgency of reform. Giving credence to Deuteronomy's own assertions about its antiquity as Sinaitic legislation allows the Deuteronomist to present Josiah's innovation as intrinsic to the original revelation. The commitment of the elders, priests, prophets, and people -- under the aegis of Josiah -- to implement the terms of the torah scroll vindicates the Deuteronomist's program. Josiah's reign represents not so much the triumph of Deuteronomy as the triumph of deuteronomistic ideology.

CHAPTER 6

JOSIAH'S REFORMS: RECOVERING THE DAVIDIC-SOLOMONIC KINGDOM

The king, and his faithful subjects, the lords and the commons of this realm, -- the triple cord, which no man can break. (Edmund Burke, *A Letter to a Noble Lord*, 1796.)

Introduction: Josiah and his Modern Interpreters

A number of recent scholars call attention to the critical role Josiah plays in the Deuteronomistic History.[1] Mayes comments that in three figures -- Moses, David, and Josiah -- "the authentic expression of the will of Yahweh is to be found" (1983:132). Tagliacarne (1989:411-21) thinks that the author promotes Josiah as a model of piety to his exilic or early postexilic audience. For Cross (1973:279-80), the reign of Josiah is the climax to the David theme in Kings.

[1] Cross (1973:281-84); Friedman (1981a:1-26); Gerbrandt (1986:46-68); Halpern (1988:207-35); Mayes (1983:133-39); Nelson (1981a: 120-28); O'Brien (1989:237); Spieckermann (1982:41-46, 78-79). Provan acknowledges Josiah's importance in the exilic version of Kings (1988:147).

Observing parallels between Moses the lawgiver and Josiah the law-enforcer, Friedman concludes that these two exemplary figures form an *inclusio* around the first edition of the Deuteronomistic History (1981a:8-10). Hoffmann combines theme and structure. Like Cross and Friedman, he argues that Josiah's role is structurally important -- Josiah reverses the sins of previous monarchs (1980:78-169, 201-203). But, like Tagliacarne, Hoffmann views Josiah's purification and unification of cult as completely idealistic, an exilic or postexilic encomium to the first commandment (1980:269-70).

Another group of commentators (e.g., Long 1984:28-29; Hobbs 1985:xxv) question whether Josiah is as revered a figure as the aforementioned scholars claim. These critics point out that the Deuteronomist commends other reformer kings such as Jehu in the North and Asa, Jehoshaphat, Jotham, and Hezekiah in the South. Provan contends that the reforms of Hezekiah, and not the reforms of Josiah, climax the original version of the Deuteronomistic History (1988:153-56). Long and Hobbs also question whether Jeroboam's role is structurally crucial.[2] They allege that although Jeroboam is a villain in the drama of the divided monarchy, other kings, such as Ahab in the North and Manasseh in the South, introduce further apostasy and are singled out by the Deuteronomist for condemnation. Savran argues, in fact, that the perfidy of the Omride dynasty, in general, and Ahab, in particular, centers the chiastically arranged Book of Kings (1987:148-55). Hence, for Savran, the interaction of king and prophet in the time of Ahab, and not the sins of Jeroboam or

2 In contrast, Mullen argues that the sins of Jeroboam are structurally significant in the exilic Deuteronomistic History (1987:212-32).

the promises to David, is critical to understanding the deuteronomistic history of the monarchy.

The foregoing scholars raise issues that need to be distinguished. If the Deuteronomist upholds the achievements of a variety of kings, what precisely are their achievements and on what grounds does he laud these monarchs? Are the criteria of evaluation sustained throughout the entire history, or are they geared toward a particular monarch? If a criterion is not sustained, what function does it have in the overall history? Does the Deuteronomist structure his treatment of kings to set one monarch apart from other kings and, if so, how and why? Finally, what is the most likely provenance for the Deuteronomist's presentation of Josiah's reforms -- the late seventh century, the Babylonian exile, or the early postexilic period?

I would readily acknowledge that the Deuteronomist upholds the accomplishments of a number of kings in addition to Josiah, but I do not see this as detracting from Josiah's structural and thematic significance. Scholars, in my view, have not adequately classified the criteria by which the Deuteronomists praise certain kings. The Deuteronomists laud Solomon's wealth and wisdom (vol. 1: chaps. 2 and 3) and praise Hezekiah's fortitude, but they do not judge other kings by these criteria.[3] Recognition of particular royal virtues enables the Deuteronomists to distinguish between the accomplishments of various kings without having these achievements detract from their overall literary strategy. Hence, the presence of a wealthy Solomon or a trusting Hezekiah does not entail that the deutero-

[3] I speak of Deuteronomists, because I maintain that an exilic Deuteronomist is responsible for the incomparability formulae applied to Solomon, Hezekiah, and Josiah (1992:411-31). This writer accents, however, motifs that are already present in his *Vorlage*.

nomistic presentation lacks consistent themes or a crescendo. We have seen that the major issues which the Deuteronomist posits in the monarchy are royal support for the temple and, concomitantly, royal suppression of all rival cults. Because of the author's pervasive interest in these matters, the reign of Josiah is vitally important to his history of the monarchy.

The Deuteronomist calls attention to the wrongdoing of deviant kings and the achievements of reformer kings, but the comparison between reformers only flatters Josiah. Far from comprising counterexamples to a unique role for Josiah, the reigns of other reformers are configured to heighten Josiah's exemplary status. Those kings whom Dtr^1 singles out for praise as reformers -- Asa, Jehoshaphat, Jotham, and Hezekiah in Judah and Joram and Jehu in Israel -- are precursors to Josiah. The heteropraxis which endures in spite of their reforms is corrected by Josiah. Hence, the Deuteronomist not only presents Josiah's reforms as the definitive divine retribution against Jeroboam's transgressions, but also against the unrequited transgressions of all of Josiah's predecessors.

Having ascertained Josiah's critical role, how does one explain it? The choice of one king as the peerless reformer does not strike me as arbitrary. I will argue that the depiction of Josiah's reforms is best understood as the work of a preexilic Deuteronomist (Dtr^1) who promotes Josianic ambitions to enhancing Jerusalem's influence in Judah and the former northern kingdom. 2 Kgs 23:1-23 valorizes the tremendous upheaval Josiah causes in the lives of his people by championing Josiah's actions as a quest to bridge the gap between the glory of the united kingdom and the decline of the divided monarchy. For Dtr^1, Josiah's returning his state to its heyday does not mean so much a restoration of an Israel encamped on the Plains of Moab (Deuteronomy), as a restoration and extension of the ideals abetted during Solomon's reign -- one people, one cult, one sanctuary, one king, and one god. Indeed, the very structure which the Deuteronomist imposes upon Solomon's rule and the dual monarchies points toward Josiah's reforms as the answer to the problems which lead to the disruption of the united kingdom, the demise of Israel, and the decline of Judah.

The second movement in Josiah's reign, like the first (chap. 5), consists of three parts: (I) Josiah's southern reforms (2 Kgs 23:4-14), (II) Josiah's northern reforms (2 Kgs 23:15-20), and (III) his celebration of Passover (2 Kgs 23:21-23). Implementing the covenant oath of 2 Kgs 23:3, Josiah's southern reforms systematically redress the sins of his forefathers. Having canceled the outstanding sins of previous royalty, including the one responsible for disunion (Solomon), Josiah redresses the sins of the monarch associated with the Assyrian exile (Jeroboam). The story of these two campaigns climaxes in the celebration of a national Passover.

I. JOSIAH'S SOUTHERN REFORMS

The account of Josiah's reforms in 2 Kgs 23:4-20 has been the subject of a long and lively debate. Geographic detail, cultic nomenclature, textual variants, and irregular grammatical features all appear in 2 Kgs 23:4-14. Compared with the relatively smooth narrative of vv 1-3, the description of Josiah's reforms in vv 4-14 is highly compressed, containing only sparse narrative transitions. Explanations for this catalogue of disparate reforms vary.

Some commentators see the paratactic style, the abundance of cultic and geographic detail, and the surprising grammatical forms as evidence of an annalistic source. Other critics see these same qualities as evidence for a series of redactions. Historians debate whether this catalogue is fiction in the guise of history, an authentic description of a Josianic revolution, or something in between.[4] Both sets of critics therefore engage in similar operations. Historians make literary-critical decisions about a dense text and literary critics come to conclusions about the historical implications of their reconstructions. Whatever the historical reality of Josiah's reforms, I will argue that the complex features of 2 Kgs 24:4-14 are not best explained by positing a series of systematic redactions. Rather, the terse sequence of royal initiatives is intentionally designed to communicate an impression of swift and decisive action.

A. THE COMPOSITION OF 2 KGS 23:4-14

I would agree with Oestreicher and Lohfink (chap. 5) that the Deuteronomist employed a *Reformbericht* in composing 2 Kgs 23:4-14.[5] The strongest criticism of this theory comes from Hoffmann. He sees 2 Kgs 23:4-14 as the product of a deuteronomistic author who

---

4 Ahlström (1993:763-81); Bright (1981:316-24); Herrmann (1981:263-72); Hölscher (1923:212-13); Jepsen (1959:107-08); Malamat (1987:287-314); Miller and Hayes (1986:392-401); Montgomery (1951:541-48); Noth (1960:272-78); Soggin (1984:241-47); Spieckermann (1982:376-81); Stade (1887:641-71); Wellhausen (1885:23-28); Würthwein (1976:398-406). See also chap. 5.

5 Definitions of this source vary greatly: Burney (1920:355); Gray (1970:729); Gressmann (1924:322, 327-28); Hölscher (1923:208-13); Jones (1984:616); Lohfink (1987:465, 471); Mayes (1983:130); Montgomery (1951:534); Nelson (1981a:79-83); O'Brien (1989:258-61); Oestreicher (1923:30-56); Weinfeld (1991:70-73); Würthwein (1976:412-21; 1984:455-61).

culls references to royal reforms from various reform notices within his history and Deuteronomy and projects them into the reign of Josiah.[6] The staccato style, which other scholars see as evidence for the Deuteronomist's dependence upon an annalistic chronicle or *Reformbericht*, Hoffmann attributes to the Deuteronomist's citation of his own reform notices.

I have three criticisms of Hoffmann's theory. First, there are expressions within these verses that are unparalleled within the Deuteronomistic History.[7] This would not make any sense if the description of reforms is an artfully concocted presentation. Second, a number of Josiah's reforms correct cultic abuses, which are not previously described in either the Deuteronomistic History or Deuteronomy (see below). Again, this contradicts Hoffmann's theory. Third, according to Hoffmann's reconstruction, one would expect the reforms to correspond or allude to the crimes. But the parallels are

---

6 1980:250-52, 264-70. Levin (1984:371), Rose (1977:51-62), and Van Seters (1983:317-20) also deem reconstructing a pre-deuteronomistic stratum in 2 Kgs 23:4-20 to be a dubious enterprise.

7 The following list is not exhaustive: in v 4: "the vessels made for Ba'l..." (הכלים העשׂוים לבעל...); in v 5, "environs of Jerusalem" (מסבי ירושלם) and "the idolatrous priests" (הכמרים); in v 7, "vestments for Asherah" (בתים לאשרה) and "shrines of the sacred males" (במות הקדשים); in v 8, "shrines of the [Jerusalem] gates" (במות השערים); in v 11, "the horses which the kings of Judah dedicated to the Sun" (הסוסים אשר נתנו מלכי יהודה לשמש) and "the chariots of the Sun" (מרכבות השמש). See also the comments of Weinfeld (1991:71). I am quoting these expressions from KM. For the textual criticism of the relevant verses, see below.

often at best imprecise.[8] Josiah's destruction of temple shrines for the sacred males (הקדשים; 2 Kgs 23:7) does not match Asa's expelling (1 Kgs 15:12) and Jehoshaphat's banishing (1 Kgs 22:47) these officiants. In v 12 Josiah "tears down the roof-top altars made by the kings of Judah," but no other text in the Deuteronomistic History mentions such altars (cf. Jer 7:18; 19:13; 32:29; 44:17; Zeph 1:5).[9] Similarly, no previous text in Deuteronomy or in the Deuteronomistic History depicts the establishment of "high places of the gates" (2 Kgs 23:8). Since the punishment in some cases does not mirror the crime or mirror any crime at all, the Deuteronomist is doing more than compiling and rephrasing reform records.

The use of a *Reformbericht* would explain, at least in part, both the unparalleled language and the unparalleled reforms. Even so, there is clear evidence that Dtr[1] shaped and supplemented his source. First, there are deuteronomistic phrases in v 5 (המקטרים לבעל לשמש ולירח ולמזלות ולכל צבא השמים), v 10 (העביר איש את-בנו ואת-בתו

---

8 Hoffmann (1980:251-52) categorizes the correspondences as parallels, allusions, and anticipations, but he does not explain why a Deuteronomist who takes such great care to compose an intricately unified account would be so loose in his terminology.

9 KM of 2 Kgs 23:12 adds, עלית אחז. This may be an explicative gloss, because of both the article (הגג) and the following relative clause, אשר-עשו מלכי יהודה (Stade and Schwally 1904:295). Hoffmann (1980:248-49) appeals to KM 2 Kgs 20:11 for a parallel, במעלות אחז (lacking in KG[B] of 2 Kgs 20:11, but appearing as במעלות עלת אחז in certain textual traditions of Isa 38:8 [the LXX, *Tg. Isa*, the Vg, and IQIsa[a]]; see Iwry 1957:27-33). Even if the text-critical obstacles could be removed, there still is no clear parallel. Neither 2 Kgs 16:11 (the reign of Ahaz) nor 2 Kgs 20:11 (and Isa 38:8) mention roof-top altars.

באש), and v 13 (תועבה) and (שקץ).[10] Second, several of Josiah's reforms conform to or resonate with the instructions of Deuteronomy. Preuss (1982:4-12) notes the following parallels.[11]

2 Kgs 23:4f.	Deut 17:3
2 Kgs 23:4,6,7,14	Deut 16:21f.; 12:3; 7:5
2 Kgs 23:4,5,8,12,13,15,16,19	Deut 12:1-7
2 Kgs 23:7	Deut 23:18
2 Kgs 23:7f.	Deut 23:17f.
2 Kgs 23:9	Deut 18:1-8
2 Kgs 23:10	Deut 18:10

These acts are mostly written in the same catalogue style as the rest of Josiah's reforms. This suggests that either Dtr[1] retouched his source to conform to Deuteronomy or that he composed the reforms himself, imitating the style of his source. In either case, one has to reckon with an active deuteronomistic hand in 2 Kgs 23:4-14.

---

[10] On these idioms, see Weinfeld (1972:321, 322, and 323, respectively), Hoffmann (1980:333, 337, 359-61), and Rose (1977:53).

[11] See also Friedman (1981a:8-9), Nicholson (1967:3), and Paton (1928:325-26). A few cautions are in order. Some of the parallels are imprecise (e.g., between 2 Kgs 23:4, 5, 8, 12, 13, 15, 16, 19 and Deut 12:1-7). As Hölscher (1922:182) and Mullen (1987:218-19) observe, Deuteronomy (except for the poems in chaps. 32 and 33) never mentions high places. Given the consistent concern with high places in Kings, the discrepancy is intriguing. Second, Josiah's cutting down the *asherahs* (ויכרת את-האשרים) in 2 Kgs 23:14 explicitly conforms to the polemic against Canaanite religion in Exod 34:13 (ואת-אשריו תכרתון). Deut 7:5 commands cutting down *asherahs* (ואשירהם תגדעון), while Deut 12:3 commands burning *asherahs* with fire (ואשריהם תשרפון באש). Third, at least one of the parallels (Deut 18:1-8) is really a contrast. See also Ahlström (1993:775-77), although I do not agree with all of his observations.

The question of style should not be the sole concern of source criticism. Instead, one should press the discussion further. Given the existence of a source, why does the Deuteronomist incorporate this source into his narrative? Why does he supplement and not completely rewrite the *Reformbericht*? As Mayes points out, appealing to a sequence of deuteronomistic redactions in these verses only magnifies this issue (1983:130). Viewing the present narrative as the product of three or more editors means that each of these different writers perpetuated or increased the stylistic problems in his *Vorlage*.[12] The disadvantages to multiple authorship therefore seem to outweigh the advantages, because the interpreter is obliged to account for both the complication (or perpetuation) of style and the multiplication of incoherence.

The style, detail, and organization of 2 Kgs 23:4-14 offer a number of advantages to the Deuteronomist. First, as we saw in chap. 5, the Deuteronomist prefaces a covenant renewal to his description of Josiah's reforms, creating the impression that the latter is a natural consequence of the former. Second, the staccato style implies swift and decisive action. This concurs with the Deuteronomist's claim that all of the events in 2 Kgs 22:1-23:23 occur within the span of a single year. Third, the mixture of radically different kinds of reforms creates the impression that all of the crimes addressed by Josiah are related. Hoffmann points out (1980:220-23) that reforms centered on

12 Hollenstein (1977:326-36); Jones (1984:616-17); Levin (1984:356-64); O'Brien (1989:251-64); Spieckermann (1982:79-112); Würthwein (1984:453-60).

Yahwistic high places and priests (2 Kgs 23:8) are framed by reforms affecting alien cults (2 Kgs 23:4-7, 10-14).[13]

Fourth, the reforms proceed according to a certain logic. Josiah begins with reforms which are chronologically and geographically more immediate (2 Kgs 23:5-6) and then progresses to other reforms which are chronologically (e.g., Solomon: 2 Kgs 23:13) and geographically (e.g., Jeroboam: 2 Kgs 23:15) more distant. Josiah's reformation begins in the Jerusalem temple, encompasses towns in Benjamin and Judah, "from Geba to Beersheba" (2 Kgs 23:8), and eventually embraces the former northern kingdom (2 Kgs 23:15-20). The record of Josiah's campaign in Jerusalem and Judah is therefore best explained not as an accumulation of several major levels of composition, but as the complex presentation of an author who edits and augments his source.

B. THE STRUCTURAL DIMENSION OF JOSIAH'S REFORMS

Hoffmann provides the most thorough analysis of how Josiah's reforms relate to the pattern of regression and reform in the reigns of previous kings (1980:169-270). He argues, I think convincingly, that Josiah's campaigns cancel the abuses of his forefathers. But Hoffmann's thesis smoothes over certain difficulties (see above) and leaves other critical issues unresolved. If the writer is painstakingly collecting all previous reforms in Deuteronomy and the Deuteronomistic History and placing them in the tenure of one king (Hoffmann 1980:

---

[13] Lohfink (1985:39) observes that this organization is not unique to Kings. In Deuteronomy 12, vv 2-3 mandate the destruction of foreign sanctuaries, vv 4-28 mandate centralization, and vv 29-31 warn against the survival of foreign cult practices.

251), why are the sins so heavily weighed in Israel's favor? In other words, how does one explain the high number (ten) of Josiah's reforms in Judah in comparison with the paucity of his reforms in the territory of the ten northern tribes? Why are there both clear parallels and substantial discrepancies between the apostasy of previous kings and Josiah's reforms? Why do some of Josiah's reforms go beyond annulling documented sins? To account for the complexity of 2 Kgs 23:4-14, one needs to explain both the parallels and the discrepancies, the retribution against past transgressions and the excess in dealing with those transgressions, the configuration of Josiah's reforms and the distribution of those reforms.

In my judgment, the Deuteronomist's compositional strategy is not so much to fit Josiah's reforms to previous perfidy, as it is to fit previous perfidy to Josiah's reforms. In other words, I do not believe that one can divorce what the Deuteronomist wishes to say about Josiah's reforms from what he believed Josiah did. The deuteronomistic portrayal of Josiah's reforms is schematic and tendentious, but not "an entirely fictional deuteronomistic composition" (contra Hoffmann 1980:268). What the Deuteronomist believes about what happened in the past places some constraints upon what he says about the past.[14] Hence, his *modus operandi* is not so much to invent

---

[14] We know that the Deuteronomist does not invent the Assyrian crisis out of whole cloth, even though his reconstruction of the Assyrian invasion of Judah differs markedly from that of Sennacherib's annals (Camp 1990:264-317; Childs 1967; Gonçalves 1986; Luckenbill 1924; Tadmor and Cogan 1988:246-51). The *bruta facta* of history limit the extent to which writers of historiographic works in both realms fabricate the past. How the Assyrian and Judahite scribes construe characters and events are matters in which they exercise considerable creativity. But both the Assyrians and the Judahites acknowledge the reality of major players (Hezekiah, Sen-

history as it is to shape history to conform to his own agenda.[15] This explains the great imbalance between northern and southern reforms. It also explains why the Deuteronomist heightens the sins of certain monarchs (e.g., Jeroboam in the North and Manasseh in the South) and downplays the lasting importance of previous reform efforts (e.g., Jehu in the North and Hezekiah in the South). The Deuteronomist adapts his account of previous kings to enhance Josiah's prestige.

The Deuteronomist sets Josiah apart from all of his forefathers in three related ways. First, Josiah's reforms dominate the deuteronomistic coverage of his reign (Cross 1973:283). The attention most other reformers receive is a few verses (e.g., 1 Kgs 22:47; 2 Kgs 3:2; 10:25-27; 15:35; 18:4). Second, Josiah's reforms are definitive, because they assail the institutional foundations of prohibited cult practices. In some cases Josiah goes beyond what Deuteronomy stipulates and in other cases Josiah's reforms are more severe than previous reforms. Third, Josiah's reforms are cultically and geographically pervasive, affecting heteropraxis in both South and North. Josiah corrects the documented sins of his forefathers, but also negates previously unmentioned malfeasance. The first point, I believe, is self-evident, but the second and third points require explication.

The Deuteronomist depicts Josiah as suppressing or deposing the personnel of illegitimate cults, destroying their sacred paraphernalia,

---

nacherib) and events (the destruction of Judahite cities, the campaign against Jerusalem, Hezekiah's indemnities, and Jerusalem's survival).

[15] As even White (1978:121), who is concerned with interpretation in history and "the fictions of factual representation," acknowledges, "Historians are concerned with events which can be assigned to specific time-space locations, events which are (or were) in principle observable or perceivable...."

and rendering their cult sites unfit for reuse. These actions are structural, intended not simply to stop people from frequenting certain religious institutions, but to eliminate these institutions entirely (*pace* Ahlström 1982:70). Following the division, for instance, the reign of the first Judahite king, Rehoboam, is marked by cultic defection: high places (במות), male officiants (קדשים),[16] and pillars (מצבות).[17] The reformers Asa (1 Kgs 15:12) and Jehoshaphat (1 Kgs 22:47) expel and banish these male officiants. Similarly, the reformer Hezekiah breaks down the pillars (מצבות; 2 Kgs 18:4), but Josiah both breaks down the pillars and desecrates the sites of those pillars by filling them with human bones (2 Kgs 23:14). In this manner, he preempts their reuse.

A similar institutional concern is evident in the Deuteronomist's treatment of high places (1 Kgs 14:23). All of Rehoboam's successors perpetuate their existence.[18] Finally, two centuries after Rehoboam, Hezekiah removes the high places (2 Kgs 18:4). While the Deuteronomist hails Hezekiah's reforms, he devotes only one verse (2 Kgs 18:4) to them. He also praises Hezekiah for obeying "the commandments YHWH gave to Moses," but does not elaborate upon these claims (2 Kgs 18:6).[19] The Deuteronomist instead turns

---

16 1 Kgs 14:23-24. The term, קדשים, is often translated "male temple prostitutes" (e.g., NRSV), or "male prostitutes" (e.g., REB, NJPS). But there are difficulties with these translations from the standpoint of comparative Semitic philology (Gruber 1986:133-48).

17 1 Kgs 14:23-24 are textually uncertain (cf. 3 Rgns 12:24a; 2 Chr 12:14; Knoppers 1990:424).

18 1 Kgs 15:3, 14; 22:44; 2 Kgs 8:18; 12:4; 14:4; 15:4, 35; 16:4.

19 2 Kgs 18:4. The contrast with Chronicles is startling (Dillard 1987:219-30; Japhet 1993:910-98; Knoppers 1989:79-83; Lowery 1991:142-68; Throntveit 1987:120-25; Williamson 1977:119-25). The Chronicler devotes most of his coverage of Hezekiah to his reforms (2 Chr 29:3-31:21) and less than one chapter to Sennacherib's

to a copious treatment of the Assyrian crisis. In any event, Hezekiah's reforms are short-lived: Manasseh "rebuilt the high places which Hezekiah his father had destroyed" (2 Kgs 21:3).[20] However, Josiah "demolishes the shrines of the male officiants which were in the temple of YHWH, where the women were weaving vestments for Asherah."[21]

Josiah's approach to the high places is both revolutionary and definitive. Josiah "brought all the priests from the cities of Judah and defiled the high places where the priests had burned incense, from Geba to Beersheba" (2 Kgs 23:8).[22] By defiling the high places, Josiah averts their reuse and by importing their Yahwistic clergy into Jerusalem, Josiah co-opts their institutional sanction. McKenzie points out that the Deuteronomist mentions the high places ten times

---

invasion (2 Chr 32:1-23). As Rosenbaum argues, one reason for the lack of attention to the Hezekian reforms in Kings is that the Deuteronomist wishes to call attention to Josiah's accomplishments as a reformer (1979:23-44). I therefore agree with Spieckermann that Hezekiah is a "Vorreformator" in Kings (1982:170-74).

20 The Chronicler's Ahaz does far worse than the Deuteronomist's Ahaz (Ackroyd 1984:251-57; Knoppers 1989:75-79). But the Chronicler's Manasseh recants and is restored (2 Chr 33:11-13; Schniedewind 1991:450-61). Hence, Josiah does not occupy as critical a position in Chronicles as he does in Kings (Williamson 1982b:396; Throntveit 1987:115-20).

21 In 2 Kgs 23:7 KM reads בתים, "houses." KG^{B} transliterates *χεττιειν* (= כתנת?), while KS transliterates *bettieim*. KL (Lucifer) reads *ad stolas*, "robes." Šanda's proposal, developed by Driver (1936:107), that the Hebrew may be related to Arabic *batt*, "garment," accounts for the testimony of some of the versions.

22 In 2 Kgs 23:8 KG^{B} reads *απο Γαιβαλ*(!) *εως Βηρσαβεε*.

in his account of Josiah's reforms (1991:125). Josiah's reign clearly marks the climax to the במות theme in Kings.

The structural dimension of Josiah's offensive against illicit religious practices is also evident in his treatment of child sacrifice. Recreant Ahaz implements this practice (2 Kgs 16:3) and Manasseh continues it (2 Kgs 21:6). The corresponding reform would be to stop this rite, but Josiah's reform goes beyond paralleling the crime. He acts to impede its revival: "he defiled the Topheth, which is in the Valley of Ben-Hinnom,[23] for passing one's son or daughter through the fire for Molek."[24] Similarly, Josiah launches a decisive campaign against the *asherahs* (האשׁרים; 2 Kgs 23:14) bequeathed to him from the time of Rehoboam (1 Kgs 14:23).[25] He cuts them down and fills their sites with human bones (2 Kgs 23:14).

---

23 Reading בן־הנם with the *Qere*, some Hebrew mss, and the versions. The *Kethib* has בני־הנם. I omit KM's לבלתי, which is syntactically difficult before להעביר and lacking in KG^B. As Stade and Schwally (1904:294) observe, the text explains the purpose of the Topheth (KG^B Ταφεθ), not the reason for its destruction.

24 2 Kgs 23:10. The translation and significance of מֹלֶךְ is disputed. Previous references to child sacrifice in the Deuteronomistic History (2 Kgs 16:3; 21:6; cf. Deut 18:10; 2 Kgs 17:17) do not mention Molek. Eissfeldt's (1935) interpretation of מֹלֶךְ as a sacrificial term (cf. Phoenician *molk*) has been defended by Mosca (1975). Heider contends that Molek is the name of a chthonic deity (1985:282-301), but Olyan doubts whether there is sufficient evidence for this interpretation (1988:11-12).

25 1 Kgs 14:23 and 2 Kgs 23:14 are the only occurrences of the masc pl אשׁרים in the Deuteronomist's depiction of the southern kingdom. I am distinguishing between the image (פסל) of Asherah (האשׁרה) in Jerusalem (a likeness of the goddess) set up by Manasseh (2 Kgs 23:6; cf. 2 Kgs 21:3, 7) and these stylized trees or poles (Olyan 1988:1-3).

Josiah's campaign against alien cult symbols also includes his methodical purge of the *Asherah*, which Manasseh "set up...as Ahab king of Israel had done" (2 Kgs 21:3, 7). In his treatment of this cult object, Josiah goes beyond what deuteronomic regulations require: "consign their *asherahs* to the fire, cut down the images of their gods (פסלי אלהיהם), and destroy their name from that place" (Deut 12:3; cf. 7:5). As Friedman (1981a:9) observes, Josiah treats this fixture in the Jerusalem temple as if it were the golden calf.

> He brought out the *Asherah* from YHWH's temple outside Jerusalem to the Wadi Kidron, burned (שׂרף) it in the Wadi Kidron, pulverized it into dust (דק לעפר), and cast its dust upon the graves[26] of the common people. (2 Kgs 23:6).

The *asherah(s)* are mentioned five times in Josiah's reign (2 Kgs 23:4, 6, 7, 14, 15). As with the high places, Josiah's campaigns end the problem of *asherah(s)* in the Deuteronomistic History.

C. THE EXHAUSTIVE NATURE OF JOSIAH'S REFORMS

Josiah's reforms are not only structural, but also thorough. Josiah's crusade against Manasseh's regression is amply rigorous.[27] Josiah redresses the sins of the worst southern king (2 Kgs 21:3, 4, 5, 6) by extirpating the *Asherah* (2 Kgs 23:6), demolishing the high places (2 Kgs 23:8), defiling the Topheth (2 Kgs 23:10), tearing down

---

26 Reading with KG^L, KS, and KT קברי. KM has קבר.

27 McKenzie (1991:119-23) shows that Provan's reasons (1988:151) for dating most of 2 Kings 21 to the exile are not compelling. I am largely following Friedman's literary-critical reconstruction of Manasseh's reign (1981b:176-88).

and crushing[28] the altars in the two temple courts and casting their dust into the Wadi Kidron (2 Kgs 23:12).[29]

The reforms of Josiah also eliminate the last vestiges of Ba'l worship in Judah. In this case, the Deuteronomist admits that Jehoiada deserves much of the credit. Jehoiada oversees the destruction of Ba'l's temple and the execution of its Ba'l priest, Mattan (2 Kgs 11:18). Given the severity of Jehoiada's reforms, one could argue that Jehoiada's elimination of the Ba'l temple along with its altars and images (2 Kgs 11:18) was a momentous feat, rivaling any of those carried out by Josiah. The execution of Mattan by the community conforms to deuteronomic prescriptions (Deut 13:13-19), while Josiah's deposition of "the idolatrous priests (הכמרים)" seems lenient by comparison (2 Kgs 23:5).[30] Nevertheless, the Deuteronomist elevates Josiah's reforms by qualifying Jehoiada's lasting significance. The Deuteronomist depicts Ba'l worship in Judah as a sub-theme to the inveterate high places, which Joash retains despite Jehoiada's tutelage (2 Kgs 12:4).[31] Second, Jehoiada's reforms fail in permanently eradicating Ba'l worship. One's legacy is partially determined by one's successors. Iniquitous Manasseh lapses by erecting altars to Ba'l (2 Kgs 21:3). Again, Josiah's reforms do not precisely parallel the sin, but they do supply the necessary antidote:

---

28 Reading וַיְרַצֵּם שָׁם with Rudolph (1952:215) and NJPS instead of KM's וַיָּרָץ מִשָּׁם.

29 Hoffmann sees an association between 2 Kgs 23:4, 5, 12 and 2 Kgs 21:3, 5 in that both refer to the host of heaven (1980:45, 155-64). The link is clear in 2 Kgs 23:12 and 2 Kgs 21:5, but unclear in 2 Kgs 23:4, 5 and 2 Kgs 21:3.

30 On the כמרים, see Hos 10:5, Zeph 1:4 (cf. KAI 225:1; 226:1).

31 2 Kgs 11:1-12:17. Cf. the Chronicler's more sustained attention to Ba'l worship in the history of Judah (De Vries 1987:59-77).

> Then the king enjoined Hilkiah the priest,[32] the priests of the second order,[33] and the guards of the threshold to bring out of YHWH's temple[34] all the vessels that were fashioned for Ba'l, for Asherah, and for all the host of heaven.[35] And he burned (שׂרף) them outside Jerusalem on the terraces[36] of the Kidron and carried their ashes to Bethel. (2 Kgs 23:4).

In this manner, the Deuteronomist both affirms the accomplishments of Josiah's predecessors and sets Josiah apart from them. The corrections of Josiah's precursors -- Asa, Jehoshaphat, Jehoiada, and Hezekiah -- are commendable, but sporadic and limited. They fail to address systematically the roots of Judah's decline.

Josiah also redresses a variety of sins by "the kings of Judah" (2 Kgs 23:5). The text does not identify these anonymous monarchs, nor does the Deuteronomist's history of Judah previously mention their infractions. The inclusion of these reforms is obviously not

32 KM and KG^B have הכהן הגדול, but גדול is *sub asteriscus* in SyrH. I read כהן (*lectio brevior*).
33 So KM (כהני המשנה), KG, and KS. KT has סגן הכהניא.
34 Literally, היכל, "hall" (cf. 1 Sam 1:9; 3:3; 2 Kgs 18:16; 24:13; KB 230-31).
35 KG^L (boc_2) adds *και εξηγαγον αυτα*.
36 KM reads problematic בשׁדמות. KG^B and KG^A transliterate *εν σαλημωθ* and *εν σαδημωθ* respectively. Mss boc_2e_2 (and Lucifer) read, *τω εμπυρισμω του χειμαρρου* ("in the furnace by the streambed"), while KS and KT simply read בנחלא. On the basis of KG^L and שׂיד ("lime"), Gray (1970:730, 733) proposes משׂרפות ("burning places," hence "limekilns") or משׂידות ("limekilns"). I follow Stager (1982:111-121) and Tadmor and Cogan (1988:285) in translating "terraces." See also the parallel between vineyards and שׁדמות in Deut 32:32, Isa 16:8, and Hab 3:17 (cf. Jer 31:40).

essential to the author's argument that Josiah rectifies the shortcomings of his (named) predecessors. Instead, they underscore the comprehensive nature of his campaign.

> And he put an end (והשבית)[37] to the idolatrous priests (הכמרים), whom the kings of Judah appointed to burn incense[38] at the high places in the cities of Judah and in the environs[39] of Jerusalem, and those who burned incense to Ba'l, the Sun, the moon, the constellations, and all the host of heaven. (2 Kgs 23:5).

Similarly, he puts an end to the horses which the kings of Judah dedicated to the Sun and consigns the chariot[40] of the Sun to fire (2 Kgs 23:11). Josiah also tears down the roof-top altars made by the kings of Judah and casts their dust into the Wadi Kidron (2 Kgs 23:12). Whatever the precise origins and nature of these cultic practices (McKay 1973a:167-69; 1973b:32-36; Smith 1990:115-20), the Deuteronomist presents Josiah's crusade in Jerusalem and its environs as all-pervasive.

Josiah concludes his campaign by defiling the high places which Solomon constructed for his wives. The Deuteronomist's terminology caricatures the gods of these high places and pinpoints the location of the original crime, "the high places which faced Jerusalem to the right of the Mount of Destruction" (ואת-הבמות אשר על-פני ירושלם אשר

---

37 So KM (cf. KG *και κατεκαυσεν*). V 11 offers a similar variation.

38 I am reading the infin לקטר (cf. Lucifer, mss boc_2e_2 *του θυμιαν* and KV *ad sacrificandum*). KM reads ויקטר, while KG^{B} has the pl *και εθυμιων* (= ויקטרו).

39 Reading ובמסבי (with a few Hebrew mss, KG, KT, and KV). KM has ומסבי.

40 Reading with KG^{AB} *και το αρμα* (= ואת-מרכבת). KM, KS, and KT have the pl.

מימין להר-המשחית).[41] Josiah is the only monarch in the history of Judah who has the temerity to attack the high places Solomon established. Josiah's assault against these venerable shrines is one more indication of the lengths to which he will go to abolish all heteropraxis within his realm.

D. CENTRALIZATION AND THE PURGE OF ALIEN CULTS

The build-up to Josiah's reforms is carefully contrived to maximize Josiah's accomplishments and to downplay those of his predecessors. Three previous southern kings mount successful reforms. But the Deuteronomist qualifies his praise for Asa and Jehoshaphat, because they tolerate the high places (1 Kgs 15:14; 22:44). Another king (Hezekiah) removes the high places, along with the pillars, the *Asherah*, and the Nehushtan, but the Deuteronomist devotes only terse coverage to these exploits (2 Kgs 18:4). The Chronicler praises a number of kings who renew covenant, lay claim to parts of the northern kingdom, and institute reforms, but the Deuteronomist champions only one king who does so.[42] That the Deuteronomist

---

41 2 Kgs 23:13 (cf. 1 Kgs 11:7-8). At the beginning of v 13 KG reads *τον οικον* (= הבית). Later in the verse, KM's להר-המשחית is a disparaging pun on להר-המשחה. Many of the versions (e.g., KS *Mascheth*) transliterate. Some would follow the reading of KT (לטור זיתיא), but the pun may be original.

42 Following the ratification of Johoiada's covenant, the people of the land implement reforms (2 Kgs 11:18). Renewing covenant, embarking on northern campaigns, making overtures to Israel, and instituting reforms are major themes in the Chronicler's history of Judah (Baltzer 1971:51-52, 72-78; Japhet 1989:105-116; Knoppers 1989:74-88; McCarthy 1982:92-111; Williamson 1977:97-131). The dichotomy some posit between the Deuteronomist (history) and the

does not provide any sustained coverage of reforms prior to the reign of Josiah is deliberate. The Deuteronomist suppresses the achievements of Josiah's predecessors to enhance Josiah's achievements. Only Josiah's reforms are sufficiently ruthless and systematic to eliminate illicit cults.

Josiah's other achievement -- the imposition of the ancient law of the sanctuary upon Judah -- occurs in the midst of his onslaught against alien religious practices. Some find it surprising that the Deuteronomist, unlike the deuteronomic writers, devotes so little attention to centralization.[43] The two issues -- centralization of the Yahwistic cult and elimination of foreign cults -- are, after all, entirely distinct. One is, by no means, the consequence of the other. Yet the paucity of attention to centralization does not seem to be an oversight.[44] The Deuteronomist provides details about geography (e.g., 2 Kgs 23:5, 8, 11, 13) and cultic *matériel* (e.g., 2 Kgs 23:7, 10, 11). But the only clue which the Deuteronomist provides to distinguish between Yahwistic and non-Yahwistic high places appears, because the Deuteronomist needs to explain why Josiah imports deposed priests into Jerusalem to assist in temple worship (2 Kgs

---

Chronicler (theology) is facile, if not false. Whatever the problems in the Chronicler's presentation, and they are many (*Tendenz*, sources, etc.), the witness of Chronicles should not be dismissed either for reconstructing history or for discerning the *Tendenz* of the Deuteronomist (Graham 1990; Japhet 1985:83-107; Knoppers 1988:143-201, 300-471; Wright 1992:20-42).

43 Cf. Deut 12:4-25 (centralization) and Deuteronomy 16-18 (the effects of centralization upon cultic calendar and public polity).

44 Nor does the lack of detailed coverage to centralization entail that Josiah's reforms were only directed against foreign cults (contra Oestreicher 1923:37-58, Hoppe 1985:107-110, *et al.*).

23:9-10). Many commentators identify these priests as (rural) Levites and contrast this text with the provisions for levitical priests in Deut 18:1-8, but the Kings text does not identify the pedigree of these officiants.[45] Nor does the text claim that these priests stem from (merely) rural areas.[46] Josiah imports "all the priests of the towns (or cities) of Judah" (2 Kgs 23:8). Again, even though the author mentions that the *kōhᵃnê habbāmôt* did not ascend the altar of YHWH in Jerusalem, but did eat *maṣṣôt* with their kinsmen (2 Kgs 23:9), the author does not specify the identity of these high place priests.[47]

In my judgment, the Deuteronomist's manner of presentation abets his ideology. Like the authors of Deuteronomy, the Deuteronomist associates centralization (Deut 12:4-28) with the elimination of foreign cults (Deut 12:1-3, 29-31). But unlike the authors of Deuteronomy, the Deuteronomist does not argue for centralization. Rather,

---

45 See, for instance, Gramberg (1829:67), Hölscher (1922:229), Kennett (1906:486), Paton (1928:352-55), Wellhausen (1885:124, 140), and White (1990:150).

46 Nelson (1991:142-43) distinguishes between Yahwistic priests serving at the high places who were not allowed to receive priestly appointments (2 Kgs 23:8) and Yahwistic priests not connected with the high places who were assigned priestly duties in Jerusalem (2 Kgs 23:9). I am unsure whether 2 Kgs 23:8-9 supports this distinction.

47 This imprecision constitutes, in my judgment, one further indication that the ideological concerns of the Deuteronomist diverge from those of the authors of Deuteronomy. The authors of Deuteronomy term a priest a levitical priest and valorize Levi (e.g., Deut 27:9-14; 33:8-11; Emerton 1962:129-38), but the Deuteronomist exhibits no consternation at either the Zadokite ascent to exclusive power during the time of Solomon (1 Kgs 2:26-27; cf. 1 Sam 2:35) or the subservient role of imported Yahwistic priests during the reformation of King Josiah.

he extends the deuteronomic trope. Josiah's actions assume the veracity of "the scroll of the torah" (chap. 5). Consistent with deuteronomic demands for cultic unity and cultic purity, Josiah's campaign against Yahwistic sanctuaries is continuous with his campaign against Canaanite cults. He thereby levels the differences between *Kultusreinheit* and *Kultuseinheit*. As a catalogue of reforms 2 Kgs 23:4-14 stigmatizes with broad strokes, allowing few distinctions between what historically must have been a complex range of discrete religious practices.[48] The contiguity of measures aimed at eradicating prohibited cult practices and measures aimed at centralizing Yahwistic worship therefore casts aspersions on the Yahwistic practices and personnel Josiah corrects.

Conclusions

Josiah may be "a cult reformer, nothing more" (Lohfink 1987: 460), but in the ancient Near East religious, economic, social, and geo-political issues are not easily disentangled. Indeed, if the Deuteronomist's interpretation of history is cultic (Halpern 1988:220-28), then the practice of cult is decisive for politics and society. Viewing Josiah's reforms as economically motivated (Bentzen 1926: 68-72; Claburn 1973:11-22) is reductive, but this does not warrant

48 For instance, the polemic against *asherah(s)* within biblical literature is, as Olyan points out (1988:3-14), largely confined to deuteronomic and deuteronomistic circles. See also the observations of Ackerman (1992:5-217) on the various forms of popular religion in sixth-century Judah. Epigraphic and archaeological evidence therefore suggests a much more complex picture of what constituted orthopraxis for various groups within ancient Israel.

overlooking the profound economic consequences of Josiah's reforms. In this respect, one needs to distinguish between the stance of an author, who wishes to present Josiah as the apotheosis of a reformer, and the preexilic issues which this presentation is meant to address. To see Josiah as simply a pious paragon for an exilic audience discounts the royalist features of the Deuteronomist's presentation and overlooks the predicament of Jerusalem and Judah in the late seventh century (Halpern 1991:77-91).

In the Deuteronomistic History Josiah's destruction of the sanctuaries established by Solomon has overt geo-political consequences. Since Solomon squanders the united kingdom due to his construction of and worship at the high places, Josiah's reforms situate him in a unique position to lay claim to the heritage of the united kingdom.[49] Similarly, his undoing all the damage done by his southern forefathers returns his state to a pristine (pre-division) cultic condition. This can only bode well for Judah. The deuteronomistic record of Josiah's southern campaigns evinces logic. Josiah's requiting the sins of his forefathers, especially Solomon, sets the scene for the next stage in his reforms: the former northern kingdom.

The portrayal of centralization as a natural component of Josiah's reforms is one more indication that 2 Kgs 23:4-14 is Josianic propaganda. Josiah's reforms represent the long overdue fulfillment of Israel's ancient charter. If, according to this charter, there is only one legitimate Yahwistic sanctuary, all other cult sites are by their very existence illicit. Pursuing details, such as the nature of the Yahwistic priests Josiah imports into Jerusalem, would therefore detract from

[49] 1 Kgs 11:1-13; 2 Kgs 23:13; vol 1: chaps. 4-5.

the Deuteronomist's agenda. Centralization occurs not because Josiah innovates, but because Josiah's reforms are definitive and exhaustive.

II. JOSIAH'S NORTHERN REFORMS

If the Deuteronomist presents Josiah's southern reforms against the sweep of Solomonic and Judahite history, he presents Josiah's northern reforms against the background of one event in Israelite history: Jeroboam's sins. Nevertheless, I would argue that the Deuteronomist's literary strategy in depicting Josiah's northern reforms is similar to his literary strategy in depicting Josiah's southern reforms. Because the Deuteronomist presents the sins of Jeroboam as a cipher for the downfall of northern monarchy, the Deuteronomist has the entire cultic history of Israel in view when he composes 2 Kgs 23:15-20. As with his portrayal of Josiah's reforms in Jerusalem and Judah, the Deuteronomist's compositional technique is not so much to fit Josiah's reforms to past wrongdoing as it is to fit previous wrongdoing to Josiah's reforms.

The desire to shape past wrongs to Josiah's rectification of those wrongs elucidates the disparity between the number of southern reforms and northern reforms. Conversely, failing to recognize the programmatic nature of the Deuteronomist's work leads to curious results. Scholars mistake the Deuteronomist's vehement denunciations of Jeroboam's cultus for evidence that the northern kingdom was more heterodox than the southern kingdom. Commentators present the treatment of northern history in Kings as more negative than it actually is or present the deuteronomistic treatment of southern history as more positive than it actually is. Pfeiffer, for instance, claims that the preexilic Deuteronomist contrasts "the virtue and security of Judah with the sinfulness and ruin of Israel" (1948:152). Similarly, historians compare the relative isolation of Judah with religious syncretism in cosmopolitan Israel.[50]

But the Deuteronomist's depiction of outstanding northern recreancy from 1 Kings 12 through 2 Kings 17 is associated with Jeroboam and is written with a view to its elimination by Josiah in 2 Kgs 23:15-20. In his portrayal of Israelite declension the Deuteronomist actually attributes a relatively small number of sins to northern kings. In contrast, the Deuteronomist posits a diverse configuration of religious sites, rituals, and symbols in pre-Josianic Judah.[51] The Judah Josiah confronts appears much more cosmopolitan than Samaria. When Josiah institutes his reforms, he confronts five times as many unrequited sins in Judah as in all of the former northern kingdom.

A. THE COMPOSITION OF 2 KGS 23:15-20

The description of Josiah's northern reforms clearly responds to Jeroboam's establishment of his counter-cultus (1 Kgs 12:28-33) and the prophetic reactions to the Bethel cultus (1 Kings 13). In fact, there is a clear parallel between the description of Josiah's reforms at Bethel in 2 Kgs 23:16-18 and the prediction of the man of God from Judah in 1 Kgs 13:2. The transition from 2 Kgs 23:15 to 2 Kgs 23:16

---

50 E.g., Bright (1981:260-62, 272-73) and Miller and Hayes (1986:234-35).

51 I see one of the additions (vv 7aβ-17) to the Deuteronomist's editorial in 2 Kings 17 as an attempt to rectify this imbalance. As Burney (1920:331), Viviano (1987:552), *et al.* demonstrate, vv 11-17 ascribe for the first time many of Judah's sins to Israel.

is, however, problematic. In v 15 Josiah destroys the Bethel altar, but in v 16 he burns human bones upon this same altar.

These two facts -- the parallel and the contradiction -- have led many commentators to view 2 Kgs 23:16-18 as a source originally associated with the narrative of 1 Kings 13.[52] Some then view v 15 and vv 19-20 as part of either the original *Reformbericht* or another source.[53] Others view v 15 and vv 19-20 as deuteronomistic.[54] Still others see most, if not all, of 2 Kgs 23:15-20 as a deuteronomistic creation.[55] A second group of scholars takes quite a different approach to the composition of 2 Kgs 23:15-20. They excise vv 16-

---

52 Burney (1920:355-56); Crenshaw (1971:43); Jepsen (1959:103; 1971:171-76); Klopfenstein (1966:646-52); Šanda (1911-12:361); Simon (1976:84-85, 101); Tadmor and Cogan (1988:299); Wilson (1980:188). Eynikel (1990:237) views vv 16-18 and 1 Kgs 13:1b, 2, 8b, 9aβ, 11-32 as stemming from the same hand. Van Dorp argues that all of vv 15-20 belong together with 1 Kings 13 (1987:64-77).

53 So, for instance, Eissfeldt (1965:297), Eynikel (1990:236), and Noth (1981:80). Oestreicher sees two traditions represented in 2 Kgs 23:15-24 (vv 15, 19; vv 16-18, 20, 21-24) neither of which belongs to the original *Reformbericht* (1923:58-60).

54 Nielsen (1959:197-98); Tadmor and Cogan (1988:299-300). McKenzie sees 2 Kgs 23:15bβ-18 as stemming from the same editor, who wrote 1 Kgs 13:32 (1991:123-25). Though not denying the possibility of a source for vv 16-18, Nelson (1981a:82-83) attributes vv 15-18 to Dtr^1 and vv 19-20 to Dtr^2.

55 Dietrich (1972:117-120 [DtrP]); Halpern (1988:249-50 [Dtr^1]); Hobbs (1985:319); Hoffmann (1980:212-19, 261-63); Hollenstein (1977:335 [DtrP]); Jones (1984:616-617, 624 [DtrP]); Mayes (1983: 131 [Dtr^1]); Van Seters (1983:319). Spieckermann sees four levels of composition in 2 Kgs 23:15-20 (1982:112-118).

18,[56] vv 16-20,[57] or all of vv 15-20 (e.g, Montgomery 1951:546 and O'Brien 1989:261-64) as late additions. How one views the compositional history on vv 16-18 is, of course, related to how one dates the prophetic narratives within 1 Kings 13. Hence, those scholars who see 1 Kings 13 as post-deuteronomistic also view most, if not all, of 2 Kgs 23:15-20 as post-deuteronomistic.

In my view, v 15 is not easily separable from v 16 and vv 16-18 are not easily separable from vv 19-20. Not only vv 16-18, but also v 15 and vv 19-20 specifically recall elements within 1 Kings 13. The description of the Bethel altar in 2 Kgs 23:15 is based upon the earlier descriptions in 1 Kings 13.

1 Kgs 12:33:	ויעל על-המזבח אשר-עשׂה בבית-אל
1 Kgs 13:32:	קרא בדבר יהוה על-המזבח אשר בבית-אל
2 Kgs 23:15:	גם את-המזבח אשר בבית-אל

The very attention in v 15 to the Bethel altar as representating Jeroboam's malfeasance reflects the focus of the man of God in 1 Kgs 13:1-5*. In contrast, the narration of Jeroboam's cultus in 1 Kgs 12:28-33 mentions his fashioning of two golden calves, his enfranchisement of Bethel and Dan, his festival, his construction of the cult places, his appointment of priests of the high places, and his ascent

56 Dozeman (1982:381); Herrmann (1981:266); McKenzie (1991: 113-114). Rofé (1974:163-64) dates 1 Kings 13 and its outcome in 2 Kings 23 to the postexilic era, but he does not, to my knowledge, identify which verses constitute this conclusion.

57 Kittel (1900:303); Ogden (1978:31-33); Gray (1970:738-39). Gray concedes that these verses may stem from the deuteronomistic redactor himself. Würthwein (1973:188; 1976:419-21; 1984:454-61) sees v 16 as an insertion by DtrP, vv 17-20 as a later addition, and v 15 as insertion made in the early Persian age.

upon the Bethel altar he constructed. Given both the deuteronomistic cliché in v 15 (אשר החטיא ישׂראל) and the concentration upon the Bethel altar, it is highly unlikely that this verse stems from a *Reformbericht*. It evinces deuteronomistic editing and introduces the focus upon the Bethel altar in the verses which follow.

I would also argue that vv 16-18 and vv 19-20 belong together. These two units resonate with a sequence of pericopes in 1 Kings 13. 2 Kgs 23:16-18 recall the prophecy of the man of God from Judah (1 Kgs 13:1-2) and the burial instructions given by the prophet from Bethel (1 Kgs 13:26-31). 2 Kgs 23:19-20, in turn, recall the asseveration of the prophet from Bethel in 1 Kgs 13:31-32. As we saw in chaps. 2 and 3, part of 1 Kgs 13:32 and all of 1 Kgs 13:33-34 are deuteronomistic. There is no need, then, to see more than one deuteronomistic hand in 2 Kgs 23:16-20. It seems more likely that a single deuteronomistic editor employed the conclusion (2 Kgs 23:16-18) of the prophetic narratives in 1 Kings 13 as the base for his own composition. In my judgment, vv 16-18* stem from an earlier source and vv 15 and 19-20, both introduced by וגם, stem from deuteronomistic composition. This editor does not simply incorporate vv 16-18 into his narrative, but retouches and updates them. This explains the anachronism in v 18 (הנביא אשר־בא משמרון in v 18) as well as the similarities between the manner of Josiah's northern reforms in v 16 and his southern reforms.[58]

As to dating, I do not see any compelling reason to jettison vv 15-20 as the work of a late Deuteronomist or post-deuteronomistic glos-

---

58 The Deuteronomist's use of the conclusion to 1 Kings 13 (2 Kgs 23:16-18) may shed light on his use of a *Reformbericht*. He likely shaped and supplemented this source in similar ways.

sator. There is, in fact, strong evidence that the same (Josianic) Deuteronomist composed both 2 Kgs 23:15-20 and 2 Kgs 23:4-14. First, there are parallels between the manner and means of Josiah's northern reforms and his southern reforms (contra Oestreicher 1923: 57). In 2 Kgs 23:15 Josiah pulverizes the Bethel altar to dust, just as he pulverizes the *Asherah* to dust in Judah (2 Kgs 23:6-7). Josiah defiles the Bethel altar (ויטמאהו; 2 Kgs 23:16), just as he defiles the high places (2 Kgs 23:8, 13) and the Tophet (2 Kgs 23:10) in Judah. Such actions do not correspond, however, to the prophecies in 1 Kings 13. 1 Kgs 13:2 predicts the slaughter of priests and the burning of human bones upon the altar, but does not overtly refer to the defilement of the altar itself. 2 Kgs 23:19 implies that Josiah also defiles the northern high places.[59] Again, this would correspond to Josiah's southern reforms, but not to 1 Kgs 13:32 which expands the prophecy of 1 Kgs 13:2 to include the high places in Samaria.

The Deuteronomist's establishing continuity between Josiah's southern and northern reforms is not limited to his shaping the latter to fit the former. There is also evidence that the Deuteronomist tailors the last of Josiah's southern reforms to resonate with Josiah's northern reforms. In 2 Kgs 23:14 Josiah "shatters the pillars" (המצבות) and "cuts down the *asherahs*" (האשׁרים), filling their sites with human bones" (2 Kgs 23:14). Neither the instructions of Deuteronomy (7:5; 12:3) nor the pattern of earlier reforms affecting "(the) *Asherah*" ((ה)אשׁרה; 1 Kgs 15:13; 2 Kgs 18:4) and "the pillars" (המצבות; 2 Kgs 3:2; 10:26, 27; 18:4) mention desecrating such cult sites with human bones. But Josiah's doing so in 2 Kgs 23:14 corre-

59 The claim that Josiah did to the northern high places "just as he had done to Bethel" (2 Kgs 23:19) implies that he defiled these shrines as well (2 Kgs 23:16).

lates with his northern reforms. Josiah uses human bones to defile both the Bethel altar and the Samarian high places (1 Kgs 13:2, 32; 2 Kgs 23:16, 19-20). Hence, the character of Josiah's final southern reforms anticipates the character of his northern reforms.

Second, Josiah's northern reforms cohere with the consistent deuteronomistic polemic against the failings of the northern monarchy, epitomized in the sins of Jeroboam. As we have seen (chap. 4), this polemic is central to his construction of Israelite history. Third, the placement of Josiah's northern forays makes sense thematically. After rectifying Solomon's sins, the cause of disunion (1 Kgs 11:1-13, 26-39), Josiah can attend to Jeroboam's sins, the ruin of the northern kingdom (1 Kgs 12:26-33; 13:33-34; 14:7-18).

B. INTRODUCTION AND OVERVIEW

If the Deuteronomist is responsible for 2 Kgs 23:15-20, how does one explain the contradiction between v 15 and v 16? Wilson (1980: 188) sees 2 Kgs 23:15 as an interpretation of the prophetic sign in 1 Kgs 13:3, (5).[60] I agree that the Deuteronomist has 1 Kings 13 in view, but there are two problems with Wilson's approach. First, 2 Kgs 23:15 does not mention any sign. Second, the phraseology of 2 Kgs 23:15 (המזבח...נתץ וישׂרף...הדק לעפר) simply does not correspond to the man of God's assertion in 1 Kgs 13:3 (המזבח נקרע

[60] I agree with Hoffmann that scholars occasionally misapply modern standards of logic to ancient writings (1980:261-62), but the tension between v 15 and v 16 is stark even by deuteronomistic standards. Hence, I find his explanation -- 1 Kgs 13:5 is a proleptic fulfillment of 2 Kgs 23:16ff. -- inadequate.

(ונשפך הדשן אשר-עליו).[61] Nelson (1987:258) advocates a different approach, describing vv 16-18 as "a flashback which considers the events of verse 15 more closely." The suggestion that the author employs 2 Kgs 23:15 to introduce the narrative of vv 16-18 has merit, but I believe the Deuteronomist's compositional strategy is more complex than Nelson indicates.

The deuteronomistic presentation of Josiah's northern reforms reflects multiple concerns and must be seen in the broader context of his depiction of Josiah's reign. First, Dtr^1 wishes to demonstrate a continuity between Josianic activity in the South and Josianic activity in the North, hence the parallels between 2 Kgs 23:15, 16, 19 and 2 Kgs 23:6-7, 8, 10, 13, 14. Josiah corrects southern and northern sins in similar ways. Second, he wishes to demonstrate that Josiah's northern reforms cancel the unrequited sins of the northern monarchy, most prominently the apostasy of Jeroboam. Hence, he adds his own introduction (v 15) and conclusion (vv 19-20) to the tradition bequeathed to him (vv 16-18*). The Deuteronomist's composition of 2 Kgs 23:15-20 is historical, exegetical, and theological -- he writes with both 1 Kgs 13:1-32 and 2 Kgs 23:4-14 fully in view.

The problem for the Deuteronomist is that Josiah's actions in his source conform to the man of God's prophecy (1 Kgs 13:2), but not to the pattern of Josiah's reforms. The interdiction of 1 Kgs 13:2 justifies Josiah's slaughter of the priests of the high places and the incineration of human bones upon the Bethel altar, but it does not say anything about Josiah's destroying the altar itself. Similarly, the Deuteronomist's expansion of the man of God's declamation (1 Kgs

61 KG 2 Kgs 23:15 differs somewhat from KM (see above), but this does not ease the the disparity between v 15 and 1 Kgs 13:3.

13:32) succeeds in extending the interdiction of 1 Kgs 13:2 to the northern high places and their attendant priests, but not in justifying the decimation of those high places.

Prefacing an account of Josiah's demolishing the altar (v 15) before taking up the source (vv 16-18*) and recounting Josiah's realization of an ancient prediction accomplishes a number of strategic ends. Josiah demolishes the Bethel altar in conformity with the *Vernichtungssymbolik* in 2 Kgs 23:4-14 and he incinerates the אשרה so that Josiah corrects the only sin remaining from the time of Ahab. Moreover, by virtue of the statement in his source: "he [the man of God] pronounced these things which you are doing against the Bethel altar" (2 Kgs 23:17), the Deuteronomist's contextualization of v 15 implies that Josiah's destruction of the Bethel altar fulfills an ancient prophecy. The Deuteronomist's reuse of tradition therefore makes that tradition speak with a new voice. The *traditio* becomes a new *traditum*. Not only are Josiah's actions consistent in both South and North, but his northern iconoclasm comports with prophetic tradition.

Similarly, by situating vv 19-20 (the fulfillment of 1 Kgs 13:32) after his source (vv 16-18*), the Deuteronomist implies that Josiah's destruction of the northern high places is fully warranted. The Deuteronomist acknowledges that these high places were built by a number of different Israelite kings, but he sanctions their abolition by recourse to a northern prophecy which predates their establishment (1 Kgs 13:32; 2 Kgs 23:19). Note the intriguing, but somewhat ambiguous assertion about the high places in the cities of Samaria, "he did to them according to all the works he performed at Bethel" (2 Kgs 23:19). Is the antecedent simply Josiah's actions in vv 16-18 or the totality of Josiah's actions in vv 15-18? It would seem, given the use of the adjective "all" before "the works" (ככל-המעשׂים), that the latter possibility is more likely.

Consistent with the Deuteronomist's concentration upon the Bethel cultus as the nexus of Jeroboam's sin in 1 Kings 13, he correlates the Bethel altar with Jeroboam's transgression, "the altar...which Jeroboam ben-Nebat made by which he caused Israel to sin" (המזבח...אשר ירבעם בן-נבט אשר החטיא ישׂראל; 2 Kgs 23:15).[62] If the Deuteronomist associates Jeroboam's sin with the Bethel shrine, the manner of Josiah's demolishing this shrine resembles Josiah's destruction of the *Asherah* in the Jerusalem temple (2 Kgs 23:6-7). This is all the more remarkable, because the altar, unlike the golden calf (Exod 32:20; Deut 9:21), the golden calves (1 Kgs 12:28-30), and the *Asherah* (2 Kgs 23:6), does not represent a deity.[63] Like Moses, Josiah destroys and pulverizes the cult objects he finds inimical (Friedman 1981a:6-7).

Exod 32:20:	וישׂרף באשׁ ויטחן עד אשׁר-דק
Deut 9:21:	ואשׂרף אתו באשׁ ואכת אתו טחון היטב אד אשׁר-דק לעפר
2 Kgs 23:15:	[64]נתץ וישׁבר את-אבניו וידק לעפר

---

[62] The cliché first occurs in Ahijah's reproof of Jeroboam (ואשׁר החטיא ישׂראל; 1 Kgs 14:16). The phrase הזה לחטאת בית ירבעם occurs in 1 Kgs 13:34 (cf. הטאות ירבעם אשׁר חטא in 1 Kgs 14:16).

[63] Had the golden calves already disappeared from Bethel and Dan (Halpern 1988:249)?

[64] 2 Kgs 23:15. I am following KG^{AB}, *κατεσπασεν και συνετριψεν τους λιθους αυτου και ελεπτυνεν εις χουν* (maximum variation). KM reads נתץ וישׂרף את-הבמה הדק לעפר. Since the locutions in both KM and KG are unusual, it does not make sense to dismiss the KG reading out of hand (*pace* Tadmor and Cogan 1988:289). KM's reading may have been influenced either by the locutions of Exod 32:20 and Deut 9:21 or by the appearance of וישׂרף later in v 15.

2 Kgs 23:15 also introduces Josiah's northern reforms by referring to Josiah's burning (שׂרף) of (the) *Asherah*.[65] Many commentators delete this assertion as a gloss, because earlier references to (ה)אשׁרה apparently associate it with the Ba'l temple in Samaria.[66] Excising the phrase as late, however, simply defers explanation. The reference is allusive, but I agree with Hoffmann (1980:78-81) and Tagliacarne (1989:239-46) that it need not be deleted. In attacking this cult symbol, Josiah is removing the last symbol of Ahab's recreancy. Olyan (1988:6) observes that the Deuteronomist's original assertion about the *Asherah* is also allusive, "he went and served Ba'l, worshiped him, and erected an altar for Ba'l in the temple of Ba'l, which he built in Samaria. Ahab also made the *Asherah*" (1 Kgs 16:31b-33). Whereas the Deuteronomist speaks of the location of Ba'l's temple and the location of Ba'l altars within this temple, he seems to associate this religious artifact with Samaria. Yet he does not pinpoint its location. The deuteronomistic configuration of this sin suggests a concern more with typology than with geography.

Ahab's sins earn him a severe condemnation from the Deuteronomist (1 Kgs 16:33), more severe than that accorded to Jeroboam (1 Kgs 14:9). But, unlike the sins of Jeroboam, all but one of the sins of Ahab do not last. The reformer "Jehu eradicates Ba'l from Israel" (2 Kgs 10:28). He destroys the Ba'l temple and the altar for Ba'l. Jehu

---

65 Thus honoring the mandate of Deut 12:3, "and their *asherahs* you shall consign to fire" (ואשׁריהם תשׂרפון באשׁ).

66 Hoffmann also calls attention to 2 Kgs 17:10, 16 (1980:127-32). But these verses are probably later additions to the reflection of the Deuteronomist on Israel's exile (n. 51).

also massacres the Ba'l priests (2 Kgs 10:25-27) in conformity with the mandate of Deut 13:13-19. The Deuteronomist qualifies his praise for Jehu, however, because he "did not desist from the sins which Jeroboam caused Israel to commit" (2 Kgs 10:31). Even in portraying the struggle of Israel's greatest reformer against the unprecedented perfidy of the Omride dynasty, the Deuteronomist's long range thematic concerns are evident. Ahab's transgressions are worse than those of Jeroboam, but Jehu's reforms only succeed in returning his nation to a pre-Ahab plight. The sins of Jeroboam endure as the dominant problem of the northern monarchy.

In his depiction of Jehoahaz' reign the Deuteronomist observes another unresolved legacy of Ahab: "the *Asherah* remained standing in Samaria" (2 Kgs 13:6). This failing goes uncorrected until Josiah's northern campaign: he "burned (the) *Asherah*" (2 Kgs 23:15b). He completes what Jehu leaves undone. Josiah's actions in the North resonate with his actions in the South. In both cases he corrects the unrequited sins of previous monarchs.

C. JOSIAH AND THE MAN OF GOD FROM JUDAH

Having introduced Josiah's northern campaign, the Deuteronomist recounts Josiah's destruction of the Bethel altar. Dtr^1 presents the sequence of Josiah's northern reforms in 2 Kgs 23:16-20 as echoing the sequence of events in the prophetic narratives of 1 Kings 13. Drawing upon tradition (2 Kgs 23:16-18*), the Deuteronomist writes 2 Kgs 23:16-20 so that Josiah fulfills the prediction of the man of God from Judah (1 Kgs 13:2; 2 Kgs 23:16-17), as well as both the hopes (1 Kgs 13:26-31; 2 Kgs 23:18) and the assessment (1 Kgs 13:32; 2 Kgs 23:19-20) of the prophet from Bethel.

Josiah begins actualizing the man of God's prophecy by burning human bones upon the Bethel altar.[67]

1 Kgs 13:2:	[68]ועצמות אדם ישׂרף עליך
2 Kgs 23:16:	העצמות מן-הקברים וישׂרף על-המזבח

If the lexical congruence between the description of Josiah's actions and the ancient prophecy was not explicit enough, 2 Kgs 23:16 cites Josiah's actions as fulfilling the man of God's interdiction against the Bethel altar.[69]

1 Kgs 13:2:	ויקרא בדבר יהוה על-המזבח
1 Kgs 13:32:	הדבר אשר קרא בדבר יהוה על-המזבח אשר בבית-אל
2 Kgs 23:16:	כדבר יהוה אשר קרא איש האלהים אשר קרא את-הדברים האלה

The citation of 1 Kgs 13:1-2 in 2 Kgs 23:16 is even more conspicuous, given that the reading of KG in 2 Kgs 23:16 is superior to the reading of KM.[70]

---

67 2 Kgs 23:16 does not mention, however, Josiah sacrificing the priests of the high places upon the Bethel altar (cf. 1 Kgs 13:2).

68 I am following KG and KS. KM has ישׂרפו.

69 I am transcribing 2 Kgs 23:16 according to KM. On the textual criticism of this verse, see below.

70 KG 2 Kgs 23:16 reads, *εν τω εσταναι* Ιεροβοαμ *εν τη εορτη επι το θυσιαστηριον και επιστρεψας ηρεν τους οφθαλμους αυτου επι τον ταφον του ανθρωπου του θεου* (= בעמד ירבעם בחג על-המזבח ויפן וישׂא את-עיניו על-קבר איש אלהים). KM has evidently suffered a haplography by *homoioteleuton* (from איש האלהים to איש האלהים).

1 Kgs 13:1: וירבעם עמד על־המזבח
2 Kgs 23:16: בעמד ירבעם בחג על־המזבח

Josiah's fulfillment of ancient revelation is surprisingly unwitting. Until he is confronted with the prophecy Josiah has no familiarity with the traditions predicting the demise of the Bethel sanctuary (2 Kgs 23:17). The theme in 1 Kings 13 that YHWH's word is inexorable, triumphing over both its opponents and its subjects, has been decisively validated (Simon 1976:86).

In deuteronomistic perspective Josiah's reforms signify more than a string of successes for a particular king. Josiah's uncontrived actions have metaphysical implications. The coherence between an age-old prophecy and its fulfillment approximately three centuries later involves human characters, but is not reducible to them. The deity continues to be active in the former northern kingdom, employing Josiah as his instrument. Josiah's cultic initiatives also have political ramifications. By negation Josiah's reforms reaffirm Israel's election. If Jeroboam's enfranchisement of a cultus at Bethel (and Dan) violates the exclusive claims of the Jerusalem temple, Josiah's abolition of the Bethel cultus reestablishes Jerusalem's exclusive status. Josiah's success manifests the deity's reassertion of sovereignty over land, history, and people.

D. JOSIAH AND THE PROPHET FROM BETHEL

Josiah's actions (2 Kgs 23:18-20), upon hearing of the Judahite man of God's prophecy, are no less remarkable than his unwitting actualization of this prophecy. The implementation of Josiah's commands concerning the bones of the man of God condones the Bethel prophet's actions three centuries earlier. The attention which the

Deuteronomist accords to the Bethel prophet marks a shift from the focus of 1 Kings 13, the oracle of the man of God against the Bethel altar, to a sub-theme within 1 Kings 13, the instructions and asseveration of the Bethel prophet (1 Kgs 13:27-32). In my view, the Deuteronomist engineers this shift to legitimate Josiah's campaign against the northern high places and his massacre of their priests.

The reverence with which the men of the town treat the bones of both the man of God from Judah and the prophet from Samaria signals the beginning of this focus on the Bethel prophet (2 Kgs 23:18). The Bethel prophet is responsible for this peculiar burial arrangement. Having heard that his judgment against the man of God has come true in the very manner he predicted (1 Kgs 13:18-22), the Bethel prophet has his sons bury the corpse of the Judahite man of God in his own grave with the proviso that upon his death they bury him in this same tomb. The Bethel prophet bases his unusual request on the phenomenal sequence of events he had just experienced. The man of God's prophecy about Josiah's burning human bones upon the Bethel altar will surely come true (1 Kgs 13:31-32); nevertheless, the man of God never specified whose bones would be burned (1 Kgs 13:2). Nor did he describe the geographical derivation of these bones (1 Kgs 13:2).

2 Kgs 23:18 conveys that not only the Judahite man of God, but also the Bethel prophet were prescient. The Bethel prophet's premonition that the fate of his bones would only be secure if he linked his fate with that of the man of God turns out to be correct. Josiah's instructions to the local men, "let him rest; do not disturb his bones" recall the Bethel prophet's own instructions to his sons, "next to his bones rest my bones."

1 Kgs 13:31:	אצל עצמתיו הניחו את־עצמותי
2 Kgs 23:18:	הניחו לו איש אל־ינע עצמתיו

The exoneration of the Bethel prophet's funereal directives (1 Kgs 13:31), in turn, validates the Bethel prophet's asseveration, justifying the destruction of all northern shrines (1 Kgs 13:32).

1 Kgs 13:2:	קרא בדבר יהוה על-המזבח
1 Kgs 13:32:	קרא בדבר יהוה על-המזבח אשר בבית-אל ועל כל-בתי הבמות אשר בשמרון[71]

Through an addendum to 1 Kgs 13:32 the Deuteronomist transforms a denunciation of one altar to a denunciation of all northern high places. Since the original declamation also predicted the slaughter of the priests of the high places upon the Bethel altar, this expansion legitimates Josiah's slaughter of all the priests of the high places upon their own altars. Finally, as we have seen, the Deuteronomist's contextualization (2 Kgs 23:15-18) of Josiah's campaign against the northern high places (2 Kgs 23:19-20) justifies their extirpation. Hence, the Deuteronomist's contextualization and transformation of his source authorize a devastating Josianic purge in the former northern kingdom.

We have seen that the introduction of Assyrian sponsored immigrants into Samaria following the northern exile reinvigorates the cultus Jeroboam established (chap. 3). When he ventures to Bethel Josiah confronts a long, but consistent, tradition of transgression. Josiah's abolition of the high places, his execution of "all the priests of the high places," and his burning of human bones upon the high

---

71 So KG. KM's בערי שמרון assimilates to the formulation בערי שמרון in 2 Kgs 23:19 (cf. 2 Kgs 17:24 and see chap. 3).

places (2 Kgs 23:20) explicitly ratify the man of God's prophecy (1 Kgs 13:2) and the Bethel prophet's asseveration (1 Kgs 13:32).

1 Kgs 13:32:	[72]ועל-כל בתי הבמות אשר בשׁמרון
2 Kgs 23:19:	וגם את-כל בתי הבמות אשר בערי שׁמרון
1 Kgs 13:2:	וזבח עליך את-כהני הבמות המקטרים עליך
2 Kgs 23:20:	וזבח את-כל-כהני הבמות אשר-שׁם על-המזבחות
1 Kgs 13:2:	ועצמות אדם ישׂרף עליך
2 Kgs 23:20:	וישׂרף את-עצמות אדם עליהם

In the deuteronomistic presentation, the independent cultic history of the northern realm only ends with the advent of Josiah's reforms. The inauguration of Jeroboam's cultus and the destruction of that cultus by Josiah constitutes an *inclusio*, enclosing the entire deuteronomistic treatment of northern cultic affairs. Both components within the *inclusio* call attention to Josiah's achievements.

Conclusions

Ahlström (1982:70-71) queries how a Judahite king could justify interfering with the cult of another realm. Denying that Josiah's northern campaign amounts to any form of annexation, Ahlström (1982:72) proposes that Josiah's northern campaign is simply punitive. I would suggest that the question Ahlström raises would be most acute in the context of the seventh century. By the time of Josiah, the northern and southern tribes had been separated far longer than they

---

72 Reading with KG (see n. 71).

had been together. I have argued that the deuteronomistic presentation of Josiah's northern crusade is but the last part of a deuteronomistic *apologia* for Josiah's unprecedented intrusion into northern affairs. The Deuteronomist lays the foundation for Josiah's northern expedition in his presentation of the united monarchy, construing the Jerusalem temple as the divinely chosen and popularly endorsed sanctuary for all Israelites (1 Kgs 8:1-2, 62-64). Because Israelite participation in the Jerusalem temple dedication is geographically inclusive and uniformly enthusiastic (1 Kgs 8:65-66), the Deuteronomist effectively incriminates any one who would deviate from this orthopraxy. The Deuteronomist never concedes that any northern king has any right to invest or support any sanctuary except the Jerusalem temple. "Yahweh of Jerusalem" is owed the exclusive allegiance of all Israelites.[73]

The Deuteronomist also defends Josiah's northern campaign by appealing to northern history. In fulfilling the prophecies of the man of God and the Bethel prophet, Josiah becomes the protector of northern traditions (Herrmann 1981:268). He doe not impinge upon the sovereign territory of another realm and its deity in attempting to reclaim a united kingdom. On the contrary, the history of the northern kingdom begs for such action. 2 Kgs 23:15-20 legitimates Josiah's incursions into northern Israel, because these incursions represent a resolution to a great impediment hindering a return to

---

[73] *Pace* Ahlström (1982:71; 1993:777-81). Handy (1990:18-35) argues that when YHWH is accepted as the sole ruling deity in Jerusalem other major and minor deities (except messenger deities) -- however the followers of these deities construed the relationship of these deities to YHWH -- are to be abandoned.

Israel's ancient grandeur. Josiah liberates the former northern kingdom from its own past.

Josiah's actions cannot therefore be understood as simply punitive. Josiah's northern reforms are, in fact, absolutely ruthless. Presented as history, Josiah's destruction of cult objects in South and North has mythological depth. The attacks against or capture of certain cult objects by Assyrian kings do more than punish a subject people: they symbolize victory for the Assyrians and their deities.[74] If Mot's slaying of Ba'l leads to havoc in nature and chaos in society (*KTU* 1.5.6:8-32), Anat's obliteration of Mot (*KTU* 1.6.2:26-35) contributes to the renewal of nature and of human society itself.[75] Inasmuch as Manasseh's construction of the *Asherah* and other cultic symbols endangers the future of Judah, Josiah's obliteration of this *Asherah* and other cultic symbols promises renaissance for Judah.

---

74 Assyrian royal inscriptions contain numerous examples of monarchs deporting religious artefacts to Assyria or, in a few cases, destroying them altogether. See, for instance, the letter of Sargon II rehearsing his destruction of the temple of Haldia (Luckenbill 1927:91 [#166]), Sennacherib's account of his destruction of Babylon's temples and gods (Luckenbill 1927:152 [#340, #341]), and Assurbanipal's crusade against the sanctuaries and deities of Elam (Luckenbill 1927:308-309 [#808, #809]). These actions involve cultic symbols from conquered territories (Cogan 1974:24; Rüterswörden 1977:16-22; Spieckermann 1982:347-54; Hallo 1983:13-17; Begg 1985a:225-26). Begg also discusses Egyptian, Sumerian, and Hittite evidence, but he points out that the Assyrian parallels are closest chronologically to the date of Deuteronomy and the Deuteronomistic History (1985a:227).

75 *KTU* 1.6.3:10-22 (Clifford 1983:183-201; Loewenstamm 1967:481-90; 1975:330-48).

For the protagonist in each of these battles, victory epitomizes the triumph of what she or he represents. Josiah's successful campaign against foreign cult objects and illicit Yahwistic cult objects therefore exonerates and promotes deuteronomistic values. The construction of Jeroboam's cultus portends northern declension and eventual ruin (1 Kgs 13:1-3, 33-34; 14:7-16; 2 Kgs 17:21-23), but Josiah's stunning obliteration of that cultus facilitates a return to a Jerusalem-centered united monarchy. Josiah's destruction of "all the cult places in the cities of Samaria" enables the Jerusalem temple to extend its influence northward. There is a method to Josiah's madness. The Deuteronomist promotes Josiah's systematic campaigns as the severe, but necessary, means to revitalize his society and recover past glory.

III. KING, CULT, AND KINGDOM

Josiah's return to Jerusalem (2 Kgs 23:20) marks his success in reunifying Judah and Samaria under the aegis of the Davidids' royal shrine. The celebration of a national Passover at the Jerusalem temple is the capstone to Josiah's southern and northern reforms (2 Kgs 23:21-23). The rest of 2 Kgs 23:21-30 falls into four sections: 1) new Josianic reforms (v 24), 2) a new evaluation (v 25), 3) a declaration of YHWH's irrevocable wrath (vv 26-37), and 4) a notice of Josiah's death and burial (vv 28-30). I maintain that only 2 Kgs 23:21-23 stem from Dtr^1. The rest of 2 Kings 23 (vv 24-30) are later deuteronomistic additions stemming from the Babylonian exile.

A. THE COMPOSITION OF 2 KGS 23:21-30

Most critics see the pericope of 2 Kgs 23:21-23 as a deuteronomistic composition, though a few commentators (e.g., Lohfink 1963:267-75; 1978:320-42; Nelson 1981a:83) believe that a source underlies the deuteronomistic editing of 2 Kgs 23:21-23.[76] In this case, I agree with the majority. My reasons do not so much center on distinctive phraseology as on content. First, the narrator of 2 Kgs 23:21-23 depicts a king leading a national Passover, while citing the stipulations of the covenant scroll as warrant (ככתוב על ספר הברית הזה; 2 Kgs 23:21). This linkage between Deuteronomy (16:1-8) and royal authority is entirely congruent with deuteronomistic ideology. Second, the author of 2 Kgs 23:21 creates an *inclusio* centering upon the discovery of the law and its implementation (2 Kgs 22:8 and 23:21). Since this literary device unifies the reign of Josiah, it more likely stems from an editor than from a source. Third, the commendation of Josiah's Passover as unrivalled since the eras of Judges and kings (2 Kgs 23:22) presupposes centralization and hence familiarity with the demands of Deuteronomy. Fourth, as Noth (1981:137) notes, the periodization of history reflected in the distinction between judges and kings is deuteronomistic. The most parsimonious explanation of all these factors is to see 2 Kgs 23:21-23 as the work of Dtr^1.

If 2 Kgs 23:21-23 is to be attributed to deuteronomistic authorship, is there any evidence that a series of deuteronomistic or later

---

[76] Those who attribute 2 Kgs 23:21-23 to deuteronomistic composition include Gray (1970:728), Hölscher (1923:208), Jepsen (1956:26-28), Jones (1984:626), Mayes (1983:174 [an exilic Deuteronomist]), McKenzie (1991:114), Noth (1981:73), O'Brien (1989:265), Spieckermann (1982:130-37 [DtrN]), Tadmor and Cogan (1988:294-96).

writers contributed to this pericope? Würthwein recognizes the deuteronomistic authorship of 2 Kgs 23:21 and views 2 Kgs 23:22-23 as a later addition, because all of Josiah's reforms could not have taken place in a single year (2 Kgs 23:23).[77] Yet, as Lohfink (1987:466) and McKenzie (1991:114) observe, the account of Josiah's reign is highly stylized. One must distinguish between literary representation and historical reality. On the basis of the former, I see no reason to attribute 2 Kgs 23:22-23 to a later hand.

Many scholars suspect that the report of a new Josianic campaign in 2 Kgs 23:24 is not original to the first edition of the Deuteronomistic History.[78] I share this suspicion. 2 Kgs 23:24 seems to be a contribution by a later, probably exilic, Deuteronomist, who wishes to round out Josiah's reforms. This writer has Josiah cancel those abuses of Manasseh which the earlier Deuteronomist forgot to include in 2 Kgs 23:4-14. Josiah rids the land of Judah and Jerusalem of necromancers, mediums, idols, festishes, and "all the detestable things" (2 Kgs 23:24).[79] O'Brien notes that this writer integrates his insertion into the narrative by reversing the sequence of earlier events within his interpolation. Beginning with his portrayal of Josiah undertaking new reforms (cf. 2 Kgs 23:4-20), this writer affirms that Josiah honors the covenant oath (2 Kgs 23:3), which is based on the torah scroll Hilkiah discovered in the temple (2 Kgs 22:8).

77 In his article on Josiah, Würthwein sees all of 2 Kgs 23:21-23 as an addition (1976:407-409), but in his commentary he assigns 2 Kgs 23:21 to DtrN (1984:454, 461).

78 Hölscher (1923:208); Jones (1984:628); Lohfink (1987:462); Mayes (1983:174); Nelson (1981a:83); O'Brien (1989:266); Spieckermann (1982:137-38 [post-deuteronomistic]); Würthwein (1976:409; 1984:454, 461). On the nature of האבות ואת-הידענים ואת-התרפים

2 Kgs 23:24:	למען הקים את-דברי התורה הכתבים על-הספר
2 Kgs 23:3:	להקים את-דברי הברית הזאת הכתבים על-הספר הזה
2 Kgs 23:24:	הספר הזה אשר מצא חלקיהו הכהן בבית יהוה
2 Kgs 22:8:	חלקיהו הכהן הגדול...ספר התורה מצאתי בבית יהוה

By positing an inverse sequence to the events in his *Vorlage* (Zeidel's Law), the editor of 2 Kgs 23:24 creates another *inclusio* framing the discovery of the law and its implementation (2 Kgs 22:8 and 23:21, 24). As Würthwein points out, the author of 2 Kgs 23:24 may also have Deut 18:10ff. in mind, because this text forbids the presence of augurs, soothsayers, necromancers, and sorcerers in the Israelite community (1976:409). Josiah's (additional) reforms signify that he completely confirms the terms of the torah scroll.[80]

Many proponents of a Josianic redaction view the commendation of Josiah's uniqueness in 2 Kgs 23:25 as the Deuteronomist's final word on Josiah, but I disagree.[81] A Josianic historian would not claim that Josiah was unmatched among all the kings who succeeded him. The incomparability formula applied to Josiah (2 Kgs 23:25) dates to a later time than the reign of Josiah, most probably the exile.[82] The author of v 25 is aware of a succession of kings after

---

ואת-הגללים mentioned in 2 Kgs 23:24, see the discussion of Lewis (1989:124-26).

79 The text alludes to, yet goes beyond (התרפים), the sins of Manasseh (2 Kgs 21:6, 11).

80 This writer may be responsible for 2 Kgs 21:11 or have this verse in his *Vorlage* (cp. 2 Kgs 23:24 with 2 Kgs 21:11).

81 Cross (1973:287); Friedman (1981a:7-8); Lohfink (1987:463,

Josiah and lives at a time when that succession had come to an end. The incomparability formulae are one means by which an exilic Deuteronomist highlights the exceptional accomplishments of major figures within his history: Moses (archetypal prophecy; Deut 34:10), Solomon (wisdom, wealth, and glory; 1 Kgs 3:12), Hezekiah (trust; 2 Kgs 18:5), and Josiah (reforms; 2 Kgs 23:25).[83] The author of 2 Kgs 23:25 is probably also the author of 2 Kgs 23:24, given the concern with reforms in both verses.

The author of 2 Kgs 23:26-27 (the disparagement of Manasseh) is most probably not identical to the author of 2 Kgs 23:24-25.[84] Camp (1990:20-23) claims that there are no signs of discontinuity in vv 25-30, but he fails to explain the awkward interjection of vv 26-27.

> Only (אך) YHWH would not turn from the heat of his great wrath by which he was incensed with Judah on account of all the vexations with which Manasseh vexed him. And YHWH said, "I shall turn away even Judah from my face as I turned my face from Israel. I shall reject Jerusalem, this city which I have chosen, and the temple, of which I said, 'my name shall be there.'" (2 Kgs 23:26-27).[85]

---

472); Nelson (1981a:83-84); Tadmor and Cogan (1988:300).

82 Cross and Nelson see v 25b, "and after him none arose like him," as a later addition; but, as Nelson notes, "Strangely, no literary seam is visible between 25a and 25b" (1981a:84).

83 In each case, this Deuteronomist links the king or prophet's uniqueness with specific features of his tenure. Rather than a key to separating redactional layers in the Deuteronomistic History, the incomparability formulae are a means through which an exilic writer unifies and focuses his *Vorlage* (Knoppers 1992:411-31).

84 So also Lohfink (1985:44-45) and O'Brien (1989:266-67).

85 The author of this interjection combines what McCarthy (1974:100) calls the provocation formula (הכעיס את־יהוה) with the anger formula (חרה אף יהוה ב- \ התאנף יהוה ב-). Manasseh's sins vex

As Nelson comments, "The attitude changes suddenly from the completely positive evaluation of the semi-messianic Josiah to one adamantly negative towards the nation as a whole" (1981a:84). Moreover, a close reading of Josiah's reforms (2 Kgs 23:8, 10, 12) reveals that he cancelled Manasseh's sins (2 Kgs 21:3-6)! 2 Kgs 23:26-27 therefore conflicts with the (earlier) author's consistent claims that reformer kings can avert divine wrath and effect blessing by correcting the sins of their predecessors.

Faulting Manasseh for the destruction of Judah and the rejection of Jerusalem (2 Kgs 23:26-27) presupposes the Babylonian exile.[86] 2 Kgs 23:26-27 are therefore best understood as a *deus ex machina* introduced by an exilic writer, who attempts to reconcile Josiah's accomplishments with the catastrophe of 586 BCE. Given the stigmatization of Manasseh and the conscious deployment of deuteronomistic clichés to impugn Jerusalem and its temple, the author of this passage is most likely Dtr^2.[87]

YHWH so that he becomes incensed and rejects his elected temple and city. Judg 2:11-14 and 2 Kgs 22:17 are the only two other instances in the Deuteronomistic History, that I am aware of, which feature similar combinations of these two formulas.

86 Burney (1920:355-56); Cross (1973:286); Friedman (1981b:186); Gray (1970:715); Kittel (1900:297); McKenzie (1985:191; 1991:125-26, 136); O'Brien (1989:268); Provan (1988:151); Stade and Schwally (1904:56). Spieckermann (1982:138) ascribes 2 Kgs 23:26-27 to DtrN. Similarly, Würthwein ascribes these verses to someone within the DtrN circle (1984:462).

87 For Cross (1973:285-87), the sins of Manasseh are the major theme of the exilic Deuteronomist. On the deuteronomistic clichés in 2 Kgs 23:27, see Weinfeld (1972:324, 325, 347).

The irregular concluding notices about Josiah's death and burial (2 Kgs 23:28-30) evince the work of a later author.[88] This author neither explains Josiah's death, nor explicitly reconciles Josiah's untimely demise with the prophecy of Huldah. Hence, it is unclear why Necho kills Josiah.[89] The laconic description of Josiah's unexpected death and burial (2 Kgs 23:29) befits the style and perspective of Dtr^2 (Cross 1973:285-87). All of the material subsequent to 2 Kgs 23:23 therefore dates to the exile (or later). 2 Kgs 23:24-25 stem from an exilic Deuteronomist, while 2 Kgs 23:26-30 are the work of Dtr^2.

B. THE LITERARY STRUCTURE OF JOSIAH'S REIGN

Literary analysis confirms that 2 Kgs 23:23 marks the end of the first edition of the Deuteronomistic History. Dtr^1 employs a double *inclusio* to conclude his depiction of Josiah (2 Kgs 22:3-10 and 2 Kgs 23:21-23). Josiah begins the eighteenth regnal year by renovating the temple (2 Kgs 22:3-7) and he ends this year celebrating a Paschal

---

88 The reference to "the rest of the acts of Josiah and all that he did" is uncharacteristically placed before his death (2 Kgs 23:28). See Halpern and Vanderhooft (1991:194-97), who extensively discuss the spare death and burial fomula for Josiah.

89 Malamat (1950:218-21; 1973:268-78) and Aharoni (1982:269-70) argue that Josiah fails in a military maneuver. Herrmann believes that Josiah was ambushed (1981:272), while Noth follows Welch (1925: 255-60) in holding that Josiah was court-martialed and executed (1960:278-80). Nelson thinks that Josiah was double-crossed by his ally, Necho (1983:183-89). Both 2 Chr 35:22 and 1 Esdr 1:28-29 provide more explanation, but the relation of these two texts to 2 Kgs 23:29 is disputed. See the comments of McKenzie (1985:184) on the Chronicler's *Vorlage* and the debate between Williamson (1982a:242-47; 1987:9-15) and Begg (1987a:1-8).

Feast at the temple with all his people (Lohfink 1963:267). This first *inclusio* marks a progression from a temple in disrepair to a restored temple -- the one and only focal point of the nation's worship. The second *inclusio* marks a progression from the discovery of the torah scroll (2 Kgs 22:8) to its implementation (2 Kgs 23:21).

The Deuteronomist also creates more immediate correspondences by describing this Passover in terms which resonate with his description of Josiah's covenant renewal. Both convocations take place at the Jerusalem temple (2 Kgs 23:3, 23). Like the national ratification of covenant, the national observance of the Paschal sacrifice is an ideal scene attended by "all the people" (2 Kgs 23:21). Consistent with deuteronomistic ideology, Josiah takes a leading role in both rites (2 Kgs 23:1-2, 21). Both observances adhere to the terms of the covenant scroll (2 Kgs 23:2-3, 21). In fact, the antecedent to "this scroll of the covenant" in 2 Kgs 23:21 is "the scroll" in 2 Kgs 23:3 (Lohfink 1963:269-71). The discovery of "the book of the torah" leads Josiah to seek prophetic counsel and to ratify a national covenant based on this book. The national covenant signals renewed popular commitment to the terms of the book (2 Kgs 23:3). The Passover marks Josiah's success in returning his people to obeying the terms of this torah scroll. Indeed, the very prospect of holding a national Passover testifies to the people's reorientation toward (deuteronomic) torah. Hence, the commemoration of the Paschal sacrifice forms a natural conclusion to the deuteronomistic account of Josiah's reign.[90]

---

[90] O'Brien (1989:267-68) also sees 2 Kgs 23:23 as the end of the original Deuteronomistic History. In his study of the Chronicler's use of the Deuteronomistic History, McKenzie proposed seeing 2 Kgs 23:23 as the end of the preexilic Deuteronomist's history (1985:181-88, 191). In his more recent study of Kings. McKenzie posits 2 Kgs 23:25 as the end of the first edition (1991:114-115, 136-37).

C. A NATIONAL PASCHAL FEAST IN JERUSALEM

Aside from the observance of Passover at Gilgal during the conquest (Josh 5:10-12), Josiah's Passover is the only Passover mentioned in the Deuteronomistic History.[91] Nevertheless, the long-range and short-range parallels to this event as a national convocation demonstrate its importance in the deuteronomistic presentation. First, as O'Brien (1989:266) points out, this assembly reclaims the temple-centered worship established by Solomon. Indeed, one can argue the case even more strongly than O'Brien does. Josiah completes what Solomon and his successors leave undone. Josiah makes the temple the sole sanctuary of the nation.

Second, Josiah successfully restores the unanimity of support for the temple, which characterizes the temple's dedication (1 Kgs 8:1-2, 62-64). The popular support for Josiah's centralized Passover, in turn, legitimates Josiah's recently completed campaign for centralization. Third, if purifying both the South and the North is essential to recovering the glory of the united kingdom, covenant renewal and Passover observance recall a time before the advent of the united

---

91 Rose notes some parallels between 2 Kgs 23:21-23 and the Passover described in Josh 5:10-12, both of which he regards as deuteronomistic (1981:32-33). But there are problems with this linkage. First, there are substantial differences between the two accounts (O'Brien 1989:265). Second, it is unclear whether Josh 5:10-12 are deuteronomistic. Noth (1987:111) ascribes these verses to the Priestly source. I am inclined to follow Brekelmans (1989:89-95), Cross (1973:103-105), Soggin (1972:73-76), and Boling and Wright (1982:190-94) in discerning a number of levels in the Joshua account.

kingdom itself. The Deuteronomist comments that "no Passover such[92] as this had been offered since the days of the Judges who judged Israel or[93] (during) all the days of the kings of Israel and the kings of Judah" (2 Kgs 23:22).

The Deuteronomist appeals to the past to acclaim Josiah's Passover, but the notion that the commemoration of Passover truly marks a return to pre-monarchic conditions represents a facile reading of the text. The very possibility of holding a national Passover in Jerusalem assumes centralization. Moreover, this Passover, like the ratification of covenant, is mandated by royalty. Rather than a simple return to a traditional institution, Josiah's Passover evinces the metamorphosis of an institution. The Deuteronomist neither denies the existence of older cultic arrangements nor ignores them. He enlists and transforms the past to commend the present.

If the deuteronomic (16:1-8, 13-17) presentation of Passover modifies its significance (Weinfeld (1972:216-17; Levinson 1991: 235-44), the Deuteronomist advances this transformation one step further by tying the Paschal sacrifice to kingship.[94] In this regard, the deuteronomic interpretation of Passover as a celebration of liberation from Egypt (Deut 16:1, 3, 6) is surely relevant (Haran 1978:321; von Rad 1966a:110-13). Josiah's victories against foreign cults are

---

92 Reading with KM, KG^L, KS, and KT. KG^B reads *το πασχα τουτο* (= הפסח הזה), implying that no Passover had been observed since the time of the Judges.

93 So KM and KG^{AB}. A few Hebrew mss and KE lack the copula.

94 Conversely, 2 Kgs 23:21-23 does not mention the festival of unleavened bread, as one might expect, given the regulations of Exod 13:1-16; 34:18-21. Levinson points out that this omission is in keeping with the deuteronomic transformation of unleavened bread from a pilgrimage feast to a local celebration (1991a:254-60).

followed by a celebration of YHWH's definitive victory against the Egyptian domination of Israel. Hence, YHWH's definitive deliverance of Israel becomes associated with the temple in Jerusalem and its royal patron. The Deuteronomist simultaneously adopts and modifies Deuteronomy's program to his own advantage. Josiah's revitalization of an older institution confirms the new arrangement.

Conclusions

However successful Josiah may have been in eliminating rival cults, Yahwistic or otherwise, to the Jerusalem temple, rarely is the force of arms sufficient alone to assuage the strong feelings of competing groups within a society or to ensure control over particular areas and their populations (Whitelam 1984:61-71). Josiah's efforts at cultic centralization were undoubtedly controversial and subject to a variety of interpretations. Since temples played vital economic and administrative functions in the ancient Near East, any attempt to eliminate sanctuaries or to centralize a given cultus would have profound economic, social, political, and religious consequences. The antiquity of other shrines and their attendant cults would likely lead their adherents to view Josiah's reforms with disapprobation.

> What this prohibition of the high places amounted to at the time was: the denial of religious experience to the majority of the population and the creation of a religious vacuum in their midst. (Weinfeld 1964:202-203).

Allowing for secular slaughter (Deut 12:15) as a means to manage the consequences of having only one site for sacrifice would in itself constitute a direct challenge to the practices of many traditional Yahwists

(Exod 20:24; Levinson (1991:169-77). Indeed, as we have seen (chap. 5), in the Deuteronomist's very stress on Josiah's uniqueness, he implicitly concedes that he holds a minority view of orthopraxis. Hence, Josiah's imperialism may even have been questioned by the elite within his own capital.

If Josiah's reforms were controversial in Judah, his forays into northern territory could scarcely have been more popular. Josiah's attempts to extirpate northern cults must have been viewed by many residents of the former northern kingdom, especially those who were descendants of foreign immigrants, as an unsolicited and merciless intrusion into their affairs.[95] The systematic desecration of ancient shrines and the execution of their priests in Samarian cities would have greatly embittered their supporters.

In the light of probable objections to Josiah's actions, it is understandable that the Deuteronomist makes a literary effort to convince disparate constituencies within his audience of the need for reform. The Deuteronomist situates the Josianic revolution within a historical context, arguing that the horrendous conditions Josiah inherited from his predecessors militate against incremental change. Josiah's campaigns systematically root out those very evils which are responsible for the demise of Israel and the ills of Judah. His conduct has political and economic consequences, but is not politically or economically motivated. Nor does Josiah eschew religious tradition. Rather, the traditions Josiah upholds predate the anomalous traditions observed by many of his predecessors.

---

95 Conversely, there may have been some who supported the deuteronomic or the deuteronomistic movements and welcomed Josiah's reforms (see below).

The Deuteronomist specifically appeals to proponents of the deuteronomic movement by positing a convergence between Josiah's achievements and the ancient law of the sanctuary. If, as many scholars believe, the deuteronomic movement originally stemmed from the North and subsequently attained some popularity in the South, the continuity between Josiah's southern and northern campaigns would appeal to supporters in both areas. Josiah upholds the unity and distinctiveness of Israel. For members of the deuteronomistic movement, Josiah's reforms reaffirm the value of Davidic kingship and the benefits of a strong monarchy.[96] In this manner, the Deuteronomist casts Josiah's actions in the most favorable light possible. One year in the reign of a single king marks the extermination of every alien cult object and category of cultic personnel left over from 300 years of northern and southern history.

By structuring three centuries of Israelite and Judahite experience to anticipate and justify Josiah's campaigns, the Deuteronomist promotes Josiah as a curator of his people's most sacred beliefs and customs. What appears as highly innovative is actually conservative, designed to recover Israel's normative past. The author defends Josiah's methodical extermination of rival cult sites to the Jerusalem temple as a reassertion of Yahwistic hegemony, thereby stigmatizing these sanctuaries as fundamentally un-Israelite. The Deuteronomist does not claim that Josiah has already successfully retrieved the golden age of David and Solomon; nor does he maintain that Josiah brings peace. Rather, it is only by solving the cultic problems left

96 Hence, the Deuteronomist negotiates a *via media* between the traditions represented by the deuteronomic movement and those represented in royal Judahite ideology (see chap. 7).

unaddressed by his forefathers that Josiah can arrest his people's decline and enable his people to make a new beginning.

The people enjoy a privileged relationship with YHWH, but the Deuteronomist structures history to show that progress in this relationship is neither inevitable nor inexorable. Renascence is contingent upon reform. The depiction of Josiah's reign evinces confidence in the future precisely because the Deuteronomist links the people's future to a recovery of their past. To Josiah's credit, he recognizes the import of the torah scroll, renews covenant, reforms Jerusalem, Judah, and the former northern kingdom, and celebrates a centralized Passover. The kingdom Josiah heads therefore stands on the threshold of a new era.

CHAPTER 7

CULT AND KINGDOM: THE DEUTERONOMISTIC PRESENTATION OF THE MONARCHY

I know, and all the world knows, that
revolutions never go backward.
(William Seward, on the Irrepressible
Conflict, October 1858).

Recognition that 1 Kings 11-14 and 2 Kings 22-23 envelop the history of the dual monarchies calls for a reexamination of Noth's influential presentation of monarchical history (1981:5-11). My argument in this chapter is not simply that the deuteronomistic presentation of Solomon's reign, disunion, the reign of Jeroboam, the fall of Israel, and the reign of Josiah is more positive and evinces a different structure than Noth acknowledged. I also want to show that the structure the Deuteronomist imposes upon the reign of Solomon and the course of the dual monarchies addresses predominately preexilic issues and is predicated upon preexilic verities. In coverage, organization, and thematic development the deuteronomistic history of Solomon and the dual monarchies finds its most likely *Sitz im Leben* in the reign of King Josiah.[1]

For Noth there are three major deuteronomistic passages marking the record of the monarchy: 1) the institution of kingship (1 Samuel 12), 2) the dedication of the temple (1 Kings 8), and 3) the end of the monarchy (2 Kings 17). The point of 1 Samuel 12 was, according to Noth (1981:91), that kingship was born in sin, but once established it should have a chance to prove itself. The completion of the temple (1 Kings 8) is the historical and theological highpoint of Israelite existence in the land. But the monarchy itself proves to be a dismal failure (Noth 1981:80). The history of Israel is a disaster, a record of "ever-intensifying decline" (Noth 1981:79).

Some scholars (e.g., von Rad 1966b:205-16; Wolff 1961:171-86; Levenson 1984:353-61) have found Noth's thematic analysis too pessimistic, while others (e.g., McCarthy 1965:131-38 and Cross 1973: 249-57) have emended Noth's list of major deuteronomistic reflections.[2] But no scholar, that I am aware of, has offered a systematic reevaluation of the structure Noth imputes to the history of the monarchy. In what follows I will concentrate upon those deuteronomistic orations which orchestrate the movement of history in the united and divided monarchies, paying special attention to the ways the Deuteronomist shapes his narrative to place Josiah's reforms in a most positive light.

---

[1] I do not assert that the Deuteronomist wrote his entire history for this purpose, but I do claim that he wrote his history of the divided monarchy with Josiah's reforms in view.

[2] Scholars have documented other literary devices by which the Deuteronomist unifies his history (vol. 1: chap. 1).

2 Samuel 7	The Promises to David; the Prayer of David
1 Kings 8*	Solomon's Temple Dedication and Prayer
1 Kings 11*	Introduction to the Dual Monarchies
1 Kgs 13:1-3 1 Kgs 13:31-34	The Prophecies against the Bethel Cultus
1 Kgs 14:7-16*	The Condemnations of Jeroboam and the Israelite Kingdom
2 Kgs 17:7ff.*	The Fall of the Northern Kingdom
2 Kgs 19:15-19 2 Kgs 20:2-3	The Prayers of Hezekiah
2 Kings 22-23*	Josiah's Reforms

Each of these speeches, prayers, and reflections, like earlier deuteronomistic editorials, comments upon a major event in Israelite history.[3] The discourses treat disparate subjects and characters, but

---

3 Readers can find discussions of the Deuteronomist's composition of most of the above reflections in previous chapters of this volume and volume 1. Note that this list is not exhaustive. It is clear, for example, that the judgment oracles against the other northern royal houses have been edited by the Deuteronomist(s); see Dietrich (1972); Wallace (1986), and McKenzie (1991). My concern in this overview is to address the overall structure of the Deuteronomist's history of the dual monarchies and not to assemble a complete tally of all deuteronomistically authored or edited pericopes.

exhibit consistency in some basic historiographic conceptions. First, the Deuteronomist composes a history of the monarchy with the thesis that its fate is cultically derivative. History is driven by the religious practices which Israel's kings observe.[4] As two minor kingdoms, strategically situated in the Near East but surrounded by a number of more powerful kingdoms, Israel and Judah paradoxically determine their fate -- through their royal representatives -- by how they relate to the Jerusalem temple. The battles without -- of kings against foreign powers -- are therefore not as important as the battles within -- of kings against foreign cults and rival Yahwistic sanctuaries.

Second, the Deuteronomist portrays the united monarchy as Israel's normative age even though he acknowledges that the united kingdom was, in many respects, anomalous. Compared with the length of time the northern tribes and the southern tribe(s) are independent nations after the time of David and Solomon, the time during which they comprise a united kingdom is relatively brief. The very depiction of the first period in Solomon's reign as a time of untrammeled peace and prosperity contrasts with the succeeding two to three centuries of Israelite and Judahite history. Hence, there is merit in both of the positions we discussed at the beginning of volume 1. The Deuteronomist's united monarchy is both idealistic and aberrant.

The Deuteronomist's stress on David as an ideal king and the first period of Solomon's reign as glorious forms a striking contrast to the historical summaries one finds in the prophets and in some of the

---

4 This is not to say that the Deuteronomist evinces a sustained interest in the *minutiae* of cultic practice; see Milgrom (1973:156-61), Noth (1981:91-94), and Weinfeld (1972:190-243). In this regard, the interests of the Deuteronomist are very different from those of the Chronicler (Ackroyd 1970:297-310; Hanson 1979:269-79; 1986:300-311; Japhet 1989:199-265; Welch 1939:55-96).

historical psalms. Isaiah (5:1-7) compares YHWH to a vintner who meticulously prepares his plot and YHWH's people to a unproductive vineyard. Jeremiah (2:2-13) contrasts the devotion of Israel, the bride of YHWH, to YHWH in the wilderness with Israel's subsequent history of insolence. For Jeremiah, Israel's entire existence in the land comprises a long period of regression. Similarly, the author of Psalm 80 contrasts the glories of the Exodus and Israel's emergence in the land (vv 9-12) with present difficulties and strife, imploring YHWH to restore his people, to appear before Ephraim, Benjamin, and Manasseh (vv 1-8, 15-20).

For the Deuteronomist, however, the story of Israel's existence in the land is not one-dimensional.[5] He upholds not Israel's experience in the wilderness but the eras of conquest and the united monarchy as Israel's finest.[6] The Deuteronomist's more nuanced perspective on the history of his people has its advantages. His highly positive estimation of David's rule and the first period in Solomon's rule establishes a context by which readers can evaluate subsequent transgression and reform. By depicting events in the divided monarchy as

---

[5] The Deuteronomist's construction of the united monarchy is both similar to and different from that of the Chronicler. Like the Deuteronomist, the Chronicler sees the united kingdom as a normative age. Unlike the Deuteronomist, the Chronicler does not posit a second, regressive stage in Solomon's reign (Japhet 1989:395-411; Braun 1973:503-16; 1976:581-90; Williamson 1976:351-61; Knoppers 1990). Moreover, unlike the Deuteronomist, the Chronicler, through his use of genealogies, emphasizes Israel's uninterrupted existence in the land (Japhet 1979:205-18; 1989:363-93)

[6] Similarly, the author of Psalm 78 sees a lesson (vv 1-8) in the election of Judah, David, and Zion (vv 65-72). This divine action represents a solution to a history of popular defiance (vv 9-64).

challenges to and departures from an earlier norm, the Deuteronomist maintains this norm as an ideal for his own generation.

The third point is related to the first two. Cult and kingdom are distinct but related institutions.[7] Cult and kingdom are obviously meant to complement one another and do so during the first period in Solomon's reign. But if a king compromises or abrogates the exclusive allegiance due the Jerusalem temple, political consequences may follow.[8] Yet such consequences, even if they involve political fragmentation, free neither the kings of Israel nor the kings of Judah from their fundamental obligations to eliminate non-Yahwistic cults and sustain the Jerusalem cult.[9] However much the standard is challenged, the standard endures. Hence, the Deuteronomist can blame a Davidid for disunion and still expect northern kings to support the cult this Davidid established in Jerusalem.

---

7 In the era of the monarchy "to do that which is right in the sight of YHWH;" "to do what is right in the sight of YHWH as \ but not as his ancestor David did;" and "to do what is evil in the sight of YHWH" are tantamount to supporting the temple or failing to observe its exclusive right to the allegiance of all subjects (Weinfeld 1972:335 [#15], 354 [#5], 339 [#1]).

8 The Deuteronomist does not apply this principle of divine retribution systematically. King Manasseh, for instance, governs longer than any other king yet never encounters any particular hardship during his corrupt reign (2 Kgs 21:1-2). Josiah's consternation (2 Kgs 22:8-13) upon hearing the recitation of the torah scroll indicates, however, the plight of his people in the wake of Manasseh and Amon's (2 Kgs 21:20) regressive tenures.

9 On occasion the consequences of royal misconduct affect the course of the natural world (2 Sam 24:10-17; 1 Kgs 17:1; 18:1, 17-18). But such divinely decreed natural ramifications of royal offenses are not a productive theme in the Deuteronomist's overall presentation.

After a false start with Saul, the monarchy begins well with David. His desire for a temple occasions a series of divine assurances (2 Sam 7:5-16). David, in turn, implores YHWH to actualize these promises (2 Sam 7:18-29). The accent of 2 Samuel 7 is therefore upon the future. Through the prophet Nathan, YHWH announces that David will achieve great renown (2 Sam 7:9) and Israel will finally achieve peace and rest (2 Sam 7:11-12). YHWH associates the liberation of his people from its oppressors with his pledge of an everlasting dynasty for David's seed (2 Sam 7:12-13). David's "throne shall be established forever" (2 Sam 7:16). YHWH pledges to implement this commitment by establishing the kingdom of David's son. This Davidic offspring, in turn, will build the temple that David himself wished to build (2 Sam 7:13). The Deuteronomist ties David's house to YHWH's house and rest for Israel to the reign of David's heir.

The Deuteronomist celebrates the realization of these pronouncements in the reign of Solomon. Solomon embodies and objectifies the divine assurances to David (1 Kgs 1:37, 47; 2:24). In fact, the Deuteronomist anachronistically cites the sempiternal Davidic promises to defend the rise of Solomon (1 Kgs 1:48; 2:24, 33). The unending rule of the house of David functions retroactively as an argument against both Adonijah's failed *coup d'État* (1 Kgs 2:24) and Shimei's insubordination (1 Kgs 2:44b-45). As promised, Solomon's house and kingdom are established (1 Kgs 2:12, 33, 46). The unprecedented peace and security promised to David ensue during the reign of his hand-picked successor (1 Kgs 3:6-7; 4:20; 5:4, 17-18).

The achievement of peace creates the requisite conditions for constructing the long-awaited central sanctuary (1 Kgs 5:17-20). Solomon's erection of a house for YHWH's name fulfills yet another Davidic promise (1 Kgs 8:14-15). YHWH confirms the fruit of Solomon's labors with a theophany (1 Kgs 8:11) and Solomon blesses God for electing David and Jerusalem.[10] In contrast with the transitory cultic institutions of the past, the temple is the permanent domicile for YHWH's name (1 Kgs 8:1-9, 14-16, 21; 9:3), the divinely approved facility for sacrifice and prayer. The temple is depicted as a basis of hope for Israelites in all kinds of predicaments (1 Kgs 8:31-51) and an inducement toward fidelity (1 Kgs 8:57-58). YHWH's goodness to David becomes a cause for national thanksgiving (1 Kgs 8:66).

The consecration of the temple does not conclude the Deuteronomist's positive coverage of Solomon. On the contrary, the Deuteronomist emphasizes that Solomon's temple is well-integrated into Israel's national life, attracting praise and attention from afar (1 Kgs 10:1-10). Solomon initiates further capital projects (1 Kgs 9:15-22), trades in commodities (1 Kgs 10:26-28), and enjoys fabulous wealth and international esteem (1 Kgs 10:18-20). He rules an empire that is the envy of its neighbors and the destiny of much of their tribute (1 Kgs 9:14, 28; 10:14, 24-25). King, cult, and kingdom complement one another in harmony. The Deuteronomist asserts that Israel achieves the apex of its glory during the reign of Solomon. His success is a measure of how much YHWH loves Israel (1 Kgs 10:9).

The concord between king, cult, and people dissipates when the temple builder no longer accords the temple his exclusive allegiance (1 Kgs 11:1-13). By attributing the decline of the united monarchy to Solomon's abandonment of the temple as the sole sanctuary for his nation, the Deuteronomist admits, even champions, grounds for northern secession. But at that time when the Davidic promises would be most in doubt, the Deuteronomist repeatedly affirms that, despite the

---

[10] 1 Kgs 8:16. My reading of this verse is informed by the testimony of KG, 4QKgs, and 2 Chr 6:5-6. On the reconstruction of 1 Kgs 8:16, see vol. 1: chap. 3 and Trebolle (1992:315-17).

territorial delimitation of the Davidic promises in the division, God's promises to David (2 Sam 7:5-16) and to Zion (1 Kings 8) still obtain (1 Kgs 11:12, 13, 34, 36). In his portrayal of Judah's subsequent history, the Deuteronomist reaffirms the validity of these promises in the midst of crisis and despite the apostasy of some Judahite kings.[11]

The author's self-conscious and coherent approach to disunion serves long-range designs. Because Judah and Israel comprise two nations under one God, united by cult, but disunited by YHWH's promises to David and Jeroboam, the Deuteronomist recounts and synchronizes the histories of both kingdoms. Given that specific cultic issues, as opposed to a complex set of economic, political, and diplomatic factors, are responsible for the division, subsequent kings are not left without any clear recourse. The Deuteronomist's very configuration of two nations under God is geared toward a positive evaluation of Josiah's southern and northern campaigns.

The institution of an Israelite cultus by Jeroboam marks his abrogation of the conditions of his dynastic covenant (1 Kgs 11:36-38) and calls into question the long term viability of the northern kingdom. Consistent with his separation of cult and kingdom, the Deuteronomist addresses the implications of Jeroboam's countercultus in two stages: the prospects for this new cult (1 Kings 13) and the effects of this cult upon Jeroboam's young kingdom (1 Kings 14). In 1 Kgs 13:1-3, 31-34, the Deuteronomist predicts the demise of the Bethel cultus at the hands of Josiah. Jeroboam invests his cultus because he fears the consequences of his people's allegiance to the Jerusalem temple (1 Kgs 12:26-27), yet Jeroboam's intransigence in maintaining this cultus ironically ensures that one day it will be eradicated (1 Kgs 13:1-3, 31-34). By narrowing the issue of Jeroboam's

---

11 1 Kgs 15:4; 2 Kgs 8:19; 19:34; 20:6.

sacral initiatives to the Bethel cultus, the Deuteronomist establishes a continuity between Jeroboam's sins and Josiah's northern campaigns, a continuity which ultimately vindicates the Jerusalem cultus that Jeroboam abandoned and Josiah reformed.

Ahijah's oracles to Jeroboam's wife address the long-range political implications of Jeroboam's cultic initiatives (1 Kgs 14:7-16). Addressing the fate of king, kin, and kingdom, these speeches function as the antithesis of the Davidic promises. Far from attaining an enduring dynasty (1 Kgs 11:36-38), Jeroboam is deprived of a dynasty altogether (1 Kgs 14:10-11). The gravity of his sins dictate that Jeroboam lose not only his ill son, but also his kingdom. The Davidic promises bring blessings of dynasty, temple, and rest for God's people, but the condemnations of Jeroboam doom Israel. For the first time in the history of Israel the threat of exile becomes a verdict (1 Kgs 14:15a, 16).

The history of the dual monarchies is binary in subject matter and theme. The promises to David provide a measure of hope and restraint in Judah, but the judgment oracles against Jeroboam evoke a sense of political catastrophe for Israel. If the Deuteronomist establishes a dialectic between the conduct of David (thesis) and the misconduct of Jeroboam (antithesis), there can be no synthesis. Rather, the punishments meted out against Jeroboam and the northern kingdom confirm the thesis of royal devotion toward the Jerusalem temple. By establishing the opposition between Jeroboam and David -- a hallmark of the deuteronomistic presentation of the divided monarchy -- the Deuteronomist orchestrates a scenario in which the history of the nascent Israelite kingdom points toward both the Assyrian exile and the sweeping reforms of Josiah of Judah.

If one judges the intent of a work by coverage and theme, the Deuteronomistic History could more easily be called an etiology of

Israel's nadir than an "*Ätiologie des Nullpunkts*" of Judah and the Davidic dynasty (contra Dietrich 1972:141). The Deuteronomist is profoundly concerned with the origins, mandate, and fate of the Israelite kingdom and devotes an inordinate amount of coverage and thematic development to its history. Such a preoccupation with the early northern kingdom and how Josiah rights its wrongs would be highly surprising if the Deuteronomist wrote during the Babylonian exile, over three and a half centuries after the rise of Jeroboam ben-Nebat. The Deuteronomist's scathing criticism of northern leadership would also be startling if he lived during a period in which Judahites had just experienced the ignominious end of their own throne, temple, and kingdom. A date in the late seventh century for composition of this work accords much better with the coverage, structure, and themes of the deuteronomistic presentation of the dual monarchies.

The major events informing the Deuteronomist's presentation of the monarchy are the Assyrian conquest of Israel, the Assyrian devastation and domination of Judah, the endurance of the Davidic throne and temple in Jerusalem, and Josiah's campaign for cultic purity and cultic unity. In the deuteronomistic construction of history the Assyrian exile is, paradoxically, a manifestation of YHWH's power, exonerating his involvement in Israelite history and the standards he established at the division. 2 Kings 17 recalls both the political promises to Jeroboam in 1 Kings 11 and the condemnations of Jeroboam and his kingdom in 1 Kings 14 by reaffirming the divine establishment of the northern kingdom, lamenting its sins, and presenting its fall as logical consequence of its allegiance to Jeroboam's cultus (2 Kgs 17:21-23). The northern kingdom's problems were longstanding and endemic. The kingdom of Israel collapses as Ahijah long foretold (1 Kgs 14:15a, 16).

If 2 Kings 17 marks the definitive end of the Israelite kingdom, the same is not true for its land and cultus. In spite of Assyrian hegemony over Samerina, YHWH continues to be active. The Assyrians conquer Samaria, deport Hoshea and the Israelites, and import foreign settlers into the former northern kingdom (2 Kgs 17:5-6, 24). Yet the Deuteronomist maintains the historical and prophetic ties that bind the fate of North and South. The Assyrian exile may mark the end of the Deuteronomist's coverage of Israel, but this cessation of continuous coverage does not entail the end of Israel.[12] The nation of Israel is finished, but its people, land, and cult are not. The very trouble foreign settlers experience in worshiping their own gods, courtesy of marauding lions, implies that YHWH has not rescinded his claim to the land of Israel (2 Kgs 17:25). These émigrés only find peace when they are instructed on how to obey YHWH, "the god of the land" (2 Kgs 17:26). The consequent revival of Jeroboam's cultus (2 Kgs 17:27-33) ironically (re)creates the conditions under which the ancient prophecies of the man of God from Judah (1 Kgs 13:2) and the old prophet from Bethel (1 Kgs 13:31-32) can be realized.

The Deuteronomist's treatment of the early Israelite monarchy and his editorial upon Israel's fall make eminent sense in the context of the late seventh century. Having distanced the fate of Judah from that of Israel in his narration of the division, the Deuteronomist relativizes the entire course of northern history in his treatment of the cultic (1 Kings 13) and political (1 Kings 14) ramifications of Jeroboam's

---

[12] Contra Noth 1981:6. Similarly, as Japhet (1989:308-24) and Williamson (1977:110-114) point out, the Chronicler's omission of the independent course of the northern kingdom following the division does not imply that he writes off the people of the northern kingdom.

sins.[13] Inasmuch as the fall of Israel confirms the words of one of Israel's own prophets (Ahijah; 1 Kgs 15:15a, 16), the Deuteronomist can cite a confluence of southern and northern prophetic tradition to defend Josiah's northern campaigns (2 Kgs 23:15-20). The persistence of Jeroboam's sins in Israel, the downfall of Israel, and the persistence of Jeroboam's sins in Samaria (1 Kgs 13:1-3, 31-32; 2 Kgs 17:21-34a) all conspire toward a favorable assessment of Josiah's forays into the former northern kingdom.[14]

The Assyrian exile is mentioned again in the context of Hezekiah's reign (2 Kgs 18:9-12), suggesting that the Assyrians also posed a tremendous threat to Judah.[15] Indeed, the crisis caused by Sen-

---

13 The negative influence of Jeroboam is mentioned 16 times in 1 and 2 Kings. The "sin(s) of Jeroboam" is referred to 11 times in 2 Kings (chap. 3).

14 The first appearance of the anger formula since the division (1 Kgs 11:9) is also important (2 Kgs 17:18; see McCarthy 1974:99-110 and vol. 1: chap. 4). As in the eras of conquest (Deut 1:37; 4:21; 9:8, 20), Judges (Josh 23:16; Judg 2:14, 20), and disunion (1 Kgs 11:9), Israel's apostasy elicits divine wrath, signalled by the anger formula (2 Kgs 17:18) and an announcement of punishment. But the outpouring of wrath is never YHWH's final action. The punishment which follows the disclosure of divine wrath traduces the history of Israel until either repentance occasions salvation (e.g., Judg 3:9, 15; 6:7) or the deity appoints a new leader to deliver the people (e.g., Deut 1:37-38; Judg 2:16, 18; 1 Kgs 11:11-13, 29-38). Even though the former fails to occur (2 Kgs 17:21-33), this does not preclude the possibility that the latter will.

15 The Book of Jeremiah (3:6-11; 7:15) likewise links the fate of Judah to the fate of Israel. See also Ezek 16:44-63; 23 and the comments of Hardmeier (1990:153-54), Holladay (1986:116-18, 236-49), Seitz (1991:141-42), and Zimmerli (1979:347-53, 471-92). On the changes in material culture during this era, see the recent overview of Dearman (1992:78-99) and the conclusions to chapter 4.

nacherib's invasion and devastation of Judah dominates the deuteronomistic coverage of Hezekiah's reign.[16] In his second speech (2 Kgs 18:28-35; cf. 2 Kgs 19:10-13), the Rabshakeh pointedly asks whether the gods of other nations, including the gods of Samaria, saved their lands (2 Kgs 18:33-34).[17] If not, would YHWH deliver Jerusalem? (2 Kgs 18:35). Yet Hezekiah clings to YHWH's promises to his temple, dynasty, and city. Hezekiah's reliance upon YHWH is especially prominent in his prayers.[18] Hezekiah's acclamations and petitions recall similar acclamations and petitions in the prayer of David (2 Sam 7:18-29) and the temple dedication of Solomon (1 Kings 8; Pratt 1987:81-90). Moreover, Hezekiah's prayers, like those of David and Solomon, appear at critical moments for the throne and cult in Jerusalem. The king places his confidence in God's promises to David and Jerusalem and pleads with YHWH to act in accordance with the acclamations and petitions of David and Solomon (2 Kgs 19:16, 19; 20:3). Isaiah's assurances to Hezekiah in 2 Kgs 19:20 and 20:5-6 that God has heeded his prayers reaffirm characteristic

---

[16] 2 Kgs 18:13-19:20, 32-36 (I follow many scholars in seeing 2 Kgs 19:21-31 as a later addition). On the deuteronomistic view(s) of this era, see the debates among Ahlström (1993:692-730), Camp (1990: 267-95), Gerbrandt (1986:68-89), Gonçalves (1986:331-487), Knoppers (1992:418-25); Lowery (1991:142-61), McKenzie (1991:101-09), Provan (1988:57-90, 133-43, 153-56), Rosenbaum 1979:23-44), Seitz (1991:47-148), Spieckermann (1982:170-74), and Tadmor and Cogan (1988:223-51).

[17] Reading ואיה אלהי ארץ שׁמרון with KG^{L} and KL in 2 Kgs 18:34. KM 2 Kgs 18:34 has הנע ועוה, but KG^{B} and Isa 36:19 lack this phrase. Anbar (1990:7-8) provides a more detailed discussion of the text-critical problems in this verse.

[18] 2 Kgs 19:15-19; 20:2-3. See also the comments of Balentine (1993:61-64, 91-97), Gonçalves (1986:332-36, 463-69), Knoppers (1992:418-23), McKenzie (1991:106-09), and Pratt (1987:63-90).

emphases of the Deuteronomist on the throne of David, the temple of Solomon, and the city of Jerusalem.

The Deuteronomist's narrative strategy is apparent. Having reaffirmed God's everlasting commitment to Jerusalem and God's promises to David (by delimiting the territorial domain of the Davidids) in his narration of disunion, the Deuteronomist can interpret Hezekiah and Jerusalem's survival in the Assyrian crisis as another public vindication of these verities. In fact, the exile of Israel coupled with the decimation of Judahite cities become arguments for the supremacy of Jerusalem, its Davidic dynasty and its temple cult (Halpern 1991). Zion wins vindication at the expense of other sanctuaries in both the former northern kingdom and Judah.

Nevertheless, the Deuteronomist does not promote the divine assurances to David and Zion as sufficient, in and of themselves, to recover past glory. The Deuteronomist employs the Davidic promises to underscore the ongoing legitimacy of Davidic rule and to explain YHWH's mercifulness in dealing with Judah. But David's house, disassociated from YHWH's house, cannot effect renewal. For southern kings, even doing "what is right in the eyes of YHWH," but tolerating the high places is not enough.[19] Divided loyalties lead to ambiguous results. The force of history points toward the need for comprehensive change. In this regard, Hezekiah's reforms (2 Kgs 18:4), occurring two centuries after the fall of Solomon, augur well for Judah. But Hezekiah's reforms are undone by his son Manasseh, whose rule is entirely retrograde (2 Kgs 21:1-7). His unprecedented apostasy calls for strong counter-measures. The build-up to Josiah's reign is carefully contrived. The dialectical structure the Deuteronomist imposes on the epoch of the divided kingdom, his evalua-

[19] 1 Kgs 15:14; 22:44; 2 Kgs 12:4; 14:4; 15:4, 35.

tion of individual monarchs, his commentary on the Assyrian exile, and his narration of Manasseh and Amon's sins (2 Kgs 21:20-22) coalesce in heralding the reign of the king who "walked in all the ways of his father David" (2 Kgs 22:2).

The narration of the beginning of Josiah's eighteenth regnal year creates a sense of crisis. The discovery of "the scroll of the torah" takes place in Josiah's eighteenth regnal year, implying that the conditions obtaining in Manasseh and Amon's reigns continue well into Josiah's reign (Ginsberg 1982:41-42). Josiah's abject reaction to the recitation of this scroll and Huldah's (original) oracle dramatizes the need for radical change. Accepting Deuteronomy's assertions of antique authority, the Deuteronomist uses the torah scroll to legitimate pervasive royal intervention in the cultic affairs of the population. The historical context, as presented in 2 Kings 22-23, valorizes Josiah's swift attempt to restore what was lost in centuries past. He restores his people to their ancient charter and undoes the damage caused by his predecessors. If the history of the dual monarchies makes the long-range argument, the description of Josiah's eighteenth regnal year steers readers toward the appropriate conclusion.

The author commends Josiah's iconoclastic campaigns as fulfilling the requisite conditions for renewal. It is only by solving the cultic problems left unaddressed by his ancestors that Josiah can arrest his people's decline. Josiah therefore redresses the remaining sins of all of his southern predecessors. He destroys cultic sites, demolishes cultic objects, suppresses non-Yahwistic priests, and incorporates Yahwistic priests from the towns of Judah in the Jerusalem cultus.[20]

---

[20] Josiah's suppression (השבית) of הכמרים (2 Kgs 23:5) is thus more lenient than his slaughter (זבח) of the Samarian priests and his incineration of their bones upon their altars (2 Kgs 23:20).

The force of the Deuteronomist's presentation is unmistakable. By removing Solomon's *bāmôt*, Josiah removes the cause of disunion. In his zeal and the comprehensiveness of his reforms Josiah is peerless.

Josiah's northern campaigns are also geared toward the past. In his reworking of the prophetic tales incorporated into 1 Kings 13, the Deuteronomist expands Josiah's mandate from extirpating the Bethel cultus (1 Kgs 13:2) to destroying all of Samaria's shrines and priests (1 Kgs 13:31-32). Josiah's reforms punctiliously follow course. Having documented the revival of Jeroboam's cult in the wake of the Assyrian exile, the Deuteronomist can explain Josiah's decimation of the Bethel altar, his extirpation of the Samarian shrines, and his slaughter of their priests by recourse to ancient prophecy (2 Kgs 23:15-20).[21] To cite the major categories employed by the Göttingen school, history, prophecy, and law converge in acclaiming Josiah's initiatives. In this manner, the Deuteronomist justifies Josiah's intervention into northern affairs and at the same time appeals to both Judahites and the inhabitants of the former northern kingdom to rally behind this David *redivivus*.

---

21 One wonders whether the Deuteronomist assumed the commands of Deut 13:7-19 (cf. Deut 17:2-7). Deuteronomy 13 mandates the death of any Israelite person (vv 9-11) or residents of any Israelite town (vv 16-18), should that person or community advocate or indulge in the worship of other gods. The Deuteronomist classifies Jeroboam's cult as the worship of other gods (1 Kgs 14:9; cf. 1 Kgs 12:28; see chaps. 2 and 4). Yet if the Deuteronomist knew of the commands of Deuteronomy 13, these commands do not overtly function as productive themes in his narration of Josiah's northern reforms. The Deuteronomist uses 1 Kings 13 as the main justification for Josiah's northern campaigns (chap. 3). On the stipulations of Deuteronomy 13, see the thorough discussion of Dion (1991).

If Josiah's reforms recall the sins of his predecessors, his public ratification of the covenant (2 Kgs 23:1-3) and his national Passover (2 Kgs 23:21-23) recall the solidarity and commitment of an earlier age. Both the covenant and the Passover clearly resonate with the pre-monarchic period. But, however much the Deuteronomist depicts Josiah's reign as reviving and implementing the mandate of *Urdeuteronomium*, Josiah's reign does not return Judah to the Plains of Moab. In the Deuteronomistic History the standards established at Sinai are mediated by the standards of the united monarchy. Consistent with his claim that Israel achieves its full definition as a temple-centered monarchy, the Deuteronomist promotes Josiah's reign as an approximation and extension of the standards established in Solomon's reign.

In a Josianic context YHWH demonstrates his fidelity to his people, actualizing the petition in Solomon's second blessing: both people and king commit to torah (1 Kgs 8:57-59). Josiah repairs the temple and reclaims its position as the center of national life. Similarly, royal and popular compliance with the torah scroll confirms Solomon's assertion that the temple could function as an inducement toward royal and popular piety.[22] Josiah therefore creates a propitious setting for a new day in the history of God's people. The future holds considerable promise, because for the first time the deuteronomistic ideals of one cult, one sanctuary, and one king -- all devoted to one deity -- have been realized.

---

[22] 1 Kgs 8:54-61; 2 Kgs 23:1-3, 4-20. At both the dedication of the temple in the time of Solomon and at the national convocation at the temple in the time of Josiah, the king leads the people in the celebration of a major feast: "the festival" (of Booths; 1 Kgs 8:65-66) and the Passover (2 Kgs 23:21-23).

Conclusions

Recognition that the Deuteronomistic History of the monarchy is a Josianic work illumines the character of Israelite religion during the late preexilic period. Scholars have proposed widely divergent reconstructions of ancient Israelite attitudes toward kingship. Some studies draw a sharp distinction between the kingship of Israel and that of its ancient Near Eastern neighbors.

> The relation between the Hebrew monarch and his people was as nearly secular as is possible in a society wherein religion is a living force. (Frankfort 1948:341).

A second group of scholars advocates a more nuanced approach, contrasting what they see as the critical (preexilic) sentiment of 1 Sam 8:10-18 and 12:1-25 with a later more favorable estimation of kingship.

> The concept of kingship, an important category for sacral history, was not integrated until late in Israel's history, and then only in a reduced format acceptable to Yahwism. (Becker 1980:17).[23]

Hence, both of these groups of scholars doubt whether kingship in (preexilic) ancient Israel was ever sacral.[24]

---

23 See also Alt (1967:225-309, 313-35), Bernhardt (1961:91-182), Weiser (1962), Crüsemann (1978), and Weinfeld (1972:169-71).

24 Frankfort (1948:339-41); Becker (1980:14-17). The choice of terminology is unfortunate, because it imports modern distinctions between the sacred and the secular into the ancient world. Moreover, definitions of sacral kingship vary (Mowinckel 1941:129-58; Bernhardt 1961:67-90; Engnell 1967; Gray 1969:289-302; Cazelles

A third group of scholars takes the opposite point of view: anti-monarchical sentiment stems chiefly from a later period, usually defined as the exile.[25] Similarly, a fourth group (e.g., Mowinckel 1962:50-80; Widengren 1955) distinguishes between the highly positive ideology of kingship prevalent in the united monarchy and the demise of this royal ideology during the late monarchy and exile. Cazelles (1978:59-124; 1992:865-66), for instance, asserts that the prophetic attacks on the monarchy and governmental officials during the divided monarchy effectively desacralized kingship.

This study suggests, however, that the makeup of late preexilic religion is more diverse than any of these theories would indicate. One has to reckon with a variety of competing views already within the preexilic period.[26] Within the spectrum of anti-monarchical, moderating, and pro-monarchical positions, the Deuteronomist advocates a decidedly pro-monarchical stance. Consistent with ancient Near Eastern royal ideology, he depicts the king as fulfilling a

---

1992:863-66; Whitelam 1992:40-48). In so far as I use the term sacral kingship, I refer to the mediatory role of the king as a bridge between divine and human realms. In this role the king is expected to patronize the cult and fulfill certain cultic responsibilities.

25 The literature is voluminous. See, for instance, Mettinger (1976:80-97), Noth (1981), and Wellhausen (1885:246-94).

26 Campbell (1986); Cross (1973:217-89); Gerbrandt (1986:189-94); Halpern (1988:181-204; 1991:11-107); Hanson (1986:148-208); Lemaire (1981; 1986); Lohfink (1981:87-100); McCarter (1980:12-30); O'Brien (1989); Rendtorff (1986:29-31, 171-74); Soggin (1972:9-26); Weippert (1985:213-49). Although some of these scholars deal with the early monarchy, my interest is chiefly in the attitudes toward the monarchy during the late preexilic period.

mediatory role between God and people.[27] In the era of the monarchy, he ties the fate of Israel and Judah to the practices of their kings. Kings mediate blessing (David, Solomon, Hezekiah, Josiah) or curse (Solomon, Jeroboam, Ahab) to their people. To maintain that an author does not adhere to royal ideology, simply because that author shows the ill effects of certain royal actions upon his land or people misconstrues the evidence.[28] Whether for good or for ill, monarchs are critical to the well-being of the people they govern.

Consistent with ancient Near Eastern royal ideology, the Deuteronomist expects kings to support the (Jerusalem temple) cultus. In fact, he endows kings with major responsibility for controlling the practice of religion within their realms. In so doing, the Deuteronomist does more than simply acknowledge the power that monarchs wielded historically in the area of cultic practice; he affirms this power. The author posits the need for a strong relationship between king and temple if the kingdom is to flourish. The king is to be the

---

27 *Contra* Frankfort (1948:339). There are substantial differences between ideologies of kingship in ancient Canaan (Ahlström 1982:1-25; Gray 1969; 1985; Whitelam 1992:40-48), Mesopotamia (Kramer 1974:163-76; Larsen 1974:285-300; Labat 1939), and Egypt (Frankfort 1948:15-139; Silverman 1991:9-87), but the Deuteronomist shares with scribes in each of these areas some common notions about the king as being critical to divine-human relations.

28 The author of the Kirta legend (*KTU* 1.14-16) associates this king's illness with both a drought in the land (*KTU* 1.16.3:13-16) and an attempted *coup d'État* (*KTU* 1.16.6:41-54). Yet this author never questions kingship as the normative means of governance. In fact, the negative effects of this king's troubles upon his family and land only underscore how important kingship is to society (*KTU* 1.15.4:25-27; 15.5:9-29; 15.6:3-5; 16.1:2-23, 56-62; 16.2:18-25, 37-49; 16.6:27-54; cf. *KTU* 1.5.6:23-24; 1.6.6:1-4). See my forthcoming article on the Kirta legend in *JAOS*.

guardian and overeseer of the cult: vigilant in supporting the temple and suppressing all of its Yahwistic and non-Yahwistic rivals. The fate of king (and therefore kingdom) is contingent upon the royal stance toward the Jerusalem temple.

The Deuteronomist is not unaware of prophetic critiques of kingship. He acknowledges early resistance to the rise of kingship (1 Sam 8:10-18; 12:1-25), includes several searing indictments of royal practices within his history (e.g., 1 Kgs 18:18; 21:21-24; 22:19-23; 2 Kgs 1:3-4, 16), and views the reigns of many monarchs negatively. He also shows no inclination to hide the failings of even some of his most highly esteemed kings (e.g., David: 2 Sam 12:7-12; Solomon: 1 Kgs 11:1-13; Hezekiah: 2 Kgs 20:12-19) from his readers. Yet his very assessment of royal performance is tied to how much a given monarch tolerates or supports illicit cults and how much he supports the Jerusalem temple.[29] Hence, the Deuteronomist criticizes kings who condone rival sanctuaries and applies his harshest denunciations to those monarchs, such as Jeroboam, Ahab, and Manasseh who invest them. Whether negatively (all northern kings, some southern kings) or positively (Jehoshaphat, Hezekiah, Josiah), the Deuteronomist's evaluative criteria are tied to the degree and nature of royal supervision of the cult.

The authority the Deuteronomist imputes to kings in overseeing the practice of religion within their territories is, to my knowledge, unrivalled in the ancient Near East. Kings in ancient Mesopotamia and Egypt are expected to support and sustain the various sanctuaries within their states. Occasionally in Neo-Assyrian inscriptions,

[29] I therefore believe that many scholars have placed undue weight on Samuel's speeches (1 Sam 8:10-18 and 12:1-25) in discerning the Deuteronomist's attitude toward kingship.

Assyrian monarchs punish or humiliate the cults of conquered peoples.[30] But as a rule kings of the Levant do not destroy sanctuaries within their own states.[31]

One must therefore go beyond seeking ancient Near Eastern analogies to Josiah's reforms to consider developments within Israel and Judah as comprising the context for the Deuteronomist's commendation of intrusive royal reforms. In my judgment, the Deuteronomist responds to a variety of preexilic critiques of royal government. The authors of Deut 17:14-20 are resigned to the institution of kingship, but significantly limit the powers of the king and the extent of his largesse.[32] Amos (6:1-8) derides the powerful of Samaria for enjoying a luxurious lifestyle, while ignoring the ruin of Joseph. He censures the house of Jeroboam II and predicts the demise of Israel (Amos 7:1-16).[33] Micah castigates the heads of the house of Jacob and the rulers of the house of Israel for perverting justice and building Zion with blood (Mic 3:1-3, 9-10). Employing the divine voice,

---

30 See Begg (1985a:225-29), Rüterswörden (1977:16-22), Spieckermann (1982:347-54), and the discussion in chap. 6.

31 Weinfeld (1964:204-212) sees a parallel between centralization and the unusual behavior of Nabonidus, but there are serious problems with this analogy (Cogan 1974:33).

32 On the indebtedness of the authors of Deuteronomy to earlier (northern) prophetic tradition, see Welch (1924:193-220), Alt (1953:250-75); Nicholson (1967:58-83), Ginsberg (1982:19-24), Weinfeld (1985:76-98), and the overview of Mayes (1979:103-08).

33 Scholars disagree about how much of Amos 7:1-16 is original to Amos and how much stems from a later time (Smend 1963:404-23; Wolff 1977:291-316; Andersen and Freedman 1989:611-38; Clements 1991:49-64; Paul 1991:226-52). This debate need not detain us, because most pundits agree that Amos forecast both the fall of Israel and the royal dynasty of his time (Amos 5:2; 8:2). In this regard, the title of Smend's article is pertinent, "*Das Nein des Amos*."

Hosea (8:4) complains that "they have made kings, but not with my approval; they have made officers, but not with my knowledge." The officers of Judah (שׂרי יהודה) behave like those who shift field boundaries (Hos 5:10). Similarly, Isaiah (1:23) speaks of Jerusalem's officers (שׂריך) as rebels and companions of thieves.

But some of these same figures are clearly unhappy with what they regard as the proliferation of cults and cult objects among the people. For Hosea, the multiplication of altars compounds Ephraim's guilt (8:11-14; cf. 4:12-19, 10:1-2; 11:2; 13:1-2, 6). YHWH asserts:

> I am YHWH your God,
> from the land of Egypt.
> A God apart from me you do not know,
> there is no savior apart from me.[34]

Jeremiah complains that Judah has as many gods as towns (Jer 2:28).[35] Both Amos and Hosea condemn the sanctuary at Bethel, among others.[36] The deuteronomic authors condemn what they consider as idolatry, but also take the radical step of calling for both *Kultusreinheit* and *Kultuseinheit* (Deuteronomy 12; cf. 4:25-28; 27:15; 29:15-19). For at least some, however, criticism of individual kings and opposition to the worship of sundry deities are not tantamount to opposition to kingship. Isaiah, for example, admonishes Ahaz, "is it too little O House of David that you weary humans? Must you also weary my God?" (Isa 7:13). Yet the same prophet

---

34 Hos 13:4. On the import of this claim, see Lang (1985:43-44), Andersen and Freedman (1980:634), and Wolff (1974:219-26).

35 See also Jer 2:8-13, 23-29; 3:1-5, 14-17; 5:1-3, 9-11, 20-31; 6:22-30; 8:4-8; 9:1-11.

36 Amos 4:4-5; 5:4-5; Hosea 4:15; 9:15; 10:5; 12:12; cf. 13:2.

promulgates ideals of what Davidic kingship should entail[37] and proclaims YHWH's continuing commitment to Zion.[38]

The Deuteronomist selectively draws upon a variety of competing discourses. His evaluation of the past shows an indebtedness to an assortment of traditions: prophetic attacks against idolatry, prophetic opposition to monarchical abuse, and the deuteronomic campaign for cultic unity and cultic purity. Yet the Deuteronomist's employment of the Davidic promises also shows indubitable affinities with royal Judahite ideology. Like Isaiah and the authors of Psalms 2, 45, 72, and 110 he celebrates David and Zion. Hence, the Deuteronomist's stance simply cannot be equated with any one of these other positions. The Deuteronomist is not only shaped by his historical context, he also seeks to shape that context. His ideology strikingly combines features of several disparate streams of tradition.

In the context of preexilic debates about cult, king, and people, the Deuteronomist marshalls the force of history to promote the resources which kings can unleash against cultic malfeasance. The "congeries of facts" (White 1978), which the Deuteronomist assembles, orders, and shapes serve a coherent purpose. He shares sentiments expressed by both the prophets and the authors of Proto-Deuteronomy about sundry forms of heteropraxis, yet he views massive royal intervention as the best means to address them. To those prophetic elements concerned with Judah's having as many gods as towns (Jer 2:28) Josiah's severe and pervasive reforms portend a solution. The deuteronomistic presentation of the monarchy is, therefore,

---

37 Isa 7:9, 14-16; 8:5-8; 8:23-9:6; 11:1-5; 16:1-5. The view that the positive assessments of David and Zion in Isaiah must all be later additions to the text is not compelling (*pace* Clements 1980:72-89). In this regard, see also the comments of Becker (1980:45-47).

38 E.g., Isa 2:2-4; 6:1-8; 14:32.

neither wholly pessimistic (Noth) nor simply a triumph of the divine word (von Rad 1966b:221), but programmatic. The Deuteronomist freely acknowledges that kings have been part of Israel's problem, but more than any previous Israelite or Judahite author he defends the powers of Davidic kingship as intrinsic to the solution.

BIBLIOGRAPHY

Aberbach, Moses and Leivy Smolar

1967 Aaron, Jeroboam and the Golden Calves. *JBL* 86:129-40.

1969 Jeroboam's Rise to Power. *JBL* 88:69-72.

Ackerman, Susan

1992 *Under Every Green Tree: Popular Religion in Sixth-Century Judah*. HSM 46. Atlanta: Scholars Press.

Ackroyd, Peter Runham

1970 *Israel under Babylon and Persia*. The New Clarendon Bible 4. London: Oxford University Press.

1984 The Biblical Interpretation of the Reigns of Ahaz and Hezekiah. Pp. 247-59 in *In the Shelter of Elyon*, ed. W. Boyd Barrick and J. R. Spencer. JSOTSup 31. Sheffield: JSOT Press.

1987 *Studies in the Religious Tradition of the Old Testament*. London: SCM.

Aharoni, Yohanan

1968 Arad: Its Inscriptions and Temple. *BA* 31:2-32.

1973 The Solomonic Temple, the Tabernacle and the Arad Sanctuary. Pp. 1-8 in Hoffner, ed.

1979 *The Land of the Bible*. Revised ed. Philadelphia: Westminster.

1982 *The Archaeology of the Land of Israel.* Philadelphia: Westminster.

Ahlström, Gösta W.

1982 *Royal Administration and National Religion in Ancient Palestine.* Studies in the History of the Ancient Near East I. Leiden: Brill.

1993 *The History of Ancient Palestine from the Palaeolithic Period to Alexander's Conquest.* JSOTSup 146. Sheffield: JSOT Press.

Albright, William Foxwell

1948 *From Stone Age to Christianity.* 2nd ed. Baltimore: Johns Hopkins University Press.

1964 The Original Account of the Fall of Samaria in II Kings. *BASOR* 174:66-67.

1968 *Yahweh and the Gods of Canaan.* New York: Doubleday.

Alfrink, B.

1943 L'Expression *škb 'm 'bwtyw*. *OTS* 2:106-18.

Allan, Nigel

1974 Jeroboam and Shechem. *VT* 24:353-357.

Alt, Albrecht

1925 Judas Gaue unter Josia. *Palästinajahrbuch* 21:100-16.

1953 Die Heimat des Deuteronomiums. Pp. 250-75 in his *Kleine Schriften zur Geschichte des Volkes Israel, II.* München: Beck'sche Verlagsbuchhandlung.

1967 *Essays on Old Testament History and Religion.* Trans. R. A. Wilson. New York: Doubleday.

Alter, Robert

1981 *The Art of Biblical Narrative.* New York: Basic.

1987 Introduction to the Old Testament. Pp. 11-35 in Alter and Kermode, ed.

Alter, Robert and Frank Kermode
1987 General Introduction. Pp. 1-8 in Alter and Kermode, ed.

Alter, Robert and Frank Kermode, ed.
1987 *The Literary Guide to the Bible.* Cambridge: Belknap.

Amiran, Ruth
1958 The Tumuli West of Jerusalem. *IEJ* 8:206-227.

Anbar, M.
1990 *Και που εισιν οι θεοι την χωρας Σαμαρειας*, "et où sont les dieux du pays Samarie?" *BN* 51:7-8.

Andersen, Francis I. and David N. Freedman
1980 *Hosea.* AB 24. New York: Doubleday.
1989 *Amos.* AB 24a. New York: Doubleday.

Arend, Walter
1933 *Die typischen Szenen bei Homer.* Problemata 7, Forschungen zur Klassischen Philologie. Berlin: Weidmann.

Avigad, Nahman
1986 *Hubrew Bullae from the Time of Jeremiah: Remnants of a Burnt Archive.* Jerusalem: Israel Exploration Society.

Baena, Gustavo
1973 El vocabulario de II Reyes 17,7-23. 35-39. *Est Bib* 32:357-384.
1974a Carácter literario de 2 Reyes 17,7-23. *Est Bib* 33:5-24.

1974b Carácter literario de 2 Reyes 17,13. 35-39. *Est Bib* 33:157-179.

Bailey, Lloyd R.
1971 The Golden Calf. *HUCA* 42:97-115.

Baillet, M., J. T. Milik, and R. de Vaux, ed.
1962 *Les "Petites Grottes" de Qumrân: exploration de la falaise, les grottes 2 Q, 3Q, 5Q, 6Q, 7Q a 10Q, le rouleau de cuivre.* DJD 3. Oxford: Clarendon.

Balentine, Samuel E.
1993 *Prayer in the Hebrew Bible: The Drama of Divine-Human Dialogue.* Overtures to Biblical Theology. Minneapolis: Fortress.

Baltzer, Klaus
1971 *The Covenant Formulary in Old Testament, Jewish, and Early Christian Writings.* Trans. David E. Green. Philadelphia: Fortress.

Barth, Karl
1957 *Church Dogmatics II: The Doctrine of God (Part 2).* Edinburgh: T.& T. Clark.

Barthélemy, Dominique *et al.*, ed.
1979 *Preliminary and Interim Report on the Hebrew Old Testament Text Project.* Vol. 2: Historical Books. New York: United Bible Societies.

Bauer, H., and P. Leander.
1922 *Historische Grammatik der hebräischen Sprache des Alten Testaments.* Halle.

Becker, Joachim
1980 *Messianic Expectation in the Old Testament*. Edinburgh: T. & T. Clark.

Becking, Bob
1992 *The Fall of Samaria: An Historical and Archaeological Study*. Studies in the History of the Ancient Near East II. Leiden: Brill.

Beentjes, Pancratius C.
1982 Inverted Quotations in the Bible: A Neglected Stylistic Pattern. *Bib* 63:506-523.

Begg, Christopher T.
1985a The Destruction Of The Calf. Pp. 208-251 in Lohfink, ed.
1985b Unifying Factors in 2 Kings 1.2-17a. *JSOT* 32:75-86.
1987a The Death of Josiah in Chronicles: Another View. *VT* 37:1-8.

Ben Zvi, Ehud
1991 Once the Lamp has been Kindled...: A Reconsideration of the Meaning of the MT *Nîr* in 1 Kgs 11:36; 15:4; 2 Kgs 8:19 and 2 Chr 21:7. *AusBR* 39:19-30.

Bentzen, Aage
1926 *Die Josianische Reform und ihre Voraussetzungen*. Copenhagen: Hasse & Sons.

Bernhardt, K.-H.
1961 *Das Problem der altorientalischen Königsideologie im Alten Testament*. VTSup 8. Leiden: Brill.

Beyerlin, Walter
1965 *Origins and History of the Oldest Sinaitic Traditions*. Oxford: Basil Blackwell.

Biran, Avraham
1980 Tell Dan -- Five Years Later. *BA* 43:168-182.
1987 "Dan." Pp. 101-112 in Perdue, Toombs, and Johnson, ed.

Biran, Avraham, ed.
1981 *Temple and High Places in Biblical Times*. Jerusalem: Nelson Glueck School of Biblical Archaeology.

Birch, Bruce C.
1976 *The Rise of the Israelite Monarchy: The Growth and Development of 1 Samuel 7-15*. SBLDS 27. Missoula: Scholars Press.

Blenkinsopp, Joseph
1988 *Ezra-Nehemiah: A Commentary*. OTL. Philadelphia: Westminster.

Boling, Robert G.
1974 In Those Days There Was No King in Israel. Pp. 33-48 in *A Light Unto My Path: Old Testament Studies in Honor of Jacob M. Myers*. Philadelphia: Temple University Press.
1975 *Judges*. AB 6A. New York: Doubleday.

Boling, Robert G. and Edward F. Campbell, Jr.
1987 Jeroboam and Rehoboam at Shechem. Pp. 259-272 in Perdue, Toombs, and Johnson, eds.

Boling, Robert G. and George Ernest Wright
1982 *Joshua: A New Translation with Notes and Commentary*. AB 6. Garden City: Doubleday.

Braun, Roddy L.
1973 Solomonic Apologetic in Chronicles. *JBL* 92:503-16.
1976 Solomon, the Chosen Temple Builder: The Significance of 1 Chronicles 22, 28 and 29 for the Theology of Chronicles. *JBL* 95:581-90.

Brekelmans, C.
1989 Joshua V 10-12: Another Approach. *OTS* 25:89-95

Brekelmans, C. and J. Lust, ed.
1990 *Pentateuchal and Deuteronomistic Studies: Papers Read at the XIIIth IOSOT Congress.* BETL XCIV. Leuven: Leuven University Press.

Brettler, Marc Zvi
1989 Ideology, History and Theology in 2 Kings XVII 7-23. *VT* 39:268-82.

Bright, John
1951 The Date of the Prose Sermons of Jeremiah. *JBL* 70:15-35.
1981 *A History of Israel.* 3rd ed. Philadelphia: Westminster.

Brooke, A. E., N. McLean, and H. S. J. Thackeray
1930-32 *The Old Testament in Greek, Vol. II Part II: I and II Kings Part III: I and II Chronicles.* London: Cambridge University Press.

Broshi, M.
1974 The Expansion of Jerusalem in the Reign of Hezekiah and Manasseh. *IEJ* 24:21-26.

Burney, C. F.
1920 *Notes on the Hebrew Text of the Book of Kings*. Oxford: Clarendon.

Camp, Ludger
1990 *Hiskija und Hiskijabild: Analyse und Interpretation von 2 Kön 18-20*. Münsteraner Theologische Abhandlungen 9. Altenberge: Telos.

Campbell, Antony F., S.J.
1986 *Of Prophets and Kings: A Late Ninth-Century Document (1 Samuel 1-2 Kings 10)*. CBQMS 17. Washington, DC: The Catholic Biblical Association of America.

Carlson, R. A.
1964 *David, the Chosen King*. Stockholm: Almqvist & Wiksell.

Carpenter, Joseph E.
1902 *The Composition of the Hexateuch*. London: Longmans, Green, and Co.

Cassuto, Umberto
1967 *A Commentary on the Book of Exodus*. Trans. I. Abrahams. Jerusalem: Magnes.

Cazelles, Henri
1967 Passages in the Singular within Discourse in the Plural. *CBQ* 29:207-19.
1978 *Le Messiae de la Bible*. Paris: Desclée.
1992 Sacral Kingship. *ABD* 5:863-66.

Childs, Brevard S.
1967 *Isaiah and the Assyrian Crisis*. SBT 2/3. London: SCM.

1974 *The Book of Exodus: A Critical and Theological Commentary*. OTL. Philadelphia: Westminster.

Claburn, W. E.

1973 The Fiscal Basis of Josiah's Reforms. *JBL* 92:11-22.

Clements, Ronald E.

1980 *Isaiah and the Deliverance of Jerusalem*. JSOT-Sup 13; Sheffield: JSOT Press.

1991 Amos and the Politics of Israel. Pp. 49-64 in *Storia e Tradizioni di Israele: Scritti in Onore di J. Alberto Soggin*, ed. D. Garrone and F. Moscati. Brescia: Paideia Editrice.

Clifford, Richard J.

1971 The Tent of El and the Israelite Tent of Meeting. *CBQ* 33:221-27.

1979 The Temple in the Ugaritic Myth of Baal. Pp. 137-47 in Cross, ed.

1983 Cosmogonies in the Ugaritic Texts and in the Bible. *Or* 53:183-201.

1990 Exodus. Pp. 44-60 in *NJBC*, ed. R. E. Brown, J. A. Fitzmyer, and R. E. Murphy. Englewood Cliffs: Prentice Hall.

Cogan, Mordecai

1974 *Imperialism and Religion: Assyria, Judah and Israel in the Eighth and Seventh Centuries B.C.E.* SBLMS 19. Missoula: Scholars Press.

1978 Israel in Exile--The View of a Josianic Historian. *JBL* 97:40-44.

Cogan, Mordecai and Israel Eph'al, ed.

1991 *Ah, Assyria: Studies in Assyrian history and ancient Near Eastern Historiography presented to Hayim Tadmor*. ScrHier 33. Jerusalem: Magnes.

Coggins, Richard J.

1975 — *Samaritans and Jews: The Origins of Samaritanism Reconsidered*. Atlanta: John Knox.

Cohn, Robert L.

1985a — Convention and Creativity in the Book of Kings: the Case of the Dying Monarch. *CBQ* 47:603-616.

1985b — Literary Technique in the Jeroboam Narrative. *ZAW* 97:23-35.

Crenshaw, James L.

1971 — *Prophetic Conflict. Its Effect Upon Israelite Religion*. BZAW 124. Berlin: de Gruyter.

Crenshaw, James L., ed.

1976 — *Studies in Ancient Wisdom*. New York: KTAV.

Cross, Frank Moore

1966 — The Contribution of the Discoveries at Qumran to the Study of the Biblical Text. *IEJ* 16:81-95.

1968 — The Structure of the Deuteronomic History. Pp. 9-24 in *Perspectives in Jewish Learning*, Annual of the College of Jewish Studies 3. Chicago.

1973 — *Canaanite Myth and Hebrew Epic*. Cambridge: Harvard University Press.

1974 — A Reconstruction of the Judean Restoration. *JBL* 94:4-18 (= *Int* 29 [1975] 187-203).

1979 — Two Offering Dishes with Phoenician Inscriptions from the Sanctuary of ‘ARAD. *BASOR* 235:75-78.

1981 — The Priestly Tabernacle in Light of Recent Research. Pp. 169-80 in Biran, ed.

1983 — The Ammonite Oppression of the Tribes of Gad and Reuben: Missing Verses from 1 Samuel 11 Found in 4QSamuel[a]. Pp. 148-58 in Tadmor and Weinfeld, ed.

Cross, Frank M., ed.
1979 *Symposia Celebrating the Seventy-Fifth Anniversary of the Founding of the American Schools of Oriental Research (1900-1975).* Zion Research Foundation Occasional Publications 1-2. Cambridge: American Schools of Oriental Research.

Cross, Frank M. and David N. Freedman
1953 Josiah's Revolt Against Assyria. *JNES* 12:56-58.

Cross, Frank M. and Shemaryahu Talmon, ed.
1975 *Qumran and the History of the Biblical Text.* Cambridge: Harvard University Press.

Cross, Frank M. and George E. Wright
1956 The Boundary and Province Lists of the Kingdom of Judah. *JBL* 202-226.

Crüsemann, Frank
1978 *Der Widerstand gegen das Königtum. Die antiköniglichen Texte des Alten Testaments und der Kampf um den frühen israelitischen Staat.* WMANT 49. Neukirchen: Neukirchener Verlag.

Curtis, E. L. and A. A. Madsen.
1910 *The Books of Chronicles.* ICC. Edinburgh: T. & T. Clark.

Dandamaev, M. A.
1979 State and Temple in Babylonia in the First Millennium B.C. Pp. 589-96 in Lipiński, ed.

Danielus, E.
1967 The Sins of Jeroboam Ben-Nabat. *JQR* 58:95-114, 204-23.

Davies, Philip R.
1992 *In Search of 'Ancient Israel.'* JSOTSup 148. Sheffield: JSOT Press.

Dearman, John Andrew
1992 *Religion and Culture in Ancient Israel.* Peabody: Hendrikson.

Deboys, David G.
1991 1 Kings XIII -- A "New Criterion" Reconsidered. *VT* 41:210-212.

Debus, Jörg
1967 *Die Sünde Jeroboams.* FRLANT 93. Göttingen: Vandenhoeck & Ruprecht.

Dever, William G.
1990 *Recent Archaeological Discoveries and Biblical Research.* Seattle and London: University of Washington Press.

De Vries, Simon J.
1978 *Prophet Against Prophet.* Grand Rapids: Eerdmans.
1985 *1 Kings.* WBC 12. Waco: Word.
1987 The Schema of Dynastic Endangerment in Chronicles. *Proceedings, Eastern Great lakes and Midwest Biblical Societies* 7:59-78.

Dietrich, M., O. Loretz, and J. Sanmartín
1976 *Die Keilalphabetischen Texte aus Ugarit.* AOAT 24. Neukirchen-Vluyn: Neukirchener Verlag.

Dietrich, Walter
1972 *Prophetie und Geschichte.* FRLANT 108. Göttingen: Vandenhoeck & Ruprecht.

1977a David in Überlieferung und Geschichte. *VF* 22:44-64.

1977b Josia und das Gesetzbuch (2 Reg. XXII). *VT* 27:13-35.

1987 *David, Saul, und die Propheten. Das Verhältnis von Religion und Politik nach den prophetischen Überlieferungen vom frühesten Königtum in Israel.* BWANT 122. Stuttgart: Kohlhammer.

Dillard, Raymond B.

1987 *2 Chronicles.* WBC 15. Waco: Word.

Dion, Paul E.

1988 Sennacherib's Expedition to Palestine. *Bulletin of the Canadian Society of Biblical Studies* 48:3-25.

1991 Deuteronomy 13: The Suppression of Alien Religious Propaganda during the Late Monarchical Era. Pp. 147-216 in *Law and Ideology in Monarchic Israel*, eds. B. Halpern and D. W. Hobson. JSOTSup 124. Sheffield: JSOT Press.

Doermann, Ralph W.

1987 Archaeology and Biblical Interpretation: Tell el-Hesi. Pp. 129-56 in Perdue, Toombs, and Johnson, ed.

Donner, Herbert R.

1973 "Hier sind deiner Götter Israel!" Pp. 45-50 in *Wort und Geschichte.* Fs. Karl Elliger. Ed. H. Gese and H. P. Rüger. Neukirchen-Vluyn: Neukirchener Verlag.

1977 The Separate States of Israel and Judah. Pp. 381-434 in *Israelite and Judean History*, ed. J. H. Hayes and J. M. Miller. London: SCM.

Dorp, Jaap van
1987 Wat is die steenhoop daar? Het graf van de man Gods in 2 Koningen 23. *Amsterdamse Cashiers Voor Exegese en Bijbelse Theologie* 8:64-97.

Dozeman, Thomas B.
1982 The Way of the Man of God from Judah: True and False Prophecy in the Pre-Deuteronomic Legend of 1 Kings 13. *CBQ* 44:379-393.

Driver, Godfrey R.
1936 Supposed Arabisms in the Old Testament. *JBL* 55:101-120.
1957 On 'LH "went up country" and YRD "went down country." *ZAW* 69:54-57.

Driver, Samuel R.
1895 *A Critical and Exegetical Commentary on Deuteronomy*. ICC. Edinburgh: T. & T. Clark.
1914 *An Introduction to the Literature of the Old Testament*. New ed. New York: Scribner's.

Eaton, John H.
1986 *Kingship and the Psalms*. 2nd edition. Sheffield: JSOT Press.

Eisenstadt, Shmuel N., ed.
1986 *The Origins and Diversity of Axial Age Civilizations*. Albany: State University of New York Press.

Eissfeldt, Otto
1935 *Molk als Opferbegriff im Punischen und Hebräischen und das ende des Gottes Moloch*. Beiträge zur Religionsgeschichte des Altertums 3. Halle: Max Niemeyer.

1965 *The Old Testament: An Introduction*. Trans. by P. R. Ackroyd. New York: Harper & Row.

Elitzur, Y.
1969 The Josiade Reform in the Light of Jerusalem Archaeology. The Stone Mounds in the West of the City. *Proceedings of the Fifth World Congress of Jewish Studies*, I:92-97.

Emerton, J. A.
1962 Priests and Levites in Deuteronomy. *VT* 12:129-138.

Emerton, J. A., ed.
1988 *Congress Volume: Jerusalem, 1986*. VTSup 40. Leiden: Brill.
1991 *Congress Volume: Leuven, 1989*. VTSup 43. Leiden: Brill.

Engnell, Ivan
1967 *Studies in Divine Kingship in the Ancient Near East*. 2nd ed. Oxford: Basil Blackwell.

Eph'al, Israel
1991 "The Samarian(s)" in the Assyrian Sources. Pp. 36-45 in Cogan and Eph'al, ed.

Eslinger, Lyle
1986 Josiah and the Torah Book: Comparison of 2 Kings 22:1-23:28 and 2 Chr. 34:1-35:19. *HAR* 10:37-62.
1989 *Into the Hands of the Living God*. JSOTSup 84. Bible and Literature 24. Sheffield: JSOT Press.

Evans, Carl D.
1983 Naram-Sin and Jeroboam: The Archetypal *Unheilsherrscher* in Mesopotamia and Biblical

Historiography. Pp. 97-125 in Hallo, Moyer, and Perdue.

Eynikel, Erik
1990 Prophecy and Fulfillment in the Deuteronomistic History. Pp. 227-237 in Brekelmans and Lust.

Fales, Frederick Mario, ed.
1981 *Assyrian Royal Inscriptions: New Horizons*. Orientis Antiqvi Collectio 17. Rome: Instituto per l'Oriente.

Fargo, Valerie M.
1987 Hesi in the Iron II Period: A Judean Border Fortress. Pp. 157-64 in Perdue, Toombs, and Johnson, ed.

Field, F., ed.
1785 *Origenis Hexaplorum quae supersunt sive veterum interpretum graecorum in totum vetus testamentum fragmenta*. Tom. I. Oxonii.

Finkelstein, Israel
1992 The Days of Manasseh: The Archaeological Background. Unpublished paper (read at the annual meeting of the Society of Biblical Literature in San Francisco).

Fishbane, Michael
1985 *Biblical Interpretation in Ancient Israel*. Oxford: Clarendon.

Fishbane, M. and E. Tov, ed.
1992 *Sha'arei Talmon: Studies in the Bible, Qumran, and the Ancient Near East Presented to Shemaryahu Talmon*. Winona Lake: Eisenbrauns.

Fitzmyer, J. A.
1967 *The Aramaic Inscriptions of Sefire.* Rome: Pontifical Biblical Institute.

Fohrer, Georg
1968 *Introduction to the Old Testament.* Trans. D. E. Green. Nashville: Abingdon.

Frankena, R.
1965 The Vassal Treaties of Esarhaddon and the Dating of Deuteronomy. *OTS* 14:122-54.

Frankfort, Henri
1948 *Kingship and the Gods: A Study of Ancient Near Eastern Kingship as the Integration of Society and Nature.* Chicago: University of Chicago Press.

Freedman, David Noel
1961 The Chronicler's Purpose. *CBQ* 23:432-42.
1962 Pentateuch. *IDB* 3:711-27.
1976 The Deuteronomic History. *IDBSup* 226-28.

Friedman, Richard E.
1981a *The Exile and Biblical Narrative.* HSM 22. Chico, CA: Scholars Press.
1981b From Egypt to Egypt: Dtr^1 and Dtr^2. Pp. 167-92 in Halpern and Levenson, ed.

Friedman, Richard E., ed.
1981 *The Creation of Sacred Literature, Composition and Redaction of the Biblical Text.* Near Eastern Studies 22. Berkeley: University of California Press.

Friedman, Richard E. and H. G. M. Williamson, ed.
1987 *The Future of Biblical Studies: The Hebrew Scriptures*. SBLSS. Decatur: Scholars Press.

Frisch, Amos
1988 Shemaiah the Prophet versus King Rehoboam: Two Opposed Interpretations of the Schism (1 Kings XII 21-4). *VT* 38:466-468.

Frost, S. B.
1968 The Death of Josiah: A Conspiracy of Silence. *JBL* 87:369-82.

Garelli, Paul
1981 La conception de la royauté en Assyrie. Pp. 1-11 in Fales, ed.

Garelli, Paul, ed.
1974 *Le Palais et la Royauté (Archéologie et Civilisation)*. XIX Recontre Assyriologique Internationale. Paris: Paul Geuthner.

Gerbrandt, Gerald Eddie
1986 *Kingship According to the Deuteronomistic History*. SBLDS 87. Atlanta: Scholars Press.

Ginsberg, H. Louis
1982 *The Israelian Heritage of Judaism*. New York: Jewish Theological Seminary of America.

Gonçalves, Francolino J.
1986 *L'expédition de Sennachérib en Palestine dans la littérature hebraïque ancienne*. EBib n.s.7. Paris: Librairie Lecoffre.

Gooding, D. W.
1967 The Septuagint's Rival Versions of Jeroboam's Rise to Power. *VT* 17:173-89.
1969 Problems of Text and Midrash in the Third Book of Reigns. *Textus* 7:1-29.

Goody, John Kankine
1968 Introduction. Pp. 1-26 in Goody, ed.

Goody, John Kankine, ed.
1968 *Literacy in Traditional Societies.* Cambridge: Cambridge University Press.

Goody, John Kankine and Ian Watt
1968 The Consequences of Literacy. Pp. 27-68 in Goody, ed.

Gordon, Robert P.
1973-74 Source Study in 1 Kings XII 24a-nα (LXX). *Transactions of the Glasgow University Oriental Society* 25:59-70.
1975 The Second Septuagint Account of Jeroboam: History or Midrash? *VT* 25:368-393.

Graham, Matt Patrick
1990 *The Utilization of 1 and 2 Chronicles in the Reconstruction of Israelite History in the Nineteenth Century.* SBLDS 116. Atlanta: Scholars Press.

Gramberg, C. P. W.
1829 *Kritische Geschichte der Religionsideen des alten Testaments.* Berlin: Duncker & Humbolt.

Gray, John
1963 *I & II Kings.* OTL. Philadelphia: Westminster.

1969 Sacral Kingship in Ugarit. Pp. 289-302 in *Ugaritica VI*. Mission de Ras Shamra 17. Paris: Mission Archéologique de Ras Shamra.

1970 *I & II Kings*. OTL. 2nd ed. Philadelphia: Westminster.

1985 *Near Eastern Mythology*. Revised ed. New York: Peter Bedrick.

Grayson, A. K.

1975 *Assyrian and Babylonian Chronicles*. Texts from Cuneiform Sources 5. Locust Valley: Augustin.

Greene, David, trans.

1987 *The History. Herodotus*. Chicago: University of Chicago Press.

Gressmann, Hugo

1921 *Die älteste Geschichtsschreibung und Prophetie Israels von Samuel bis Amos und Hosea*. 2nd ed. Schriften des Alten Testaments 2/1. Göttingen: Vandenhoeck & Ruprecht.

1924 Josia und das Deuteronomium. *ZAW* 42:313-37.

Grønbaek, J. H.

1965 Benjamin und Judah: Erwägungen zu 1 Kön. 12,21-24. *VT* 15:421-36.

Gross, Walter

1979 Lying Prophet and Disobedient Man of God in 1 Kings 13: Role Analysis as an Instrument of Theological Interpretation of an OT Narrative Text. *Semeia* 15:97-135.

Gruber, Mayer I.

1986 Hebrew *qĕdēšāh* and her Canaanite and Akkadian Cognates. *UF* 18:133-148.

Gunneweg, A. and O. Kaiser, ed.
1979 *Textgemäß. Aufsätze und Beiträge zur Hermeneutik des alten Testaments.* Fs. Ernst Würthwein. Göttingen: Vandenhoeck & Ruprecht.

Hallo, William W.
1983 Cult Statue and Divine Image: A Preliminary Study. Pp. 1-17 in Hallo, Moyer, and Perdue.

Hallo, William, W., J. Moyer, and L. Perdue, ed.
1983 *Scripture in Context II: More Essays on the Comparative Method.* Winona Lake: Eisenbrauns.

Halpern, Baruch
1976 Levitic Participation in the Reform Cult of Jeroboam I. *JBL* 95:31-42.
1981 *The Constitution of the Monarchy in Israel.* HSM 25. Chico, CA: Scholars Press.
1988 *The First Historians. The Hebrew Bible and History.* San Francisco: Harper & Row.
1991 Jerusalem and the Lineages in the seventh Century BCE: Kingship and the Rise of Individual Moral Liability. Pp. 11-107 in *Law and Ideology in Monarchic Israel*, eds. B. Halpern and D. W. Hobson. JSOTSup 124. Sheffield: JSOT Press.
1992 Sociological Comparativism and the Theological Imagination: The Case of the Conquest. Pp. 53-67 in Fisbane and Tov, ed.
forthcoming Sybil, or the Two Nations? Archaism, Alienation and the Elite Redefinition of Traditional Culture in Judah in the 8th-7th Centuries B.C.E. *The Study of the Near East in the Twenty-First Century*, ed. J. Cooper. Baltimore: Johns Hopkins University Press.

Halpern, Baruch and Jon Levenson, ed.
1981 *Traditions in Transformation: Turning Points in Biblical Faith. Essays Presented to Frank Moore Cross, Jr.* Winona Lake: Eisenbrauns.

Halpern, Baruch and David S. Vanderhooft
1991 The Editions of Kings in the 7th-6th Centuries B.C.E. *HUCA* 62:179-244.

Handy, Lowell K.
1990 Dissenting Deities or Obedient Angels: Divine Hierarchies in Ugarit and the Bible. *BR* 35:18-35.

Hanson, Paul D.
1968 The Song of Heshbon and David's *Nîr*. *HTR* 61:297-320.
1979 *The Dawn of Apocalyptic: The Historical and Social Roots of Jewish Apocalytic Eschatology.* Philadelphia: Fortess.
1986 *The People Called: The Growth of Community in the Bible.* San Francisco: Harper and Row.

Haran, Menahem
1978 *Temples and Temple-Service in Ancient Israel. An Inquiry into the Character of Cult Phenomena and the Historical Setting of the Priestly School.* Oxford: Oxford University Press. [repr. Eisenbrauns, 1985.]

Hardmeier, Christof
1990 *Prophetie im Streit vor dem Untergang Judas. Erzählkommunikative Studien zur Enstehungssituation der Jesaja- und Jeremiaerzählungen in II Reg 18-20 und Jer 37-40.* BZAW 187. Berlin: de Gruyter.

Hatch, Edwin, and Redpath, Henry
1897 *A Concordance to the Septuagint and the other Greek Versions of the Old Testament*. vol. I, II. Suppl. 1906. Oxford: Clarendon.

Hauer, Christian E.
1986 From Alt to Anthropology: The Rise of the Israelite State. *JSOT* 36:3-15.

Heider, George C.
1985 *The Cult of Molek: A Reassessment*. JSOTSup 43. Sheffield: JSOT Press.

Herrmann, Siegfried
1981 *A History of Israel in Old Testament Times*. 2nd ed. Trans. J. Bowden. Philadelphia: Fortress.
1984 King David's State. Pp. 261-75 in *In the Shelter of Elyon: Essays on Ancient Palestinian Life and Literature in Hnor of G. W. Ahlström*, ed. W. B. Barrick and J. R. Spencer. JSOTSup 31. Sheffield: JSOT Press.

Herzog, Zeev
1981 Israelite Sanctuaries at Arad and Beer-Sheba. Pp. 120-122 in Biran, ed.

Hillers, Delbert R.
1964 *Treaty Curses and the Old Testament Prophets*. BibOr 16. Rome: Pontifical Biblical Institute.

Hobbs, T. R.
1985 *2 Kings*. WBC 13. Waco: Word.

Hoffmann, Hans-Detlef

1980 *Reform und Reformen. Untersuchungen zu einem Grundthema der deuteronomistischen Geschichtsschreibung.* ATANT 66. Zürich: Theologischer Verlag.

Hoffner, Harry, ed.

1973 *Orient and Occident: Essays Presented to Cyrus H. Gordon on the Occasion of his Sixty-Fifth Birthday.* AOAT 22. Kevelaer: Butzon & Bercker.

Holder, John

1988 The Presuppositions, Accusations, and Threats of 1 Kings 14:1-18. *JBL* 107:27-38.

Holladay, William L.

1986 *Jeremiah 1.* Hermeneia. Philadelphia: Fortress.

1989 *Jeremiah 2.* Hermeneia. Philadelphia: Fortress.

Hollenstein, Helmut

1977 Literarkritische Erwägungen zum Bericht über die Reformmassnahmen Josias 2 Kön. XXIII 4ff. *VT* 27:321-336.

Hölscher, Gustav

1914 *Die Profeten.* Leipzig.

1922 Komposition und Ursprung des Deuteronomiums. *ZAW* 40:161-255.

1923 Das Buch der Könige, seine Quellen und seine Redaktion. Pp. 158-213 in ΕΥΧΑΡΙΣΤΗΡΙΟΝ. *Studien zur Religion und Literatur des Alten und Neuen Testaments.* Fs. Hermann Gunkel, Bd. 1, ed. H. Schmidt. FRLANT 36/1. Göttingen: Vandenhoeck & Ruprecht.

1952 *Geschichtsschreibung in Israel.* Lund: Gleerup.

Hoppe, Leslie J.
1980 The Meaning of Deuteronomy. *BTB* 10:111-117.
1985 Jerusalem in the Deuteronomistic History. Pp. 107-110 in Lohfink, ed.

Horn, Siegfried H.
1988 The Divided Monarchy: The Kingdoms of Israel and Judah. Pp. 109-149 in Shanks, ed.

Horst, Friedrich
1923 Die Kultusreform des Königs Josia (II. Rg. 22-23). *ZDMG* 77:220-35.

Hurowitz, Victor (Avidor)
1992 *I Have Built You an Exalted House: Temple Building in Light of Mesopotamian and North-west Semitic Writings.* JSOTSup 115. Sheffield: JSOT Press.

Isbell, Charles D.
1978 2 Kings 22:3-23:24 and Jeremiah 36: A Stylistic Comparison. *JSOT* 8:33-45.

Ishida, Tomoo
1977a *The Royal Dynasties in Ancient Israel. A Study on the Formation and Development of Royal-Dynastic Ideology.* BZAW 142. Berlin / New York: de Gruyter.
1977b נגיד: A Term for the Legitimization of the Kingship. *AJBI* 3:35-51.
1988 Royal succession in the kingdoms of Israel and Judah with special reference to the people under arms as a determining factor in the struggles for the throne. Pp. 96-106 in Emerton, ed.

Ishida, Tomoo, ed.
1982 *Studies in the Period of David and Solomon and Other Essays*. Winona Lake: Eisenbrauns.

Iwry, Samuel
1957 The Qumrân Isaiah and the End of the Dial of Ahaz. *BASOR* 147:27-33.

Jamieson-Drake, David W.
1991 *Scribes and Schools in Monarchic Judah*. JSOT-Sup 109. Ths Social World of Biblical Antiquity Series 9. Sheffield: Almond.

Japhet, Sara
1979 Conquest and Settlement in Chronicles. *JBL* 98:205-18.
1985 The Historical Reliability of Chronicles: The History of the Problem and Its Place in Biblical Research. *JSOT* 33:83-107.
1989 *The Ideology of the Book of Chronicles and its Place in Biblical Thought*. Trans. Anna Barber. Beiträge zur Erforschung des Alten Testaments und des Antiken Judentums 9. Frankfurt: Lang.
1993 *I & II Chronicles*. OTL. Louisville: Westminster / John Knox.

Jastrow, Morris
1903 *A Dictionary of the Targumim, the Talmud Babli and Yerushalmi, and the Midrashic Literature*. Brooklyn: Traditional.

Jepsen, Alfred
1956 *Die Quellen des Königbuches*. 2nd ed. Halle: Max Niemeyer.
1959 Die Reform des Josia. Pp. 97-108 in *Festschrift Friedrich Baumgärtel zum 70. Geburtstag 14. Januar 1958*, ed. J. Herrmann. Erlanger For-

schungen, Reihe A: Geisteswissenschaften 10. Erlangen: Universitätsbibliothek.

1970 Ahabs Buße. Ein kleiner Beitrage zur Methode lterarhistorischer Einordnung. Pp. 145-55 in *Archäologie und Altes Testament: Fs. K. Galling*, ed. A. Kuschke and E. Kutsch. Tübingen.

1971 Gottesmann und Prophet: Anmerkungen zum Kapitel 1. Kön. 13. Pp. 171-182 in *Wolff*, ed.

Jones, Gwilym H.

1984 *1 and 2 Kings*. 2 vols. NCB. Grand Rapids: Eerdmans.

Josephus (Flavius)

1934 *The Jewish Antiquities, Books V-VIII*. LCL. Trans. H. St. J. Thackeray and R. Marcus. Cambridge: Harvard University Press.

1937 *The Jewish Antiquities, Books IX-XI*. LCL. Trans. R. Marcus. Cambridge: Harvard University Press.

1943 *The Jewish Antiquities, Books XII-XIV*. LCL. Trans. P. Marcus. Cambridge: Harvard University Press.

Joüon, Paul

1912 Notes de Critique Textuelle (AT) [Kings]. *Mélanges de l'Université Saint-Joseph* 5:473-485.

1923 *Grammaire de l'hébreu biblique*. Rev. ed. Rome: Pontifical Biblical Institute.

1929 Notes philologiques sur le texte hébreu de 2 Rois. *Bib* 10:53-61.

Kallai, Zecharia

1978 Judah and Israel -- A Study in Israelite Historiography. *IEJ* 28:251-61.

Kaufmann, Yehezkel
1960 *The Religion of Israel: From Its Beginnings to the Babylonian Exile.* Trans. and abridged by M. Greenberg. Chicago: Chicago University Press.

Keil, C. F.
1877 *The Books of the Kings.* 2nd ed. Trans. J. Martin. Edinburgh: T. & T. Clark.

Kennett, R. H.
1920 *Deuteronomy and the Decalogue.* Cambridge: Cambridge University Press.

Kenyon, Kathleen M.
1974 *Digging Up Jerusalem.* New York: Praeger.

King, Philip J.
1988 *Amos, Hosea, Micah: An Archaeological Commentary.* Philadelphia: Westminster.

Kitchen, Kenneth A.
1986 *The Third Intermediate Period in Egypt (1100-650 B.C.).* 2nd ed. Warminster: Aris & Phillips.

Kittel, Rudolph
1900 *Die Bücher der Könige.* HK 1/5. Göttingen: Vandenhoeck & Ruprecht.

Klopfenstein, M. A.
1966 1. Könige 13. Pp. 639-672 in *Parrhēsia.* Fs. Karl Barth. Ed. E. Busch, J. Fangmeier, and M. Geiger. Zürich: EVZ.

Klostermann, A.
1887 *Die Bücher Samuelis und der Könige.* Kurzgefasster Kommentar zu den heiligen Schriften Alten und Neuen Testaments, 3. Nördlingen: C. H. Bech'schen Buchhandlung.

Knierim, Rolf
1971 Offenbarung im Alten Testament. Pp. 206-235 in Wolff, ed.

Knoppers, Gary N.
1987 Dynastic Oracle and Secession in 1 Kings 11. *Proceedings, Eastern Great Lakes and Midwest Biblical Societies* 7:159-72.
1988 "What Share Have We in David?": The Division of the Kingdom in Kings and Chronicles. Diss., Harvard University. Ann Arbor: UMI.
1989 A Reunited Kingdom in Chronicles? *Proceedings, Eastern Great Lakes and Midwest Biblical Societies* 9:74-88.
1990 Rehoboam in Chronicles: Villain or Victim? *JBL* 109:423-440.
1991 Reform and Regression: The Chronicler's Presentation of Jehoshaphat. *Bib* 72:500-524.
1992 "There was None Like Him": Incomparability in the Books of Kings. *CBQ* 54:411-31.
1993 *Two Nations Under God: The Deuteronomistic History of Solomon and the Dual Monarchies.* Vol. 1: *The Reign of Solomon and the Rise of Jeroboam.* HSM 52. Atlanta: Scholars Press.
1994 Jehoshaphat's Judiciary and "the Scroll of YHWH's Torah." *JBL* 113:87-108.
forthcoming Sex, Religion, and Politics: The Deuteronomist on Intermarriage. *HAR* 15.
forthcoming Prayer and Propaganda: The Dedication of Solomon's Temple and the Deuteronomist's Program. *CBQ*.

forthcoming Aaron's Calf and Jeroboam's Calves. *Fortunate the Eyes that See: Essays in Honor of David Noel Freedman in Celebration of His Seventieth Birthday*, ed. A. H. Bartelt, *et al.* Grand Rapids: Eerdmans.

forthcoming Dissonance and Disaster in the Legend of Kirta. *JAOS*.

forthcoming The Deuteronomist and the Deuteronomic Law of the King. *ZAW*.

Kramer, Samuel N.
1974 Kingship in Sumer and Akkad: The Ideal King. Pp. 163-76 in Garelli, ed.

Kropat, Arno
1909 *Die Syntax des Autors der Chronik Vergleichen mit der seiner Quellen: Ein Beitrag zur historischen Syntax des Hebräischen*. BZAW 16. Giessen: Töpelmann.

Kuenen, Abraham
1887-92 *Historisch Kritische Einleitung in die Bücher des Alten Testaments*. Leipzig: Otto Schulze.

Kugel, James
1981 On the Bible and Literary Criticism. *Prooftexts* 1:217-36.

Kuhl, Curt
1952 Die "Wiederaufnahme" --ein literarkritische Prinzip? *ZAW* 64:1-11.

Labat, René
1939 *Le caractère religieux de la royauté assyro-babylonienne*. Etudes d'assyriologie 2; Paris: Librairie d'amérique et d'orient Adrien-Maisonneuve.

Labuschagne, C. J.
1960 Some Remarks on the Prayer of David in II Sam. 7. Pp. 28-35 in *Studies on the Book of Samuel.* Papers Read at the Third Meeting of Die O. T. Werkgemeenskap in Suid-Afrika. University of Stellenbosch.

Lackenbacher, Sylvie
1990 *Le palais sans rival: le récit construction en Assyrie.* Paris: Éditions la découverte.

Lambdin, Thomas O.
1971 *An Introduction to Biblical Hebrew.* New York: Scribners.

Lance, H. D.
1967 Gezer in the Land and History. *BA* 30:34-47.

Lang, Bernhard
1985 No God but Yahweh! The Origin and Character of Biblical Monotheism. Pp. 41-49 in *Monotheism,* ed. Claude Geffré and Jean-Pierre Jossua. Edinburgh: T. & T. Clark.

Larsen, Mogens Trolle
1974 The City and its King: On the Old Assyrian Notion of Kingship. Pp. 285-300 in Garelli, ed.

Larsen, Mogens Trolle, ed.
1979 *Power and Propaganda. Mesopotamia 7.* Copenhagen: Akademisk.

Lemaire, André
1981 *Les écoles et la formation de la Bible dans l'ancien Israël.* OBO 39. Editions Universitaires Fribourg Suisse. Göttingen: Vandenhoeck & Ruprecht.

Lemke, Werner E.
1976 The Way of Obedience: I Kings 13 and the Structure of the Deuteronomistic History. Pp. 301-26 in *Magnalia Dei*, ed. F. M. Cross et al. Garden City: Doubleday.

Levenson, Jon Douglas
1979 The Davidic Covenant and its Modern Interpreters. *CBQ* 41:205-19.
1984 The Last Four Verses in Kings. *JBL* 103:353-61.
1985 *Sinai and Zion: An Entry into the Jewish Bible.* New York: Seabury.

Levin, Christoph
1984 Joschija im deuteronomistischen Geschichtswerk. *ZAW* 96:351-71.

Levinson, Bernard M.
1991 The Hermeneutics of Innovation: The Impact of Centralization Upon the Structure, Sequence, and Reformulation of Legal Material in Deuteronomy. Diss., Brandeis University. Ann Arbor, MI: UMI

Lewalski, Barbara Kiefer, ed.
1986 *Renaissance Genres: Essays on Theory, History, and Interpretation.* Cambridge: Harvard University Press.

Lewis, Theodore J.
1989 *Cults of the Dead in Ancient Israel and Ugarit.* HSM 39. Atlanta: Scholars Press.

Liddell, H. G. and Scott, R.
1968 *A Greek-English Lexicon.* Oxford: Oxford University Press.

Lindblom, J.
1962 *Prophecy in Ancient Israel.* Philadelphia: Fortress.

Lipiński, Édouard, ed.
1979 *State and Temple Economy in the Ancient Near East I-II.* Orientalia Lovaniensia Analecta 5-6: Departement Oriëntalistiek.

Loewenstamm, Samuel E.
1967 The Making and Destruction of the Golden Calf. *Bib* 48:481-490.
1975 The Making and Destruction of the Golden Calf -- a Rejoinder. *Bib* 56:330-348.

Lohfink, Norbert
1963 Die Bundesurkunde des Königs Josias (Eine Frage an die Deuteronomiums forschung). *Bib* 44:261-288.
1971 Die Sicherung der Wirksamkeit des Gotteswortes durch das Prinzip der Schriftlichkeit der Tora und das Prinzip der Gewaltenteilung nach den Ämtsetzen des Buches Deuteronomium (Dt 16, 18-18,22). Pp. 143-55 in *Testimonium Veritati*, ed. H. W. Wolff. Frankfurter Theologische Studien 7. Frankfurt: Knecht.
1978 Die Gattung der "Historischen Kurzgeschichte" in den letzten Jahren von Juda und in die Zeit des Babylonischen Exils. *ZAW* 90:319-47.
1981 Kerygmata des Deuteronomistischen Geschichtswerks. Pp. 87-100 in *Die Botschaft und die Boten*. Fs. H. W. Wolff. Ed. J. Jeremias and L. Perlitt. Neukirchen-Vluyn: Neukirchener Verlag.
1982 *Great Themes from the Old Testament*. Trans. Ronald Walls. Edinburgh: T. & T. Clark.

1984 Zur deuteronomischen Zentralisationsformel. *Bib* 65:297-329.

1985 Zur neueren Diskussion über 2 Kön 22-23. Pp. 24-48 in Lohfink, ed.

1987 The Cult Reform of Josiah of Judah: 2 Kings 22-23 as a Source for the story of Israelite Religion. Pp. 459-476 in Miller, Hanson and McBride.

1990a 2 Kön 23,3 und Dtn 6,17. *Bib* 71:34-42.

1990b Welches Orakel gab den Daviden Dauer? Ein Textproblem in 2 Kön 8,19 und das Funktionieren der dynastischen Orakel im deuteronomistischen Geschichtswerk. Pp. 349-70 in *Lingering Over Words: Studies in Ancient Near Eastern Literature in Honor of William L. Moran*, ed. T. Abusch, J. Huehnergard, and P. Steinkeller. HSS 37. Atlanta: Scholars Press.

Lohfink, Norbert, ed.

1985 *Das Deuteronomium: Entstehung, Gestalt und Botschaft*. BETL 68. Leuven: Leuven University Press.

Long, Burke O.

1973 2 Kings III and Genres of Prophetic Narrative. *VT* 23:337-48.

1984 *1 Kings*. FOTL 9. Grand Rapids: Eerdmans.

1987 Framing Repetitions in Biblical Historiography. *JBL* 106:385-99 (= *Poceedings of the Ninth World Congress of Jewish Studies* A:69-76).

1991 *2 Kings*. FOTL 10. Grand Rapids: Eerdmans.

Lowery, Richard H.

1991 *The Reforming Kings: Cult and Society in First Temple Judah*. JSOTSup 120. Sheffield: JSOT Press.

Luckenbill, Daniel David

1924 *The Annals of Sennacherib*. OIP II. Chicago: Chicago University Press.

1926 *Ancient Records of Assyria and Babylonia. Vol. I: Historical Records of Assyria from the Earliest Times to Sargon*. Chicago: Chicago University Press.

1927 *Ancient Records of Assyria and Babylonia. Vol. II: Historical Records of Assyria from Sargon to the End*. Chicago: Chicago University Press.

Lundbom, Jack R.

1976 The Lawbook of the Josianic Reform. *CBQ* 38:293-302.

MacDonald, John

1969-70 The Structure of II Kings XVII. *Glasgow University Oriental Society Transactions* 23:29-41.

Malamat, Abraham

1950 The Last Wars of the Kingdom of Judah. *JNES* 9:218-27.

1963 Kingship and Council in Israel and Sumer: A Parallel. *JNES* 22:247-253.

1973 Josiah's Bid for Armageddon. *JANESCU* 5: 267-78.

1974 Megiddo, 609 B.C.: The Conflict Re-Examined. *Acta Antiqua* 22:445-449.

1987 The Last Years of the Kingdom of Judah. Pp. 287-314 in Perdue, Toombs, and Johnson, ed.

Mandelkern, Solomon

1937 *Veteris Testamenti Concordantiae Hebraicae atque Chaldaicae*. Jerusalem: Schocken.

Mayes, A. D. H.

1978 King and covenant: a study of 2 Kings chs 22-23. *Hermathena* 125:34-47.

1979 *Deuteronomy*. NCB. Grand Rapids: Eerdmans.

1983 *The Story of Israel Between Settlement and Exile. A Redactional Study of the Deuteronomistic History*. London: SCM.

Mazar, Amihai

1982 Iron Age Fortresses in the Judaean Hills. *PEQ* 114:87-109.

1990 *Archaeology of the Land of the Bible 10,000--586 B.C.E.*. ABRL. New York: Doubleday.

Mazar, Benjamin

1957 The Campaign of Pharaoh Shishak to Palestine. VTSup 4:57-66.

McCarter, P. Kyle

1980a The Apology of David. *JBL* 90:489-504.

1980b *I Samuel*. AB 8. New York: Doubleday.

1981 Plots, True or False: The Succession Narrative as Court Apologetic. *Int* 35:355-67.

1983 The Ritual Dedication of the City of David in 2 Samuel 6. Pp. 273-77 in *The Word of the Lord Shall Go Forth: Essays in Honor of David Noel Freedman in Celebration of his Sixtieth Birthday*, ed. C. L. Meyers and M. O'Connor. Winona Lake: Eisenbrauns.

1984 *II Samuel*. AB 9. New York: Doubleday.

McCarthy, Dennis J.

1965 II Samuel 7 and the Structure of the Deuteronomic History. *JBL* 84:131-38.

1972 *B^{e}rît* in Old Testament History and Theology. *Bib* 53:110-21.

1974 The Wrath of Yahweh and the Structural Unity of the Duteronomistic History. Pp. 97-110 in *Essays in Old Testament Ethics*, ed. J. L. Crenshaw and J. T. Willis. New York: KTAV.

1978 *Treaty and Covenant*. AnBib 21A. 2nd ed. Rome: Pontifical Biblical Institute.

1982 Covenant and Law in Chronicles-Nehemiah. *CBQ* 44:25-44.

McKay, John W.

1973a Further Light on the Horses and Chariot of the Sun in the Jerusalem Temple. *PEQ* 105:167-169.

1973b *Religion in Judah under the Assyrians 732-609 B.C.* SBT 2/26. Naperville, IL: Allenson.

McKenzie, Steven L.

1985 *The Chronicler's Use of the Deuteronomistic History*. HSM 33. Atlanta: Scholars Press.

1986 1 Kings 8: A Sample Study into the Texts of Kings Used by the Chronicler and Translated by the Old Greek. *BIOSCS* 19:15-34.

1991 *The Trouble with Kings: The Composition of the Book of Kings in the Deuteronomistic History*. VTSup 42. Leiden: Brill.

Meek, Theophile

1969 The Code of Hammurabi. Pp. 163-80 in Pritchard, ed.

Meier, Samuel

1988 *The Messenger in the Ancient Semitic World*. HSM 45. Atlanta: Scholars Press.

1992 *Speaking of Speaking*. VTSup 46. Leiden: Brill.

Merendino, R. P.

1981 Kleinere Beiträge zu 2 Kön 22:3-23:15. Eine Erwiderung. *BZ* 25:249-255.

Mettinger, Tryggve N. D.

1976 *King and Messiah. The Civil and Sacral Legitimation of the Israelite Kings.* ConBOT 8. Lund: CWK Gleerup.

1982 *The Dethronement of Sebaoth: Studies in the Shem and Kabod Theologies.* ConBOT 18. Lund: CWK Gleerup.

Milgrom, Jacob

1973 The Alleged 'Demythologization and Secularization' in Deuteronomy. *IEJ* 23:156-161.

1983 The Ideological and Historical Importance of the Office of Judge in Deuteronomy. Pp. 129-39 in Rofè and Zakovitch, ed.

Miller, James Maxwell and John H. Hayes

1986 *A History of Ancient Israel and Judah.* Philadelphia: Westminister.

Miller, Patrick D., Paul D. Hanson, and S. D. McBride, ed.

1987 *Ancient Israelite Religion. Essays in Honor of Frank Moore Cross.* Philadelphia: Fortress.

Montgomery, James A.

1951 *A Critical and Exegetical Commentary on the Books of Kings.* ICC. Edinburgh: T. & T. Clark.

Moore, Mark

1990 Jeroboam's Calves: Idols or Imitations? *BT* 41: 421-24.

Moorey, P. R. S.

1971 A Bronze Statuette of a Bull. *Levant* 3:90-91.

Mosca, Paul G,

1975 Child Sacrifice in Canaanite and Israelite Religion: A Study in *Mulk* and *mlk*. Diss., Harvard University.

Mosis, Rudolph

1973 *Untersuchungen zur Theologie des chronistischen Geschichtswerkes*. Freiburg: Herder.

Mowinckel, Sigmund

1935 *Det Gamle Testamente II: De Tidligere Profeter*. Oslo: H. Aschehoug.

1941 Immanuelprofetien Jes. 7 Streiflys fra Ugarit I. *Norsk teologisk tidsskrift* 42:129-58.

1962 *The Psalms in Israel's Worship*. Oxford: Basil Blackwell.

Mullen, E. Theodore

1987 The Sins of Jeroboam: A Redactional Assessment. *CBQ* 49:212-32.

1988 The Royal Dynastic Grant to Jehu and the Structure of the Book of Kings. *JBL* 107:193-206.

Na'aman, Nadav

1974 Sennacherib's "Letter to God" on His Campaign to Judah. *BASOR* 214:25-39.

1979 Sennacherib's Campaign to Judah and the Date of the *LMLK* Stamps. *VT* 29:61-86.

1986 Hezekiah's Fortified Cities and the *LMLK* Stamps. *BASOR* 261:5-21.

Nelson, Richard D.

1981a *The Double Redaction of the Deuteronomistic History*. JSOTSup 18. Sheffield: JSOT Press.

1981b Josiah in the Book of Joshua. *JBL* 100:531-540.

1983 *Realpolitik* in Judah (687-609 B.C.E.). Pp. 177-89 in Hallo, Moyer, and Perdue, ed.

1987 *First and Second Kings*. Interpretation. Louisville: John Knox.

1991 The Role of the Priesthood in the Deuteronomistic History. Pp. 132-47 in Emerton, ed.

1993 *Raising Up a Faithful Priest: Community and Priesthood in Biblical Theology*. Louisville: Westminster / John Knox.

Nicholson, E. W.

1963 2 Kings 22,18 -- A Simple Restoration. *Hermathena* 97:94-98.

1967 *Deuteronomy and Tradition*. Philadelphia: Fortress.

1970 *Preaching to the Exiles*. Oxford: Basil Blackwell.

1991 Deuteronomy's Vision of Israel. Pp. 191-203 in *Storia e Tradizioni di Israele: Scritti in Onore di J. Alberto Soggin*, ed. D. Garrone and F. Moscati. Brescia: Paideia Editrice.

Nielsen, Eduard

1959 *Shechem. A Traditio-Historical Investigation*. 2nd ed. Copenhagen: G. E. C. Gad.

Noth, Martin

1930 *Das System der zwölf Stämme Israels*. BWANT 4/1. Stuttgart: Kohlhammer.

1938 Die Wege der Pharaonenheere in Palästina und Syrien, Untersuchungen zu dem hieroglyphischen Listen palästinischen und syrischen Stadte, IV: Die Schoschenkliste. *ZDPV* 61:277-304.

1957 Zur deuteronomistischen Geschichtsauffassung. Pp. 558-65 in *Proceedings of the Twenty-Second Congress of Orientalists*. Vol. 2. Ed. Z. V. Togan. Leiden: Brill.

1960 *The History of Israel*. 2nd ed. London/New York: A.& C. Black/Harper & Row.

1962 *Exodus*. OTL. Philadelphia: Westminster.
1966 *The laws in the Pentateuch and other studies*. Trans. D. R. Ap-Thomas. Edinburgh: Oliver & Boyd.
1967 *Überlieferungsgeschichtliche Studien: Die sammelnden und bearbeitenden Geschichtswerke im Alten Testament*. 3rd ed. Tübingen: Max Niemeyer. English translations follow below.
1968 *Könige*. BKAT 9/1. Neukirchen-Vluyn: Neukirchener Verlag.
1981 *The Deuteronomistic History*. Trans. J. Doull *et al*. JSOTSup 15. Sheffield: JSOT Press.
1987 *The Chronicler's History*. Trans. H. G. M. Williamson. JSOTSup 50. Sheffield: JSOT Press.

Nowack, Wilhelm
1925 Deuteronomium und Regum. Pp. 221-31 in *Vom Alten Testament Karl Marti zum siebzigsten Geburtstag gewidmet*, ed. K. Budde. BZAW 41. Giesen: Töpelmann.

O'Brien, Mark A.
1989 *The Deuteronomistic History Hypothesis: A Reassessment*. OBO 92. Göttingen: Vandenhoeck & Ruprecht.

Obbink, K. T.
1929 Jahwebilder. *ZAW* 47:264-79.

Oded, Bustenay
1977 Judah and the Exile. Pp. 435-88 in *Israelite and Judean History*, ed. J. H. Hayes and J. M. Miller. OTL. Philadelphia: Westminster.
1979 *Mass Deportations and Deportees in the Neo-Assyrian Empire*. Wiesbaden: Reichert.

Oestreicher, Theodor
1923 *Das deuteronomistische Grundgesetz*. BFCT 27/4. Gütersloh: Bertelsmann.

Ofer, Avi
forthcoming Judah. *Encyclopedia of Near Eastern Archaeology*, ed. E. M. Meyers *et al*. New York: Oxford University Press.

Ogden, Graham
1978 The Northern Extent of Josiah's Reform. *AusBR* 26:26-34.

Olmstead, Albert Ten Eyck
1913-14 Source Study and the Biblical Text. *AJSL* 30: 1-35.

Olyan, Saul
1982 Zadok's Origins and the Tribal Politics of David. *JBL* 101:177-93.
1988 *Asherah and the Cult of Yahweh in Israel*. SBLMS 34. Atlanta: Scholars Press.

Oppenheim, A. Leo
1977 *Ancient Mesopotamia. Portrait of a Dead Civilization*. Rev. ed. completed by Erica Reiner. Chicago: University of Chicago Press.

Paton, Lewis Bayles
1928 The Case for the Post-Exilic Origins of Deuteronomy. *JBL* 47:322-357.

Paul, Maarten J.
1990 King Josiah's Renewal of the Covenant (2 Kings 22-23). Pp. 269-276 in Brekelmans and Lust.

Paul, Shalom M.
1991 *Amos*. Hermeneia. Philadelphia: Fortress.

Perdue, Leo G.
1973 The Making and Destruction of the Golden Calf -- A Reply. *Bib* 54:237-246.

Perdue, Leo G, Lawrence E. Toombs, and Gary L. Johnson, ed.
1987 *Archaeology and Biblical Interpretation: Essays in Memory of D. Glenn Rose*. Atlanta: John Knox.

Pfeiffer, Robert H.
1948 *Introduction to the Old Testament*. 2nd ed. New York: Harper & Brothers.
1961 *Religion in the Old Testament*. New York: Harper & Brothers.

Pitard, Wayne T.
1987 *Ancient Damascus: A Historical Study of the Syrian City-State from Earliest Times until its Fall to the Assyrians in 732 B.C.E.* Winona Lake: Eisenbrauns.

Plein, Ina
1966 Erwägungen zur Überlieferung von I Reg 11:26-14:20. *ZAW* 78:8-24.

Plöger, Otto
1957 Reden und Gebete im deuteronomistischen und chronistischen Geschichtswerk. Pp. 35-49 in *Festschrift für Günther Dehn zum 75. Geburtstag*, ed. W. Schneemelcher. Neukirchen: Kries Moers.

Pohlmann, Karl-Friedrich
1978 *Studien zum Jeremiabuch: Ein Beitrag zur Frage nach der Enstehung des Jeremiabuches.* FRLANT 118. Göttingen: Vandenhoeck & Ruprecht.

Polzin, Robert
1976 *Late Biblical Hebrew: Toward an Historical Typology of Biblical Hebrew Prose.* HSM 12. Missoula: Scholars Press.
1980 *Moses and the Deuteronomist. A Literary Study of the Deuteronomic History.* Part 1: Deuteronomy, Joshua, Judges. New York: Seabury.
1989 *Samuel and the Deuteronomist. A Literary Study of the Deuteronomic History.* Part 2: 1 Samuel. San Francisco: Harper & Row.

Pratt, Richard Linwood
1987 Royal Prayer and the Chronicler's Program. Diss., Harvard Divinity School. Ann Arbor: MI: UMI.

Priest, J.
1980 Huldah's Oracle. *VT* 30:366-368.

Preuss, Horst Dietrich
1982 *Deuteronomium.* ErFor 164. Darmstadt: Wissenschaftliche Buchgesellschaft.

Pritchard, James B., ed.
1969 *Ancient Near Eastern Texts Relating to the Old Testament.* 3rd ed. Princeton: Princeton University Press.

Provan, Iain
1988 *Hezekiah and the Book of Kings.* BZAW 172. Berlin/New York: de Gruyter.

Rad, Gerhard von

1930 *Das Geschichtsbild des chronistischen Werkes.* Stuttgart: Kohlhammer.

1953 *Studies in Deuteronomy.* SBT 9. London: SCM.

1962 *Old Testament Theology.* Vol. 1. New York: Harper & Row.

1966a *Deuteronomy.* OTL. Trans. D. Barton. Philadelphia: Westminster.

1966b *The Problem of the Hexteuch and Other Essays.* New York: McGraw-Hill.

Rahlfs, Alfred

1904 *Septuaginta-Studien. 1.Heft. Studien zu den Königsbüchern.* Göttingen.

Reiner, Erica

1969 Akkadian Treaties from Syria and Assyria. Pp. 531-41 in Pritchard, ed.

Rendtorff, Rolf

1986 *The Old Testament: An Introduction.* Trans. John Bowden. Philadelphia: Fortress.

Reviv, Hanoch

1981 Popular Assemblies in the Bible. *Proceedings of the Seventh World Congress of Jewish Studies: Studies in the Bible and the Ancient Near East*: 95-98 (Hebrew).

1985 History and Historiography during the Time of the Division of the Kingdom: Toward an Understanding of the Term *Edah* in I Kings 12:20. *Zion* 50:59-63 (Hebrew).

1989 *The Elders in Ancient Israel.* Jerusalem: Magnes.

Robinson, J.
1972 *The First Book of Kings.* Cambridge: Cambridge University Press.

Rofé, Alexander
1970 The Classification of the Prophetical Stories. *JBL* 89:427-440.
1974 Classes in the Prophetical Stories: Didactic Legenda and Parable. Pp. 143-164 in *Studies in Prophecy*. VTSup 26. Leiden: Brill.
1988 *The Prophetical Stories*. Jerusalem: Magnes.

Rofè A. and Y. Zakovitch, ed.
1983 *Studies in Ancient Narrative and Historiography: Sefer Yitshak Aryeh Zeligman (Isac Leo Seeligmann Anniversary Volume)*. Vol. III. Jerusalem: Rubenstein.

Rooker, Mark
1990 *Biblical Hebrew in Transition: The Language of the Book of Ezekiel*. JSOTSup 90. Sheffield: JSOT Press.

Rose, Martin
1977 Bermerkungen zum historischen Fundament des Josia-Bildes in II Reg 22f. *ZAW* 89:55-62.
1981 *Deuteronomist und Yahwist. Untersuchungen zu den Berührungspunkten beider Literaturwerke*. ATANT 67. Zürich: Theologischer Verlag.

Rosenbaum, Jonathan
1979 Hezekiah's Reform and Deuteronomistic Tradition. *HTR* 72:23-44.

Rudolph, Wilhelm
1952 Zum Text der Königsbücher. *ZAW* 63:201-215.
1955 *Chronikbücher*. HAT 21. Tübingen: Mohr.

Rüterswörden, Udo
1977 Beiträge zur Vernichtungssymbolik. *BN* 2:16-22.
1987 Von der politischen Gemeinschaft zur Gemeinde: Studien zu Dt 16,18-18,22. BBB 65. Frankfurt am Main: Athenäum.

Šanda, Albert
1911-12 *Die Bücher der Könige*. 2 vols. Exegetisches Handbuch zum Alten Testament 9. Münster: Aschendorffsche Verlagsbuchhandlung.

Sasson, Jack M.
1968 Bovine Symbolism In The Exodus Narrative. *VT* 18:380-387.
1973 The Worship Of The Golden Calf. Pp. 151-159 in *Orient and Occident: Essays Presented to Cyrus H. Gordon on the Occasion of his Sixty-Fifth Birthday*, ed. Harry A. Hoffner, Jr. AOAT 22. Neukirchen-Vluyn: Neukirchener Verlag.

Savran, George
1987 1 and 2 Kings. Pp. 146-164 in Alter and Kermode, ed.

Schniedewind, William M.
1991 The Source Citations of Manasseh: King Manasseh in History and Homily. *VT* 41:450-61.

Seebass, Horst
1967/68 Die Verwerfung Jeroboams I. und Salomos durch die Prophetie des Ahia von Silo. *WO* 4:163-82.
1975 Tradition und Interpretation bei Jehu ben Chanani und Ahia von Silo (I Reg 16,1-4; 14,7-16). *VT* 25:175-90.

1978 Erwägungen zum altisraelitischen System der zwolf Stämme. *ZAW* 90:196-219.

Seger, Joe D.

1983 Investigations at Tell Halif, Israel, 1976-80. *BASOR* 252:1-23.

1987 Tel Gezer: Phase II Excavations 1972-1974. Pp. 113-28 in Perdue, Toombs, and Johnson, ed.

Seitz, Christopher R.

1989 *Theology in Conflict*. BZAW 176. Berlin/New York: de Gruyter.

1991 *Zion's Final Destiny: The Development of the Book of Isaiah*. Minneapolis: Fortress.

Sellin, Ernst

1910 *Einleitung in das alte Testament*. Leipzig: Quelle und Meyer.

Shanks, Hershel, ed.

1988 *Ancient Israel: A Short History from Abraham to the Roman Destruction of the Temple*. Englewood Cliffs: Prentice-Hall / Washington, DC: Biblical Archaeology Society.

Shaver, Judson R.

1989 *Torah and the Chronicler's History Work: An Inquiry into the Chronicler's References to Laws, Festivals, and Cultic Institutions in Relationship to Pentateuchal Legislation*. BJS 196. Atlanta: Scholars Press.

Shenkel, James D.

1968 *Chronology and Recensional Development in the Greek Text of Kings*. HSM 1. Cambridge: Harvard University Press.

Shiloh, Yigal
1979 Iron Age Sanctuaries and Cult Elements in Palestine. Pp. 147-157 in Cross, ed.
1987 Underground Water Systems in Eretz-Israel in the Iron Age. Pp. 203-45 in Perdue, Toombs, and Johnson, ed.
1989 Judah and Jerusalem in the Eighth-Sixth Centuries B.C.E. Pp. 97-106 in *Recent Excavations in Israel: Studies in Iron Age Archaeology*, ed. S. Gitin and W. G. Dever. ASOR 49. Winona Lake: Eisenbrauns.

Silverman, David P.
1991 Divinity and Divinities in Ancient Egypt. Pp. 58-97 in *Religion in Ancient Egypt: Gods, Myths, and Personal Practice*, ed. B. E. Shafer. Ithaca: Cornell University Press.

Simon, Uriel
1976 1 Kings 13: A Prophetic Sign--Denial and Persistance. *HUCA* 47:81-117.

Smend, Rudolf
1963 Das Nein des Amos. *EvT* 23:404-23.
1971 Das Gesetz und die Völker: Ein Beitrag zur deuteronomistischen Redaktionsgeschichte. Pp. 494-509 in Wolff, ed.
1978 *Die Enstehung des Alten Testaments*. Stuttgart: Kohlhammer.

Smith, Mark S.
1990 *The Early History of God*. New York: Harper & Row.

Soggin, J. Alberto

1967 *Das Königtum in Israel: Ursprünge, Spannungen, Entwicklung*. BZAW 104. Berlin: Töpelmann.

1972 *Joshua*. OTL. Philadelphia: Westminster.

1981 *Judges*. OTL. Philadelphia: Westminster.

1984 *A History of Israel: from the Beginnings to the Bar Kochba Revolt, AD 135*. London: SCM.

Sperber, Alexander, ed.

1959 *The Bible in Aramaic Based on Old Manuscripts and Printed Texts*. Volume II: The Former Prophets according to Targum Jonathan. Leiden: Brill.

Spieckermann, Hermann

1982 *Juda unter Assur in der Sargonidenzeit*. FRLANT 129. Göttingen: Vandenhoeck & Ruprecht.

Stade, Bernhard

1885 Miscellen 10. Anmerkungen zu 2 Kö. 10-14. *ZAW* 5:275-99.

1886 Miscellen 16. Anmerkungen zu 2 Kö. 15-21. *ZAW* 6:156-189.

1887 *Geschichte des Volkes Israel*. Erster Band. Berlin: Historischer Verlag Baumgärtel.

Stade, Bernhard and F. Schwally

1904 *The Book of Kings. Critical Edition of the Hebrew Text*. The Sacred Books of the Old Testament 9. Ed. Paul Haupt. Leipzig: Hinrichs.

Stager, Lawrence

1982 The Archaeology of the East Slope of Jerusalem. *JNES* 41:16-22.

Stern, Ephraim
1975 Israel at the Close of the Monarchy: An Archaeological Survey. *BA* 38:26-54.

Stipp, Hermann-Josef
1987 *Elischa-Propheten-Gottesmänner. Die Kompositionsgeschichte des Elischazyklus und verwandter Texte, rekonstruiert auf der Basis von Text- und Literarkritik zu 1 Kön 20.22 und 2 Kön 2-7.* ATAT 24. St. Ottilien: EOS.

Stohlmann, Stephen
1983 The Judaean Exile after 701 B.C.E. Pp. 147-75 in Hallo, Moyer, and Perdue, ed.

Streck, M.
1916 *Assurbanipal I-III.* Vorderasiatische Bibliothek 3. Leipzig: Hinrichs.

Stulman, Louis
1986 *The Prose Sermons of the Book of Jeremiah: A Redescription of the Correspondences with the Deuteronomistic Literature in Light of Recent Text-Critical Research.* SBLDS 83. Atlanta: Scholars Press.

Suzuki, Yoshihide
1987 Deuteronomic Reformation in View of the Centralization of the Administration of Justice. *AJBI* 13:22-58.

Tadmor, Hayim
1982 Traditional Institutions and the Monarchy: Social and Political Tensions in the Time of David and Solomon. Pp. 239-57 in Ishida, ed.

Tadmor, Hayim and Mordecai Cogan
1988 *II Kings*. AB 11. New York: Doubleday.

Tadmor, Hayim and Moshe Weinfeld, ed.
1983 *History, Historiography and Interpretation*. Jerusalem: Magnes.

Tagliacarne, Pierfelice
1989 *"Keiner war wie er": Untersuchung zur Struktur von 2 Könige 22-23*. ATAT 31. St. Ottilien: EOS.

Talmon, Shemaryahu
1958 Divergencies in Calendar-Reckoning in Ephraim and Judah. *VT* 8:48-74.
1981 Polemics and Apology in Biblical Historiography--2 Kings 17:24-41. Pp. 57-68 in Friedman, ed.

Talmon, Shemaryahu and Weston W. Fields.
1989 The Collocation מַשְׁתִּין בְּקִיר וְעָצוּר וְעָזוּב and its Meaning. *ZAW* 101:85-112.

Talshir, Zipora
1992 Is the Alternate Tradition of the Division of the Kingdom (3 Kgdms 12:24a-z) Non-Deuteronomistic? Pp. 599-621 in *Septuagint, Scrolls, and Cognate Writings: Papers Presented to the International Symposium on the Septuagint and Its Relations to the Dead Sea Scrolls and Other Writings*, ed. G. J. Brooke and B. Lindars. SBLSCS 33. Atlanta: Scholars Press.

Thiel, Winfried
1973 *Die deuteronomistische Redaktion von Jeremia 1-25*. WMANT 41. Neukirchen-Vluyn: Neukirchener Verlag.

1981 *Die deuteronomistische Redaktion von Jeremia 26-45*. WMANT 52. Neukirchen-Vluyn: Neukirchener Verlag.

Throntveit, Mark
1987 *When Kings Speak: Royal Speech and Royal Prayer in Chronicles*. SBLDS 93. Atlanta: Scholars Press.

Tigay, Jeffrey H.
1986 *You Shall Have No Other Gods: Israelite Religion in the Light of Hebrew Inscriptions*. HSS. Atlanta: Scholars Press.

Toorn, Karel van der
1991 The Babylonian New Year Festival: New Insights from the Cuneiform Texts and their Bearing on Old Testament Study. Pp. 331-44 in Emerton, ed.

Trebolle Barrera, Julio C.
1980 *Salomòn y Jeroboán: Historia de la recensión y redacción de 1 Reyes 2-12, 14*. Institución San Jeronimo 10. Valencia: Investigación Biblica.
1989a *Centena in Libros Samuelis et Regum. Variantes Textuales y Composición literaria en los libros de Samuel y Reyes*. Textos y Estudios "Cardinal Cisneros" 47. Madrid: Consejo Superior de Investigaciones Científicas Instituto de Filología.
1989b The Text-Critical Use of the Septuagint in the Books of Kings. Pp. 285-99 in Cox, ed.
1992 Light from 4QJudg^{a} and 4QKgs on the Text of Judges and Kings. Pp. 315-24 in *The Dead Sea Scrolls: Forty Years of Research*, ed. D. Dimant and U. Rappaport. Leiden: Brill / Jerusalem: Magnes.

Vannutelli, P.
1931 *Libri Synoptici Veteris Testamenti*. Rome: Pontifical Biblical Institute.

Vanoni, Gottfried
1984 *Literaturkritik und Grammatik. Untersuchungen der Wiederholungen und Spannungen in 1 Kön 11-12*. ATAT 21. St. Ottilien: EOS.

Van Seters, John
1981 Histories and Historians of the Ancient Near East: The Israelites. *Or* 50:137-185.
1983 *In Search of History*. New Haven: Yale University Press.
1991 The So-Called Deuteronomistic Redaction of the Pentateuch. Pp. 58-77 in Emerton, ed.

Vater, Ann M.
1979 Narrative Patterns for the Story of Commissioned Communication in the Old Testament. *JBL* 99:365-382.
1980 Story Patterns for a *Sitz*: A Form- or Literary-Critical Concern? *JSOT* 11:47-56.

Vaux, Roland Guérin de
1958 *Les Livres des Rois*. La Sainte Bible. Jerusalem. Paris: Éditions du Cerf.
1965 *Ancient Israel: Its Life and Institutions*. 2 Vols. New York: McGraw-Hill.
1971 *The Bible and the Ancient Near East*. Trans. D. McHugh. Garden City: Doubleday.

Veijola, Timo
1975 *Die ewige Dynastie. David und die Entstehung seiner Dynastie nach der deuteronomistischen*

Darstellung. Annalae Academiae Scientiarum Fennicae, série B, Tom 193. Helsinki: Suomalainen Tiedeakatemia.

1977 *Das Königtum in der Beurteilung der deuteronomistischen Historiographie*. Annalae Academiae Scientiarum Fennicae, série B, Tom 198. Helsinki: Suomalainen Tiedeakatemia.

Viviano, Pauline A.

1987 2 Kings 17: A Rhetorical and Form-Critical Assessment. *CBQ* 49:548-59.

Wallace, Howard N.

1986 The Oracles Against the Israelite Dynasties in 1 and 2 Kings. *Bib* 67:21-40.

Walsh, Jerome T.

1989 The Contexts of 1 Kings XIII. *VT* 39:3:355-70.

Weinfeld, Moshe

1964 Cult Centralization in Israel in the Light of a Neo-Babylonian Analogy. *JNES* 23:202-212.

1970 The Covenant of Grant in the Old Testament and in the Ancient Near East. *JAOS* 90:184-203.

1972 *Deuteronomy and the Deuteronomic School*. Oxford: Clarendon.

1973a ברית: *b*^e^*rîth*. *TDOT* 2:253-79.

1973b On 'Demythologization and Secularization in Deuteronomy.' *IEJ* 23:230-233.

1982 The Counsel of the "Elders" to Rehoboam and its Implications. *MAARAV* 3:27-53.

1985 The Emergence of the Deuteronomic Movement: The Historical Antecedents. Pp. 76-98 in Lohfink, ed.

1991 *Deuteronomy 1-11*. AB 5. Garden City: Doubleday.

Weippert, Helga

1972 Die 'deuteronomistischen' Beurteilungen der Könige von Israel und Juda und das Problem der Redaktion der Königsbücher. *Bib* 53:301-39.

1983 Die Ätiologie des Nordreiches und seines Königshauses (1 Reg 11:29-40). *ZAW* 95:344-75.

1985 Das deuteronomistische Geschichtswerk. Sein Ziel und Ende in der neueren Forschung. *TRu* 50:213-249.

1991 Geschichten und Geschichte: Verheißung und Erfüllung im deuteronomistischen Geschichtswerk. Pp. 116-31 in Emerton, ed.

Weiser, Artur

1962 *Samuel. Seine geschichtliche Aufgabe und religiöse Bedeutung. Traditionsgeschichtliche Untersuchungen zu 1 Samuel 7-12.* FRLANT 81. Göttingen: Vandenhoeck & Ruprecht.

Welch, Adam C.

1924 *The Code of Deuteronomy: A New Theory of Its Origin*. New York: Doran.

1925 The Death of Josiah. *ZAW* 43:255-60.

1939 *The Work of the Chronicler: Its Purpose and Date*. The Schweich Lectures 1938. London: Oxford University Press.

Wellhausen, Julius

1885 *Prolegomena to the History of Ancient Israel.* Trans. J. Sutherland Black and A. Menzies. Edinburgh: Adams and Charles Black.

1963 *Die Composition des Hexateuchs und der historischen Bücher des Alten Testaments.* Berlin: de Gruyter. [repr. of 4th ed.]

Welten, Peter
1973 *Geschichte und Geschichtsdarstellung in den Chronikbüchern.* Neukirchen: Neukirchener Verlag.

Westermann, Claus
1967 *Basic Forms of Prophetic Speech.* Trans. H. White. Philadelphia: Westminster.
1991 *Prophetic Oracles of Salvation in the Old Testament.* Louisville, KY: Westminster/John Knox.

White, Hayden
1978 *Tropics of Discourse: Essays in Cultural Criticism.* Baltimore: Johns Hopkins University Press.

White, Marsha
1990 The Elohistic Depiction of Aaron: A Study in the Levite-Zadokite Controversy. Pp. 149-59 in *Studies in the Pentateuch*, ed. J. A. Emerton. VTSup 41. Leiden: Brill.

Whitelam, Keith W.
1979 *The Just King: Monarchical Judicial Authority in Ancient Israel.* JSOTSup 12. Sheffield: JSOT Press.
1984 The Defence of David. *JSOT* 29:61-87.
1986 The Symbols of Power: Aspects of Royal Propaganda in the United Monarchy. *BA* 49:166-73.
1992 King and Kingship. *ABD* 4:40-48.

Widengren, Geo
1955 *Sakrales Konigtum im Alten Testament und im Judentum.* Stuttgart: Kohlhammer.
1957 King and Covenant. *JSS* 2:1-32.

Willi, Thomas

1972 *Die Chronik als Auslegung*. FRLANT 106. Göttingen: Vandenhoeck & Ruprecht.

Williamson, Hugh G. M.

1976 The Accession of Solomon in the Books of Chronicles. *VT* 26:351-61.

1977 *Israel in the Books of Chronicles*. Cambridge: Cambridge University Press.

1982a The Death of Josiah and the Continuing Development of the Deuteronomic History. *VT* 32: 242-47.

1982b *1 and 2 Chronicles*. NCB. Grand Rapids: Eerdmans.

1987 Reliving the Death of Josiah: A Reply to C. T. Begg. *VT* 37:9-15.

Wilson, Robert R.

1980 *Prophecy and Society in Ancient Israel*. Philadelphia: Fortress.

Winkle, D. W. van

1989 1 Kings XIII: True and False Prophecy. *VT* 29:31-43.

Wiseman, Donald J.

1958 The Vassal Treaties of Esarhaddon. *Iraq* 20:1-99.

Wolff, H. W.

1961 Das Kerygma des deuteronomistischen Geschichtswerk. *ZAW* 73:171-186. English translation follows below.

1974 *Hosea*. Hermeneia. Philadelphia: Fortress.

1975 The Kerygma of the Deuteronomic Historical Work. Pp. 83-100 in *The Vitality of Old Testament Traditions*, ed. W. Brueggeman and H. W. Wolff. Atlanta: John Knox.

1977 *Joel and Amos*. Hermeneia. Philadelphia: Fortress.

Wolff, H. W., ed.

1971 *Probleme biblischer Theologie: Festschrift Gerhard von Rad*. München: Kaiser.

Woude, A. S. van der, ed.

1990 *In Quest of the Past, Studies on Israelite Religion, Literature, and prophetism: Papers Read at the Joint British-Dutch Old Testament Conference, Held at Elspeet, 1988*. *OTS* 26. Leiden: Brill.

Wright, John Wesley

1992 From Center to Periphery: 1 Chronicles 23-27 and the Interpretation of Chronicles in the Nineteenth Century. Pp. 20-42 in *Priests, Prophets, and Scribes: Essays on the Formation and Heritage of Second Temple Judaism in Honour of Joseph Blenkinsopp*, ed. E. Ulrich, *et al.* JSOTSup 149. Sheffield: JSOT Press.

Würthwein, Ernst

1973 Die Erzählung vom Gottesman aus Juda in Bethel zur Komposition von 1 Kön 13. Pp. 182-89 in *Wort und Geschichte: Festschrift Karl Elliger*. AOAT 18. Ed. H. Gese and H. P. Rüger. Neukirchen-Vluyn: Neukirchener Verlag.

1976 Die josianische Reform und das Deuteronomium. *ZTK* 73:395-423.

1977 *Die Bücher der Könige: 1 Könige 1-16*. ATD 11/1. Göttingen: Vandenhoeck & Ruprecht.

1984 *Die Bücher der Könige: 1 Kön. 17-2 Kön. 25.* ATD 11/2. Göttingen: Vandenhoeck & Ruprecht.

Yadin, Yigael
1976 Beer-sheba: The High Place Destroyed by King Josiah. *BASOR* 222:7-17.

Zeidel, Moshe
1955-1956 Parallels between Isaiah and Psalms. *Sinai* 38:149-172, 229-240, 272-280, 335-355 (in Hebrew).

Zevit, Ziony
1985 Deuteronomistic Historiography in 1 Kings 12-2 Kings 17 and the Reinvestiture of the Israelian Cult. *JSOT* 32:57-73.

Zimmerli, Walther
1979 *Ezekiel 1.* Hermeneia. Philadelphia: Fortress.

Zobel, Hans-Jürgen
1990 יִשְׂרָאֵל: *yiśrā'ēl*. *TDOT* 6:397-420.

INDEX OF CITATIONS

HEBREW BIBLE

Deuteronomy (continued)

Deuteronomy (continued)

Deuteronomy (continued)

Deuteronomy (continued)

Joshua

Joshua (continued)

Judges

1 Samuel

1 Samuel (continued)

2 Samuel

1 Kings (continued)

1 Kings (continued)

1 Kings (continued)

1 Kings (continued)

1 Kings (continued)

1 Kings (continued)

1 Kings (continued)

1 Kings (continued)

2 Kings (continued)

2 Kings (continued)

2 Kings (continued)

1 Chronicles (continued)

2 Chronicles

2 Chronicles (continued)

SEPTUAGINT

3 Reigns

1 Esdras

QUMRÂN

4QKgs[a]

6QKgs

OTHER ANCIENT SOURCES

AR II

Assurbanipal II

Annals (continued)

VTE

INDEX OF AUTHORS

C (continued)

D

D (continued)

E

F

F (continued)

G

G (continued)

H

H (continued)

I

J

J (continued)

K

L

L (continued)

M

M (continued)

M (continued)

N

N (continued)

O

O (continued)

P

P (continued)

R

S

S (continued)

S (continued)

T

V

W

W (continued)

W (continued)

Y

Z